I0414568

The Southern African Region Historical Policies and the Land Redistribution Crisis in Zimbabwe

The Southern African Region Historical Policies and the Land Redistribution Crisis in Zimbabwe

Author—Andrew Choga

iUniverse, Inc.
New York Lincoln Shanghai

The Southern African Region Historical Policies and the Land Redistribution Crisis in Zimbabwe

Copyright © 2005 by Andrew Choga

All rights reserved. No part of this book may be used or reproduced by any means, graphic, electronic, or mechanical, including photocopying, recording, taping or by any information storage retrieval system without the written permission of the publisher except in the case of brief quotations embodied in critical articles and reviews.

iUniverse books may be ordered through booksellers or by contacting:

iUniverse
2021 Pine Lake Road, Suite 100
Lincoln, NE 68512
www.iuniverse.com
1-800-Authors (1-800-288-4677)

ISBN-13: 978-0-595-35632-4 (pbk)
ISBN-13: 978-0-595-80107-7 (ebk)
ISBN-10: 0-595-35632-X (pbk)
ISBN-10: 0-595-80107-2 (ebk)

Printed in the United States of America

Contents

1.1 Foreword

The land redistribution issue, a southern African regional problem affecting Zimbabwe, will very likely impact South Africa and Namibia in the near future, due to similar historically racial, segregation-based land allocation policies in these countries. In the interest of spreading Christianity and civilization, the colonization of southern Africa was perhaps inevitable. In addition, the industrializing nations of Europe also needed to establish sources of raw materials and markets to sustain the industrial revolution. In order to meet the increasing demand for raw materials, commercial farmland had to be acquired in the new colonies, sometimes through the displacement of the natives from the agriculturally rich areas to sandy soils considered sufficient for native subsistence farming at that time. The newly resettled colonial commercial farmers were granted legal title to the land as an incentive for resettling in what was considered the Dark Continent and to ensure the introduction of sustainable, efficient methods of agricultural mass production. At the time, the natives were excluded from commercial farming due to their lack of training, capital, and equipment. As a result, the natives found themselves confined to poor, sandy subsistence agricultural areas, while the colonial commercial farmers became owners of large tracts of productive land. In South Africa, Namibia, and Rhodesia (now Zimbabwe), racially segregated development laws ensured the mineral-rich and fertile agricultural lands remained in the hands of the descendents of the colonial commercial farmers.

After the attainment of independence and the end of racial segregation, the majority of the landless and demobilized ex-combatants expected the government to implement land redistribution policies in their favor, while the descendents of the colonial commercial farmers expected the postcolonial, majority-ruled governments to redistribute land, while considering the continuation of economically viable agricultural activities. In the case of Zimbabwe, a clause within the British-sponsored Lancaster House Constitution granted the commercial farmers protection against deprivation of property, including land, for a period of ten years after independence. After twenty years of independence without the right to land ownership, the landless and the unsuccessfully reintegrated ex-combatants started invading and occupying the commercial farms, seizing cattle and equipment. The governments of South Africa and Namibia are now in a better position to plan and prepare economically viable land redistribution programs based on lessons learned from the Zimbabwe program, which resulted in violent commercial farm invasions and illegal occupations, sometimes causing the loss of innocent lives.

Andrew Choga

2.0 European Imperialism and the British Colonization of Zimbabwe

Emerging in the early eighteenth century, European imperialism continued into the early nineteenth century. While Ancient Rome used imperialism to acquire territory and land, Modern Europe had other means and motives to justify its imperialistic behavior. Modern Europeans not only wanted to obtain land; they also wanted to achieve power—socially, politically, and economically. The majority of the motivations for imperialism were derived from the industrial revolution. The European countries strived to obtain control over colonies in order to control strategic passages, such as the Straits of Gibraltar and the Suez Canal. They also wanted the control of overseas bases to keep ships and troops supplied and ready whenever needed.

Not all European imperialistic motives were selfish though. Several Europeans went overseas to try to help unfortunate people, feeling as if they were offering their "blessings" to the "pitiful heathens." European governments imposed their laws on the people and taught them how to rule in a structured fashion. European missionaries spread Christianity, and humanitarians promoted public health and education. Many European countries also wanted to increase their wealth; therefore, they had economic reasons for their imperialistic behavior. The great economic financiers, a few wealthy men—for example, Cecil John Rhodes—used their wealth and social connections to induce the government to protect their investments through political dominance over undeveloped lands.

France, the United Kingdom, and Germany were the three main imperialist powers in Africa during the late nineteenth century. In February 1885, the main European powers signed the Berlin Act, which formalized the process of the partition of Africa. The Act included the guidelines of how each country was to define its territories. The colonies on the West Coast of Africa were a legacy of the fortunes that could be made out of the slave trade.

The French negotiated treaties with several African leaders from a powerful military position. France focused on the military direction of the expansion by going from fort to fort and taking control. Using military tactics to obtain territory, they secured themselves economically. The French, who were rather harsh in their administration and their attempts to increase their economic footholds, used forced labor and imprisonment of Africans to maintain and expand their interests. Whenever possible, the French fostered the production of groundnuts and cotton and imposed taxation.

The United Kingdom's imperialistic activities in Africa from 1869 to 1912 had different motives. The United Kingdom wanted to colonize, find new markets and materials, attain revenge and world prestige, convert natives to Christianity, and spread the English style of orderly government. The United Kingdom wanted to control Africa in order to be financially secure. They also wanted to safeguard the country and protect their landholdings from German or French invasion. The British wanted to protect the Suez Canal in northeast Africa and the Cape Route to the east. Control over the Suez Canal allowed them financial superiority and comfort.

Germany, a country formed from imperialism itself, had two main reasons for involvement in the scramble for Africa. Germany modeled itself after France and the United Kingdom and knew these two countries would not waste their time, resources, and energy on an unprofitable effort. Germany thought, if they obtained colonies in Africa, then they would also dominate, such as the two great powers did. Otto Von Bismarck, Germany's leader for imperialism, and the rest of Germany simply longed to see their country get ahead. Germany also wanted to play the "game." They felt colonization in Africa would help Germany and force others to reckon with them.[1]

The British Colonization of Zimbabwe

Long before the arrival of Arab traders, Portuguese and British missionaries, treasure hunters, and the British South Africa Company (BSAC) pioneer column, indigenous populations occupied the country now called Zimbabwe. The Tonga and Lozi were in the north. Manyika and Ndau were in the east. Karanga, Shangaan, and Venda were in the southeast. Zezuru, Korekore, and Tavara were in the central. Matebele and Kalanga were in the west. The Matebeles came later, when they escaped from the uprising against Tshaka, the Zulu of South Africa. With the assistance of Robert Moffat, the missionary, the Matebeles settled in what is now known as Matebeleland, which the Kalanga tribe sparsely occupied at that time. The Matebeles encouraged tribes under their domination to assimilate the Matebele culture and language through forced marriages and military conscription of the host tribe's young men and boys. Also escaping from the uprising against Tshaka the Zulu was Soshangana, who settled in Mozambique and southeastern Zimbabwe. The Shangaans integrated into the local tribes through intermarriage. All these tribes respected their tribal boundaries and did not go to war against one another for territorial gains. However, Matebele warriors conducted

---

1. *Black majority government or meritocracy? Bulletin 14, no. 4 (1976): 116–136.*

organized raids against other tribes for women, military conscription, cattle, and grain. The situation changed with the arrival of the BSAC-sponsored occupation force, that was composed of men from all walks of life including doctors, builders, carpenters, welders, blacksmiths, and men of war recruited from the United Kingdom, Canada, Australia, New Zealand, Europe, and so forth.

The Rudd Concession, which granted sweeping commercial and legal powers to Cecil John Rhodes, facilitated the BSAC occupation of Zimbabwe. Armed with the Concession, Rhodes used his considerable financial resources, derived from his control of De Beers and the gold fields of South Africa, to form the BSAC, which subsequently obtained a charter from Her Majesty Queen Victoria in 1899. The charter granted the BSAC the right to operate in all southern Africa, north of Bechuanaland (Botswana), north and west of the Zuid-Afrikaanse Republiek (Transvaal), and west of Portuguese East Africa. The charter did not stipulate a northern limit, facilitating the realization of Cecil John Rhodes' dream of creating a British Empire corridor from Cape to Cairo.

The original BSAC pioneer column left Kimberley, South Africa, for Rhodesia in May 1890 and established Fort Victoria in August 1890 without any recorded resistance from the local population. A party of pioneers, guided by the famous hunter, Courtney Selous, continued further north. In September 1890, they raised the British flag, the Union Jack, at Fort Salisbury (now called Harare). The BSAC pioneers immediately dispatched a party to eastern Rhodesia to obtain a concession from Chief Mutasa, thereby securing the country's eastern border with Mozambique. The Shona tribes allowed the BSAC pioneers to settle in their areas in exchange for protection against the Matebele raiders and the Portuguese. However, eastern border disputes persisted, finally leading to an armed confrontation between the BSAC pioneers and the Portuguese in 1891. The Portuguese were defeated, and the boundary dispute was settled at the Anglo-Portuguese Convention in June 1891.

In 1892, Dr. Leander Starr Jameson, a close associate and task man of Cecil John Rhodes, was appointed chief magistrate for Mashonaland. Jameson, believing the Matebele could be absorbed peacefully into the country's labor force, attempted securing a temporary method of coexistence with the Matebele based on segregation by designating a boundary between them and the Mashona. He also tried preventing the Matebele from entering Mashonaland except as laborers. Before the arrival of the BSAC, the Matebeles entered Mashonaland on protection tax collection-related issues. The Matebeles were not prepared to be deprived of their traditional raiding grounds for women, military recruits, cattle, and grain. After numerous incidents, matters finally came to a head in 1893, when a

Matebele impi raided the Fort Victoria area to punish local inhabitants for alleged cattle theft. After a skirmish between the pioneers and a Matebele impi, Jameson finally decided the Matebele had to be put down and officially declared war against the Matebeles on June 18, 1893. Despite the vast numerical superiority of the Matebele, the BSAC pioneers defeated the Matebele with their sophisticated weapons and greater mobility on horseback. King Lobengula burnt down his royal capital of Bulawayo and fled northwards. During the pursuit of the Matebele, Major Allan Wilson and thirty-one men were trapped and killed on the banks of the flooding Shangani River following a fierce engagement that ended the uprising. Lobengula died somewhere in the Wankie area during the flight of the Matebele[2].

After being satisfied with the total occupation of Zimbabwe, Dr. Jameson decided to consolidate British imperialism in southern Africa through the invasion of Afrikaans Transvaal. Unfortunately, Jameson was defeated, captured, humiliated, and jailed for his involvement in the abortive invasion in December 1895. The Jameson raid came at a time when Rhodes was vigorously campaigning for the unification of the British and Afrikaans republics under the British flag. The Mashonas and Matebeles decided to end white domination in Rhodesia due to a rinder pest epidemic, which spread throughout the country in 1896, decimating cattle herds. White veterinary officers aggravated matters by shooting cattle belonging to blacks in an effort to prevent the disease from spreading. Other causes of discontent among the blacks were BSAC's land and development labor policies and the introduction of a taxation system. In the absence of the troops who had accompanied Jameson on the invasion of the Transvaal, the second uprising proved far more serious than the 1893 rebellion. Namely, the BSAC was forced to call for reinforcements from the British Cape Colony. Sir Fredrick Carrington, setting out with a force of 2,000 white and 600 black soldiers, finally drove the remaining Matebele impis into the Matopos hills, where they were blockaded for several months. Rhodes then arrived in Rhodesia from London and decided to become personally involved in the matter. In October 1896, he went into the Matopos, held a surrender meeting with the Matebele chiefs, and persuaded them to relinquish their arms and surrender peacefully.

By that time, the rebellion against BSAC occupation had spread to Mashonaland. The Mashona rebellion led by spiritual mediums, Nehanda, Kaguvi, Mukwati, Mashayamombe, Mangwende, Gwenzi, and others, was finally put down by

---

2.   Among the Matabeles D. Carnegie (1894, repr. 1970); J. M. Selby, Shaka's Heirs
       (1971).

the BSAC police with the assistance of a force of mounted infantry under the command of Colonel Edwin Alderson, who later became Inspector General of the Canadian Forces in World War 1. Nehanda, Kaguvi, and others were sentenced to death and executed at Fort Salisbury. Although the BSAC did not discover a major gold field, numerous small mines were opened up, and steady streams of immigrants, keen to escape from the depression following the Boer War, were arriving from South Africa. While the BSAC did not do much to initially encourage agriculture, land was plentiful and handed out freely. After much trial and error, farming became established. Within twenty years of the first pioneers entering Rhodesia, the ground roots of a sound agricultural industry had been established.

After 1910, anti-BSAC sentiments mounted in Southern Rhodesia. An increasing number of settlers felt the country should be placed under British rule. However, the United Kingdom did not see the advantage of taking over the burden from the BSAC at that time. The BSAC attempted to fuse the two Rhodesias—Northern and Southern—during the years immediately after World War I. However, Southern Rhodesia was wary of the large black population she would acquire by this move, and the scheme was finally rejected in 1917. During the following year, the Privy Council handed down a long-awaited decision concerning the land question in Southern Rhodesia. Elected members of the legislature contended the BSAC did not own unallocated land in its private capacity and revenue from unallocated land should be used for the administration of the territory, instead of being appropriated by the BSAC.

Following the Privy Council's decision in favor of the legislature, the BSAC lost the economic motivation to govern the territory and made a claim for reimbursement of administrative deficits from the British government. A South African solution seemed to be the best answer to the Rhodesian dilemma. A referendum was held in 1922 to determine whether the territory should become the fifth province of South Africa. The anti-Unionist movement carried the vote by a majority of 2,785. The British government formally annexed Southern and Northern Rhodesia in 1923 and paid some compensation to the BSAC. The first general election was held in 1924, and Charles Coghlan became the first prime minister of Southern Rhodesia after the territory was granted self-government. However, the British government did retain the right of assent in matters pertaining to black rights.

A brief look at the franchise and the system of land tenure during the period of 1923 to 1953 is warranted. With the granting of self-government in 1923, Rhodesia retained the Cape Colony system, which gave voting rights to blacks and whites who owned property to the value of at least £150 equivalent USD 300 or had an annual income of at least £100 equivalent USD 200. A simple language test in English accompanied both means. These voting qualifications for a common voters' roll were maintained until 1951 when the financial qualifications were raised. The Morris Carter Commission was convened to review the land redistribution matter in 1925. Its recommendations were embodied in the Land Apportionment Act of 1930 (amended in 1941), which allocated the land. Fifty percent was given to whites. Thirty percent was given to blacks. The rest remained unallocated.

The Federation of Rhodesia and Nyasaland, established on August 1, 1953, was a short-lived state in southern Africa. Existing until the end of 1963, it was composed of the former British colonies of Northern Rhodesia, Southern Rhodesia, and the Nyasaland Protectorate. The goal was to create a midway between the newly independent and socialist black independent states and the white-dominated governments of South Africa, Rhodesia, Angola, and Mozambique. The Federation ultimately floundered because the black African nationalists wanted a greater share of power than the white-dominated settler population was willing to concede. Sir Godfrey Martin Huggins was prime minister of the Federation of Rhodesia and Nyasaland from 1953 to 1956. Sir Roy Welensky followed from 1956 until the Federation's dissolution in 1963. The Federation officially collapsed December 31, 1963, when Northern Rhodesia was granted independence from the United Kingdom as Zambia, under Kenneth Kaunda, while Nyasaland gained independence as Malawi, under the leadership of Life President Hastings Kamuzu Banda. The remaining British colony of Southern Rhodesia simply became Rhodesia.

The British refused to grant independence to minority-ruled Rhodesia. As a last resort, Rhodesia unilaterally declared independence, triggering a civil war that did not end until 1980. The British government was fully aware of the direction of events in Rhodesia and attempted preventing the Unilateral Declaration of Independence. The British Prime Minister, Sir Harold Wilson, dispatched two of his ministers to Rhodesia and invited the Rhodesian prime minister, Ian Douglas Smith, to visit London in October 1965. When this failed, Sir Harold Wilson personally visited Rhodesia towards the end of October 1965, making an eleventh hour bid to avert the Unilateral Declaration of Independence. His efforts failed, and Ian Smith announced Rhodesia's Unilateral Declaration of Independence on November 11, 1965. In retaliation, the British government removed Rhodesia from the sterling area. British exports of capital goods to Rhodesia were banned. The purchase of Rhodesian tobacco was discontinued. Rhodesia was denied access to the London capital market. The Commonwealth Sugar Agreement was terminated, insofar it impacted Rhodesia. Rhodesian passports were declared illegal documents. The Southern Rhodesia Act outlawed most trade with Rhodesia on November 16. On December 5, 1965, the British government seized Rhodesian assets worth £9 million equivalent to USD 18 million in the British Reserve Bank.

In spite of these measures, Wilson's predictions that the Rhodesian government would collapse "within a matter of weeks"[3] did not prove true. The United Kingdom took the Rhodesian matter to the United Nations Security Council on April 9, 1966, and obtained the world body's consent to impose the Beira blockade to prevent oil destined for Rhodesia from reaching the Mozambique port of Beira. The British oil blockade was confined to the Port of Beira while the port of Maputo and South African ports remained accessible to Rhodesian oil imports. The British government expected the oil embargo to bring the Rhodesian government to its knees. At the Commonwealth Conference held in January 1967, Sir Harold Wilson again emphasized the rebel government could not survive an oil embargo for long and the rebellion would end in weeks rather than months. British warships prevented several tankers from reaching Beira during April 1966, but most of Rhodesia's oil requirements had been at that time rerouted through the then-apartheid South African ports of Durban and Port Elizabeth. Surprising enough, based on the assumption that sanctions would harm the majority Africans more than the minority whites, the British government voted against a United Nations resolution on mandatory sanctions against Rhodesia.

While the Land Apportionment Act did guarantee the land rights of blacks, thereby protecting them from exploitation, it created much bitterness and remained a most contentious issue in Rhodesia. Legislation by the Smith government amending the Land Apportionment Act to give blacks access to agricultural, industrial, and commercial land resulted in the most critical test of the Ian Smith regime leadership since the Unilateral Declaration of Independence when twelve members of the Rhodesia Front party opposed the prime minister in parliament. The Land Apportionment Act was redrafted in 1969 and renamed the Land Tenure Act. In terms of the new Act, blacks and whites were allocated an equal area of 45 million acres (18,210,000 hectares) apiece. The remaining land, approximately 10 million acres (4,047,000 hectares), was designated national land for use as parks, nature reserves, and so forth.[4]

---

3.   Commonwealth Conference, Nigeria, Lagos.1966 Sir Harold Wilson speech

The Second Chimurenga Struggle and Apartheid South Africa Peace Initiatives

In 1966, armed Zimbabwe African National Liberation Army (ZANLA) guerrillas fought a fierce battle against the Rhodesian security forces at Chinhoyi in which all the seven fighters, including David Guzuzu, perished. This battle—now referred to as the Chinhoyi battle—signaled the beginning of the Second Chimurenga armed struggle. Six years later, on December 21, 1972, armed guerrillas attacked a white farm in the Centenary area. This incident marked the beginning of a protracted guerrilla war. As tension mounted throughout the northern areas of the country, the government in Salisbury decided to close the country's border with Zambia until the Zambian authorities gave the assurance that no anti-Rhodesian terrorists would be harbored in their country. Zambia closed her border with Rhodesia on February 1, 1973, and kept it closed, despite Rhodesia's decision three days later to reopen her side of the border. The border area remained tense as an increasing number of land mine and shooting incidents were reported. The most significant of these encounters occurred in the vicinity of the Victoria Falls on May 15, 1973, when rifle fire from the Zambian side of the Zambezi River killed two innocent Canadian tourists.

On July 5, 1973, a large group of armed freedom fighters abducted 295 African pupils and teachers from the St. Albert's Mission School in the northeast region of the country. Rhodesian security forces succeeded in rescuing all but eight of those abducted.[5] In August 1973, serious unrest erupted on the campus of the University of Rhodesia, following initial student protest about low wages paid to African workers at the university. The increased guerrilla activity also forced the Rhodesian government to extend national service from nine months to one year. In June 1973, while the Victoria Falls incident was still clear in every mind, several officials from the British Foreign Office arrived in Rhodesia for talks with the Rhodesian government and leaders of the African National Council (ANC). During the last months of 1973, further guerrilla incursions finally became such a menace that the Rhodesian government started offering cash rewards for information leading to the capture or death of freedom fighters. The most notable of those who gallantly participated in the northeastern offensive were guerrilla commanders Kid Ma Wrong of the Centenary area, Mudzimundi-

---

4.   Black majority government or meritocracy Rhodesia Bulletin 14, no. 4 (1976): 116–136.
5.   Terrorists abduct school childrenand teachers fron St Albert's Mission—Rhodesia Herald News Paper 6 July 1973.

ringe of Bindura, and others. Freedom fighters launched a rocket and mortar attack on the Harare fuel tank depot, creating an inferno over Harare and thereby prompting the apartheid government of South Africa to send firefighting reinforcements to the aid of the Rhodesian government.

The Portuguese coup on April 25, 1974, had an immediate, wide-ranging impact on the political landscape of southern Africa. By the middle of the year, a Frelimo-led caretaker government had been installed in Lourengo Marques, resulting in the unavailability of the port of Beira and Lourenco Marques, which were Rhodesia's main trade outlets. A new railway link from Rutenga to Beit Bridge was completed and became Rhodesia's lifeline to the outside world. This provided an additional railway line between Rhodesia and South Africa, the backbone of the Smith regime. The import route through the Rutenga-Beitbridge railway line became a target for daily guerrilla ambushes. In the general election held on July 31, 1974, the Rhodesia Front Party again won all fifty white constituencies.

South African Prime Minister, John Vorster launched his famous policy of détente with Africa during a speech to the senate in Cape Town on October 23, 1974. President Kenneth Kaunda of Zambia reacted a few days later, welcoming the speech as, "the voice of reason for which Africa and the world have been waiting."[6] President Kaunda of Zambia encouraged black Rhodesian nationalists to unite, with a view of negotiating with the Rhodesian government, a course he and Vorster openly favored. Several leaders, including Ndabaningi Sithole and Joshua Nkomo, were released as a result of Vorster's détente efforts. On December 9, 1974, black leaders met in Lusaka and signed an agreement uniting the Zimbabwe African Peoples Union (ZAPU), Zimbabwe African National Union (ZANU), and the Front for the Liberation of Zimbabwe (FROLIZI), under the banner of the African National Council of Bishop Muzorewa. Two days after the meeting, Smith informed the country that the government was to hold a constitutional conference with the nationalists and nationalist leaders still in detention would be released. The prime minister indicated he expected terrorist incursions in Rhodesia to cease in reciprocation. South Africa also expected acts of terrorism to cease, and Vorster confirmed that South African police units originally sent to Rhodesia in 1967 and 1968 would be withdrawn if terrorists were to discontinue their own activities. Despite a definite lull in terrorist incursions, these soon increased again. On January 10, 1975, the Rhodesian government stopped the release of political detainees. Security measures were again tightened, and military

---

6.   Avoid secret political deals—Isaya Muriwo Sithole Financial Gazette 3/11/2004

officials later admitted their relaxed vigilance during the initial stages of détente had enabled terrorists to increase activities in certain areas of eastern and north-eastern Rhodesia. In March 1975, Sithole was again arrested on charges of plotting the assassination of the entire Rhodesian cabinet. The second arrest of Sithole caused an immediate outcry in African circles, and pressure was brought upon South Africa to bring about his release. Smith led a high-ranking Rhodesian government delegation to a conference with the South African prime minister on March 15, 1975. Political rivals assassinated Herbert Chitepo, leader of the ZANU movement, four days later in Lusaka, revealing the serious rift within the nationalist movement.

The Rhodesian Special Court renewed the detention order on Sithole at the beginning of April 1975, but, following an appeal by Muzorewa that was supported by the South African government, he was released on April 6, 1975. Efforts to unite the Rhodesian government and the various nationalists were intensified during the next two months, as the South African government played a prominent role in attempting to bring the interested parties to the conference table. Tension again mounted among supporters of the various black movements. Thirteen people were killed, and twenty-eight people were injured when the police opened fire on a crowd of several thousand blacks in the township of Highfields in Harare on June 2, 1975.

The initial talks held between Ian Douglas Smith, the Rhodesian prime minister, and the ANC leaders on June 15, 1975, ended in an impasse as the parties were unable to agree on the venue for a constitutional conference. The Rhodesian minister of information and several members of parliament flew to Lusaka ten days later for talks with Kaunda, and they reached an agreement for a conference to be held on neutral ground soon after their arrival. The conference was held on the bridge near the Victoria Falls in railway carriages provided by the South African Railways on August 25, 1975. Presidents Kaunda and Vorster attended the meeting, which may be regarded as the climax of the détente exercise, despite the fact that Smith and the black nationalists failed to reach an agreement. The ANC disintegrated after the Victoria Falls meeting, as Joshua Nkomo formed his own internal wing with Muzorewa and Sithole leading the external faction. The front line presidents, notably Julius Nyerere of Tanzania and Samora Machel of Mozambique, believed political settlement was impossible.[7] This led directly to the establishment of the Zimbabwe People's Army (ZIPA), a military group con-

---

7.   Rhodesian Black groupings in disarray. Rhodesia Bulletin 14, nos. 7–8 (1976): 268–270

sisting of former ZANU and ZAPU cadres. ZIPA forces, led by an eighteen-man high command under former ZANU field commander Rex Nhongo, launched a new offensive against Rhodesia on January 18, 1976. This onslaught was perhaps the single, most significant element in the political struggle for Rhodesia and quickly led to an escalation of the conflict, especially along the Mozambique border, where incidents became increasingly common. South African and Cuban involvement in the Angolan civil war as well as the threat of Cuban involvement in Rhodesia again fixed the international spotlight on southern Africa and the Rhodesian issue, leading to the Kissinger initiative and the abortive Geneva Conference.

Smith met Henry Kissinger, the American secretary of state, for talks in Pretoria, South Africa. Smith then returned to Rhodesia to announce he had accepted the Kissinger proposals, calling for the establishment of an interim government, and a handover to black majority rule within two years. The proposals included American-British assurances and guarantees for the white minority. The agreement called for a halt to sanctions and the terrorist war. The black nationalists and a number of front line presidents all rejected the Kissinger proposals and intimated they had never been party to them, the impression Kissinger had given according to Smith and Vorster. The Salisbury government and the black leaders assembled at Geneva under the chairmanship of Ivor Richard, a British United Nations representative, in October 1976 to try to see how the Kissinger proposals could best be implemented. However, dissent among the black delegates marked the conference from the beginning. When it broke up for Christmas, advancement had not been made. In fact, the assembly of the conference originally scheduled for mid-January 1977 had been indefinitely postponed because of the deadlock.[8]

The armed struggle intensified and escalated throughout the country, thereby forcing the British government to call for the Lancaster House peace talks in 1979. The peace talks resulted in a compromise between the Zimbabwe-Rhodesia government, the Patriotic Front, and the British government. Both parties agreed to independence under the Lancaster House Independence Constitution. It included a clause on Freedom from Deprivation of Property, which later became the source of problems that led to strained relations between the Zimbabwe government, the ex-combatants and landless natives, commercial farmers, the British government, and the international community.[9]

8.   *Rhodesian Black groupings in disarray. Bulletin 14, nos. 7–8 (1976): 268–270*
9.   *Ibid.*

Analysis of the Land-Ownership Conflict Background

The Arabs wanted to trade with the natives and spread the doctrine of Islam. Likewise, European imperialism was necessary for the spread of Christianity and civilization in the Dark Continent. The Berlin Conference held from November 1884 to February 1885 was also necessary for the establishment of an organized partition of Africa among the industrializing nations for sources of raw materials to fuel and sustain the industrial revolution in Europe. The partition of Africa took natural geographic boundaries and the ethnic distribution of the native populations of Africa into consideration. In the case of Zimbabwe, the partition of Africa and Cecil John Rhodes' ambition to establish a British imperial corridor from Cape to Cairo caused Shona tribe dialects to be spoken on both sides of the Zimbabwe and Mozambique borders. Zimbabwe Ndebele was spoken in Zimbabwe and northern South Africa, and Tonga was spoken south of the Zambezi in Zimbabwe and north of the Zambezi in Zambia.

The Kalanga people are found on both sides of the Zimbabwe and Botswana border. Before the partition of Africa, rivers and mountains were recognized boundaries. Populations concentrated in clusters based on tribe and language. In the case of Rhodesia and Mozambique, the locals could cross the artificial borders—legally or illegally—with the knowledge of the colonial power administrators on both sides of the border. The partition of Africa border demarcations was a compromise between natural borders and ethnic group distributions. The United Nations and the African Union recognized the borders demarcated and agreed upon at the Berlin Conference.

Of all the concessions given to Europeans by King Lobengula of Matabeleland, the most critical to Zimbabwe was the Rudd Concession. The Rudd Concession of 1888, which was alleged to have been fraudulently obtained from King Lobengula, became the vehicle through which colonialists obtained mineral rights in Mashonaland. The concession provided Rhodes with the momentum to obtain a royal charter in 1889, which, among other rights, granted the BSAC authority to administer and govern the region that encompasses present-day Zimbabwe. The charter was granted, despite King Lobengula's statements that he had been deceived. Lobengula repudiated the Rudd Concession, stating that he would "not recognise the paper, as it contains neither my words nor the words of those who got it."[10] Her Majesty Queen Victoria's Advisor's response to King Lobengula was that it "would be unwise to exclude white men."[11] The Rudd Concession was countered by the Lippert Land Concession of April 1889, which

10.   Zimbabwe Under Siege by Gregory Elich August 26, 2002

reflected competing British and German aspirations to acquire the same territory. The Lippert Concession was also deceitfully obtained from King Lobengula. With the collusion of the BSAC and without King Lobengula's knowledge, the BSAC soon purchased the Lippert Concession. King Lobengula voluntarily signed the Rudd Concession, but he did not know of its contents and long-term implications. He must have interpreted it as a simple treasure trophy hunting and mineral prospecting concession whose activities were to be limited to Mashonaland. King Lobengula signed the Rudd Concession, despite other European concession seekers advising him not to sign it due to its future implications on the government of his kingdom. The European civilized legal implications of signing a piece of paper did not have any meaning to King Lobengula.

BSAC pledged to give King Lobengula £100 equivalent USD 200 per month, a steamboat on the Zambezi River, or the sum of £500 equivalent USD 1,000 in lieu as compensation, as well as 1,000 rifles and 100,000 rounds of ammunition. Modern scholars view the Rudd Concession as a great trick due to the fact King Lobengula was illiterate and had never seen a steamboat before. Not only that, a journey from his capital of Bulawayo to the Zambezi River could have taken as much as one month, which was too long for a king to be out of the royal kraal. At the time of the signing of the Rudd Concession, King Lobengula had nothing to buy with £100 equivalent USD 200 per month.

At the end of the day, the pledges were never honored due to King Lobengula's involvement in the Matebeleland uprising. Based on the Rudd Concession, Cecil John Rhodes mobilized a group of men from all walks of life from the United Kingdom, America, Canada, Germany, and so forth with instructions to occupy Zimbabwe through Mashonaland. King Lobengula sent an army to intercept the pioneer column in the Fort Tuli area, but he authorized them to continue with their journey to Mashonaland under the impression that the mission was for hunting and mineral prospecting. King Lobengula was not aware the pioneer column was coming to permanently settle. However, the Shona chiefs welcomed the arrival of the pioneer column as new settlers, in exchange for protection against the Matebele raiders. Armed with intelligence on protection needs, on arrival in Mashonaland, the pioneers dispatched a party to eastern Rhodesia to obtain a concession from Chief Mutasa, who also welcomed the arrival and settlement of the pioneer column in exchange for protection against the

---

11. Queen Victoria Advisor to Lobengula replied that it was unwise to include whitemen.

Shangaan raiders and the Portuguese. The eastern boundary dispute was settled at the Anglo-Portuguese Convention in June 1891.

In order to consolidate the BSAC occupation of Mashonaland and set the stage for the invasion of Matebeleland, Dr. Leander Starr Jameson was appointed chief magistrate for Mashonaland in 1892. King Lobengula was made to understand the Rudd Concession did not include Matebeleland. Hence, this is the reason why he did not stop the pioneer column from entering Mashonaland. In order to provoke war with the Matebeles, Dr. Jameson prevented the Matebeles from entering Mashonaland except as laborers. The Matebeles were not prepared to be deprived of their traditional raiding grounds and were not prepared to work for anybody. After numerous incidents, matters finally came to a head in 1893, when a Matebele army unit raided the Fort Victoria area to punish local blacks for cattle theft. This was a golden opportunity for Jameson to attack King Lobengula and subject the Matebeles under BSAC rule. After this incident, the BSAC declared war against King Lobengula, assembled an invasion force, and advanced toward the Matebeleland capital of Bulawayo. After heavy resistance, King Lobengula set Bulawayo afire, trekked north, and fought fierce battles against the pioneer column, notably the Alan Wilson patrol.

The BSAC army was reinforced with 2,000 white infantrymen and 600 native soldiers from the British Cape Colony who blockaded the Matebele army in the Matopos area. The Matebele army finally surrendered. Cecil John Rhodes summoned the remnants of the defeated Matebele chiefs to Matopos Hills for peace talks. The chiefs accepted the surrender conditions. The Matopos Hills later became Cecil John Rhodes' burial place. The defeat of the Matebeles marked the total colonization of the country now known as Zimbabwe. In the interest of spreading Christianity and western civilization, procuring raw materials for the industrial revolution, establishing markets and building an empire, the BSAC occupation of Zimbabwe was perhaps inevitable. The BSAC could not have achieved the stated diverse objectives without the establishment of a form of civilized English type administration in Rhodesia through negotiated concessions and the occasional use of force.

In order to develop the colony of Zimbabwe, the natives were forced to pay development tax or face arrest and being drafted into forced labor camps. The natives could not have avoided participation in development labor because tax could only be paid in cash. In order to have cash, one had to volunteer to work in development labor camps. Forced labor was instrumental to the development of commercial farms as well as construction of roads, airports, dams, and railway lines. The natives did not understand the potential benefits of the development projects. In their uncivilized opinion, forced labor was slavery. The continued sei-zure of land and livestock, resulted in the Mashona rebellion of 1896 led by spir-itual mediums and fighters. The BSAC reinforced with mounted infantry troops from the Cape Colony. They then (bloodily) suppressed the uprising and pub-licly executed the resistance leaders. The BSAC was trying to enforce a civilized system on illiterate natives, thereby resulting in the clash of cultures.

The reason for joining the Second Chimurenga armed struggle was to recover the land occupied by force through negotiations propelled by the use of force. Against this background, land issue ranked highest among the grievances moti-vating the indigenous black majority to launch the Second Chimurenga/Imfazwe to free the country from colonial oppression. Notably, "*mwana wevhu/umntwana womhlabati* (child of the soil)" became the nationalists' rallying call in the period preceding the liberation war. Herbert Chitepo, chairman of the Zimbabwe Afri-can National Union (ZANU) party, stated:

> I could go into the whole theories of discrimination, in legislation, in resi-dency, in economic opportunities, in education. I could go into that, but I will restrict myself to the question of land because I think this is very basic. To us the essence of exploitation, the essence of white domination, is domination over land. That is the real issue.[12]

The armed struggle targeted commercial farmers and forced them to desert their farms to seek refuge in the cities. The struggle followed the commercial farmers into towns and cities, striking fuel depots and power stations. It also dis-rupted transport services, thereby making movement unsafe and occasionally impossible in most areas. Fighting was necessary for both sides to engage in con-structive peace negotiations and accept the concept of majority African rule before independence.

In the interest of upholding the new world order of democracy, human rights, and freedom of association, the British government gradually granted self-gov-ernment and independence to the British African colonies. Despite this progres-sive policy, the British were reluctant to grant independence to southern African colonies, especially Kenya, South Africa, and Zimbabwe, due to the favorable cli-matic conditions as well as vast mineral and agricultural resources. South Africa became a union of British and Afrikaans Republics led by the majority Afrikaans under the British flag. The union of South Africa became a republic within the

---

12. *Herbert Chitepo, Zimbabwe African National Union Chairman—Speech on a trip to Australia in 1973*

British Commonwealth. (It left the group due to its inhuman apartheid policy.) After the defeat of Germany, southwest Africa became a United Nations trustee under South African administration while Tanganyika was placed under British administration.

The British granted independence without a fight to British West Africa, Ghana, Nigeria, Sierra Leone, Gambia, and British Cameroon. The agricultural and fauna-rich Kenya was of strategic importance to the United Kingdom. Hence, a man calling himself Sir Didan Kimathi, Knight Commander of the African Empire and Prime Minister of the Southern Hemisphere, led the Mau Mau rebellion. To qualify for membership, the Mau Mau rebellion required all volunteers to present the head of their colonial master. The British understood the continuation of the Mau Mau rebellion was a major threat to the existence of British colonialism in Kenya and Africa. This is the reason why the British welcomed the emergence of the Jomo Kenyatta-led Kenya African National Union (KANU), which advocated for independence through nonviolent means. Jomo Kenyatta was allegedly a Mau Mau guerrilla commander who disowned the armed struggle and sought to attain independence through negotiations. The Mau Mau rebels were not even invited to the Lancaster House negotiations. The postindependence government of Kenya ignored the contribution made by the Mau Mau rebels toward Kenyan independence. (In fact, the Mau Mau leaders are currently not even considered national heroes.) The landlocked Malawi with its agrarian-based economy and its neocolonialist government under British-trained surgeon and president Kamuzu Banda, was granted independence after minor civil disturbances. Kamuzu Banda later became an ally of Portuguese East Africa and apartheid South Africa. Zambia was hastily added onto the independence list after the discovery of alternative power transmission mediums, resulting in the decline of the value of copper on the world market. The British protectorates of semi-desert Botswana, mountainous Lesotho, and Swaziland were granted independence on request due to the absence of known mineral resources at that time.

The independent African colonies joined other former British colonies to form the British Commonwealth. The United Kingdom found itself under heavy pressure from the international community and the British Commonwealth countries to end the war in Zimbabwe and grant independence under majority African rule. The British granted independence to Zimbabwe without the freedom to redistribute land for ten years after independence.[13]

---

13. Ibid.

3.0 Land Ownership: The Most Critical Issue in Independence Negotiations

The land issue was inevitably central to any initiatives aimed at resolving the crisis in Rhodesia. It was a major stumbling block in all pre-independence negotiations initiatives, including those held in Geneva (1976) and Malta (1978). In 1977, British Foreign and Commonwealth Secretary Lord Owen and American Ambassador to the United Nations Andrew Young proposed the Anglo-American Proposals. Under which, the British and American governments pledged to contribute toward a fund for land reform, including paying compensation to white commercial farmers whose lands would be redistributed to landless blacks.

The near collapse of the Lancaster House conference in 1979 revolved around the land question. The Patriotic Front's position at the Lancaster House negotiations was that the primary cause of the liberation struggle in Zimbabwe was the recovery of land the people had been dispossessed of. To those involved in the talks, it was brought forward that the dispossession without compensation was not a thing of the distant past. Rather, it was an occurrence still within the memories of living people. Further arguing its case, the Patriotic Front objected to British provisions in the draft bill of rights, which sought to convert the freedom from deprivation of property into a right to retain privilege and perpetuate injustice while upholding the status quo.

The pledge by the British government, which was supported by the American government, to support the new political dispensation by agreeing to the creation of a fund to finance land reform in a new Zimbabwe broke the impasse at the constitutional talks. During an interview on the British Broadcasting Corporation (BBC) *Hard Talk* program in 2002, former British Commonwealth secretary general, Sir Shridath Ramphal, highlighted this fact. In the interview, Sir Shridath stated he had "intervened through the American government."[14] That intervention secured assurances for the Patriotic Front to resume talks and accept the British constitutional proposals. He added:

> The American ambassador, Mr. K. Brewster, with the support of Cyrus Vance, the secretary of state, persuaded the president who was Jimmy Carter to make an offer of U.S. assistance in conjunction with other countries, including Britain[15].

---

14.   *British Broadcasting Corporation (BBC) Hard Talk program interview Sir Shridath Ramphal in 2002*

In its announcement of the agreement that was finally reached, the Patriotic Front said the following:

> We have now obtained assurances that Britain, the United States of America, and other countries will participate in a multinational donor effort to assist in land, agricultural, and economic development programs. These assurances go a long way in allaying the great concern we have over the whole land question arising from the great need our people have for land and our commitment to satisfy that need.[16]

Lord Carrington, government chairman of the Lancaster House conference, acknowledged the centrality of the land issue and the enormity of the resources needed to redress the colonial legacy in a statement issued on October 11, 1979:

> We recognize that the future of Zimbabwe, whatever its political complexion, will wish to extend land ownership. The costs would be very substantial indeed, well beyond the capacity, in our judgement, of any individual donor country, and the British government cannot commit itself at this stage to a specific share in them. We should, however, be ready to support the efforts of the government of independent Zimbabwe to obtain international assistance for these purposes.[17]

However, the final agreement did not address the land problem adequately. The Patriotic Front accepted it on the understanding that the United Kingdom, the United States, and other donor nations would pay for land needed for resettlement. During a press conference on October 16, 1979, the president of Tanzania, Julius Nyerere, stated the land issue would be impossible for an independent government in Zimbabwe:

> To tax Zimbabweans in order to compensate people who took it away from them through the gun. Really the British cannot have it both ways. They made this an issue, and they are now making vague remarks mixing rural development aid with the question of land compensation. The two are separate...The British paid money to Kenya. That the future government of Zim-

---

15. *British Broadcasting Corporation (BBC) Hard Talk program interview Sir Shridath Ramphal in 2002*

16. *The Zimbabwe Patriotic Front rejoins the Lancaster House Independence negotiations October 1979*

17. Lancaster House Zimbabwe IndependenceConstitution negotiations-Partial record 1979.

babwe must pay compensation is a British demand, and the British must promise in London to make the money available.

As part of the Declaration of Rights, the British inserted Section 16 of the Draft Constitution, which sought to prohibit the compulsory acquisition of property of any description except under the authority of law. This required the acquiring authority to give reasonable notice of its intention to acquire the property in question. The property could only be acquired in the interest of defense, public order, public morality, public health, and town and country planning. In the event of compulsory acquisition, the acquiring authority would be required to pay prompt, adequate compensation. As part of the Declaration of Rights, Section 16 would be entrenched for a period of ten years from the date of independence. During this period, any amendment to the constitution would be on the basis of a one hundred percent parliamentary vote. That is, every parliament member must support any such amendment. In response to this attempt to perpetuate the status quo on land ownership, the Patriotic Front vehemently objected to the restrictions imposed on land acquisition. Such entrenchment of the Declaration of Rights was unduly restrictive of the sovereignty of the parliament of Zimbabwe. It also granted a veto to the minority, which was contradictory to democratic norms and the basic objective of the national liberation struggle itself. Furthermore, the concept of a willing buyer precluded the possibility of a planned, systematic process of land reform in the country.

Freedom from Deprivation of Property Clause—Lancaster House Agreement

1. Every person will be protected from having his property compulsorily acquired except when the acquisition is in the interests of defense, public safety, public order, public morality, public health, town and country planning, the development or utilizations of that or other property in such a manner as to promote the public benefit or, in the case of underutilized land, settlement of land for agricultural purposes. When property is wanted for one of these purposes, its acquisition will be lawful only on condition that the law provides for the prompt payment of adequate compensation and, where the acquisition is contested, that a court order is obtained. A person whose property is so acquired will be guaranteed the right of access to the High Court to determine the amount of compensation.

2.   Exception will be made for the taking of possession of property during a
      period of public emergency.

3.   Compensation paid in respect of loss of land to anyone who is a citizen
      of or ordinarily resident in Zimbabwe (or to a company the majority of
      whose shareholders are such persons) will, within a reasonable time, be
      remittable to any country outside Zimbabwe, free from any deduction,
      tax or charge in respect of its remission, but subject always to

      a.   its attachment, by order of a court, in connection with civil pro-
            ceedings; and

      b.   Reasonable restrictions as to the manner in which the payment is to
            be remitted. The Constitution will, on the same basis as in other
            Declarations of Rights, make clear that a number of transactions,
            which might be considered to involve an element of compulsory
            acquisition, will not be so regarded for the purposes of the Declara-
            tion of Rights.

4.   It will be made clear, for the avoidance of doubt, that the property cov-
      ered by this constitutional guarantee includes rights, whether vested or
      contingent, of individuals to receive benefits under a law, contract or
      scheme relating to the payment of pension benefits.[18]

Land Ownership and Commercial Farmer Resistance

Zimbabwe's black majority gained independence from British colonial rule after
a long war of African resistance. Following protracted negotiations in London
between the liberation armies and the newly elected Tory government of Prime
Minister Margaret Thatcher in 1979, it culminated in the Lancaster House
Agreement. The outcome ensured black majority rule based on the Lancaster
House Constitution, which sealed the fate of the racist Rhodesia regime led by
Ian Smith. An independent Zimbabwe ("Large House of Stone") was born, and
the Zimbabwe African National Union-Patriotic Front (ZANU-PF) formed the
government under President Robert Mugabe. The roots of the conflict over land
reform and the Zimbabwe government-backed campaign by the War Veterans
Association to take white settler land led back to that agreement.

---

18.   Zimbabwe Lancaster House Independence Constitution Clause on freedom from
      deprevation of property—1979

In all the demands made, the most significant political and diplomatic struggle over the course of those talks headed by Foreign Secretary Lord Carrington, which often threatened to collapse, was centered on land reform. Rhodesia's white minority rulers were relentlessly opposed to the liberation struggle and would concede nothing. The solution was sought in what became the Lancaster House negotiations. Liberation leaders were determined to ensure the United Kingdom, which backed the Rhodesia government, would not prevent Zimbabwe from beginning the battle to address the huge vested interests of white commercial farmers in any agreement. The roots of that crisis, of course, go back to colonial days.[19]

Returning to the Lancaster House Constitution, the government of Ian Douglas Smith in the late 1970s was becoming increasingly aware of the momentum and irreversibility of the armed struggle for independence. International pressure for Smith to revoke the Unilateral Declaration of Independence for Rhodesia that had been made in November 1965 did not help his situation. On the other hand, the war was already bringing a lot of fatigue to the national economy.

He earnestly wanted change as well, except he wanted change that would make him emerge as some kind of a winner. On the other hand, the United Kingdom, as the former colonial master, wanted to remove the Rhodesian headache fast, hence its insistence on a constitution leading to new elections should be urgently implemented.

At the end of the day, the process of developing the Lancaster House Constitution reflected a plethora of interests, but the final outcome was that a compromise had to be reached in the shortest amount of time because the revolutionaries always threatened to take the next plane back to the bush to resuscitate the devastating war. But, similar to the case of the current debate, the Lancaster process focused attention on political considerations. Mostly, the preoccupation was with determining how to ensure a relatively smooth political—and by implication—leadership transition. Even those fighting for this country's liberation were easily exhausted with the momentum they saw as the chance for black rule in Zimbabwe. For this reason, they accepted a clause that made it illegal for them to compulsorily acquire property, particularly land, from white owners for a full decade.

The danger of such a compromise is largely evident in what has happened in the political field since late 1999 when both civil society and emerging political

---

19. British Colonialism, Zimbabwe's Land Reform and Settler Resistance—Steve Lawton

establishments began vigorously questioning the status quo. Today, that clause in the Lancaster House Constitution largely defines Zimbabwe's political crisis. Ever since restless Zimbabweans began moving onto farms, the country has suffered a lot of bastardization that has transformed the country into a virtual pariah state.[20]

Analysis of the Importance of Land Ownership in Independence Negotiations

The British government-sponsored Lancaster House conference agenda prioritized the end of hostilities, return to British rule, holding of elections, and establishment of a nonracial state. The British convinced the Patriotic Front leadership to attend the Lancaster House conference by promising to establish a post independence land acquisition fund for the compensation of commercial farmers, offering their farms for sale under the "willing-seller, willing-buyer" principle. At the Lancaster House conference, the British changed the goalposts and offered to fund a portion of the land acquisition fund. The Zimbabwe government, the United States, and other donors would fund the rest. Julius Nyerere, former president of Tanzania, raised some concerns on the morality of making Zimbabweans contribute toward obtaining land that was forcefully taken from them. The Patriotic Front leadership could not accept independence with freedom from deprivation of property while the Rhodesians could not accept independence without freedom from deprivation of property. The Lancaster House conference was nearly derailed on several occasions due to the land redistribution issue. The Lancaster House Agreement clause on freedom from deprivation of property was a political compromise between the two diverse positions. The Patriotic Front accepted the inclusion of the clause on freedom from deprivation of property based on post independence land acquisition pledges the British and American governments made. By agreeing to the Lancaster House Agreement clause on the freedom from deprivation of property, the Patriotic Front leadership compromised the very reason why young Zimbabweans abandoned their homes to join the armed struggle.

The Patriotic Front was a fragile alliance, whose formation was forced on the Zimbabwe nationalists by the Organization of African Unity Liberation Committee and the Southern Africa Development Committee leadership in order to ensure a united liberation front during the Lancaster House negotiations. Imme-

---

20. *Constitutional debate preoccupied with leadership change, David Moyo University of Zimbabwe Department of Political Philosophy.*

diately after the conclusion of the Lancaster House Agreement, Robert Mugabe and Joshua Nkomo flew to their respective host capitals of Maputo and Lusaka. Before the two liberation movements returned to Zimbabwe, ZANU-PF announced it was going to contest the elections separate from Patriotic Front Zimbabwe African Peoples Union (PF-ZAPU). Independent political analysts concluded the Patriotic Front alliance negotiated for independence, focusing on their individual party future political roles in an independent Zimbabwe. Suspicion and hidden post independence political agendas was one of the reasons why they did not effectively address the land issue. Although land was an important topic of the independence negotiations, the Patriotic Front alliance leadership did not want to scare the minority white commercial farmers and industrialists, hence the adoption of the policy of national reconciliation after independence.

Bishop Abel Muzorewa and Dr. Sylus Mundawarara signed the Lancaster House Agreement on behalf of the Zimbabwe-Rhodesia internal settlement illegal government. The Zimbabwe-Rhodesian group accepted all the conditions—without any amendments—the British government presented. Similar to the Zimbabwe-Rhodesia constitution, which also recognized freedom from deprivation of property, the Lancaster House Constitution contained many safeguard clauses protecting the minority population. Dr. Mundawarara, formerly of Zimbabe African National Union (ZANU), lead by Reverend Ndabaningi Sithole, turned state witness in a ZANU treason trial in which he was an accomplice in a plan to import arms of war into the country from Zambia and plotted to assassinate the entire Rhodesian cabinet. Amongst those implicated in the Ian Smith cabinet assassination plot was the Reverend Ndabaningi Sithole, who was sentenced to a prison term, which was later suspended due to pressure from the international community and Apartheid South Africa. The Zimbabwe-Rhodesian group sought an end to the war, which they knew could not be won in the battlefield. Bishop Muzorewa envisioned an independent Zimbabwe with the white minority controlling the means of production including land, industry, and commerce. The Zimbabwe-Rhodesia government accepted the idea of independence under a neocolonialist government with a majority black cabinet. Via the inclusion of the clause on freedom from deprivation of property after independence, all parties to the Lancaster House Agreement accepted the Zimbabwe-Rhodesia government principle of gradual transformation from neocolonialist to genuine independence. The British government—and the international community as well—wanted a lasting solution to the Zimbabwe independence issue. The Lancaster House Agreement did not meet the aspirations of the landless majority and the demobilized ex-combatants because it allowed for a staggered, organized land redistribution process.

The inclusion of a clause on freedom from deprivation of property and land in Zimbabwe was influenced by lessons learnt from Marxist revolutionary land and property nationalization policies implemented in neighboring, post independence Mozambique. Immediately after independence, the Popular Front for the Liberation of Mozambique (FRELIMO) Marxist government supported the masses in a socialist revolution, which resulted in most of the descendents of the former Portuguese colonial masters deserting their properties voluntarily or by force and seeking refuge in then-Rhodesia, South Africa, and Portugal. The absentee landlords—under the leadership of businessman Jorge Jardim and other capitalists as well as Rhodesian and South African governments—financially and logistically supported the launching of the Mozambique National Resistance Movement (RENAMO). The principal objective of RENAMO was to remove the FRELIMO government by force and replace it with a neocolonialist regime. The Mozambique rebel war ended with the signing of a Italian government-sponsored peace agreement in October 1992. The successful disarmament, demobilization, and reintegration of the rebel RENAMO forces into the national army and other state security institutions as well as the holding of free and fair elections resulted in the Mozambican government allowing the absentee landlords to return and participate in the economic recovery and development of Mozambique. The FRELIMO government allowed the properties' original owners to return and negotiate with the properties' current occupiers for the peaceful repossession of their properties under government mediation. At all cost, the British government and the international community wanted to prevent postindependence confrontation between the commercial farmers and the landless, which could have resulted in a brain drain and white exodus from independent Zimbabwe.

According to sources within the former Rhodesian army, General Peter Walls and other senior army officers planned to stage a coup if the Patriotic Front won the elections. For that reason, the announcement of the election results was delayed while a solution was sought to avert the planned coup. After consultations with the front line states, it was agreed that General Peter Walls would become the commander in chief of all forces loyal to the former Rhodesian government and the Patriotic Front. General Peter Walls was later declared *persona non grata* and asked to resign from the army. The British and the international community did not support the Rhodesian military coup idea because the result could have plunged the country back to a bloody civil war. It was unclear if the

Zimbabwe-Rhodesia government would have supported the planned military takeover if the Patriotic Front had won the elections. The Patriotic Front factions needed the support of the minority white community to guarantee the sustainability of the postconflict economy and, particularly, the agricultural and industrial sectors. Despite the ZANU government policy of reconciliation, some reactionary, ex-Rhodesians in the military detonated large quantities of ammunition at Inkomo barracks while those in the air force destroyed military airplanes. Those implicated in the air force sabotage were arrested, only to be released and sent home to the United Kingdom. The British government paid compensation for the destroyed aircraft and continued supplying spare parts to the Air Force of Zimbabwe.

The majority of the ex-combatants in the independence war were from rural, agricultural areas, but they were deliberately offered reintegration opportunities via trade/vocational training and cash grants. Because of inappropriate reintegration, the ex-combatants failed to transform from military to civilian life. Under the leadership of Chenjerai Hunzwi, a Polish-trained doctor, the ex-combatants staged a few demonstrations seeking government intervention on their deteriorating social welfare. The government conceded to their demands by presidential decree, thereby forcing the government to grant hefty, lump-sum pensions and monthly allowances to the ex-combatants. After realizing the government did not have the authority to redistribute land to the landless, the landless and ex-combatants who failed to adjust from military to civilian life began invading and occupying commercial farms, seizing cattle and equipment throughout the country. Recovery of the agriculturally rich land occupied by descendents of commercial farmers, which they had gained through negotiations and by use of force, was one of the reasons why ex-combatants were prepared to pay the ultimate price during the war of liberation. Although the government was not directly involved in what became land invasions, it was held responsible in its capacity as the recognized custodian of law and order in the country. The Zimbabwean government was accused of failing to protect Zimbabweans of British origin against occasionally armed ex-combatants and landless farm invaders. Some of the invasions were violent, resulting in deaths of commercial farmers and their dependents, including farm workers. These commercial farmers were Zimbabweans by birth and did not have any alternative home except Zimbabwe.

With a two-thirds majority in parliament, the Zimbabwean government began implementing constitutional amendments designed to authorize the acquisition of land without compensation, which resulted in legal battles between the government and commercial farmers. The only alternative for the commercial farmers was to support a change in government through the ballot box. In order to accelerate a constitutional regime change, the commercial farmers supported and financed the formation of the Movement for Democratic Change.

The British were correct in their capacity as the colonial masters when they pledged for the organized land acquisition program under their own conditions and at their own pace, independent from how loud the landless were demanding. For the original ex-combatants, after twenty years without being granted access to land, most had engaged in other sustainable income-generating activities instead of waiting for land that never came. Some of the ex-combatants became carpenters, teachers, lawyers, policemen, soldiers, and even businessmen during the landless, postindependence period of twenty years. The ex-combatants from agricultural-based societies felt betrayed by the Mugabe government because of its failure to deliver the land at independence. Land repossession was the most influential motivating factor for people to join the armed struggle. Those who perished during the armed struggle would have been surprised to come back to life and see the land was still under the control of the minority white commercial farmers after twenty years of independence. Basically, the Lancaster House Agreement provided political power without control of the land and means of production.

The British government was prepared to grant independence to the Zimbabwe-Rhodesia government if the Patriotic Front had decided to withdraw from the peace negotiations. The Zimbabwe-Rhodesia government had accepted the Lancaster House Agreement including the clause on freedom from deprivation of property. The British had the power to legitimize the Zimbabwe-Rhodesia government by appointing a resident governor, calling for elections, and granting independence to Zimbabwe—with or without the participation of the Patriotic Front. Under such a situation, the Patriotic Front could have found itself fighting a democratically elected and internationally recognized government. The Patriotic Front leadership did not have any alternative except acceptance of the Lancaster House Agreement, including the clause on freedom from deprivation of property. The front line states wanted to see an end to the protracted war, which was also impacting their national economies and threatening the security of their nationals.

The people of Zimbabwe voted for the Patriotic Front, ZANU, and ZAPU to bring an end to the war. The electorate was aware that voting for the Zimbabwe-Rhodesian political parties would result in the Patriotic Front refusing to accept the results of the elections and resuming the guerrilla war with bases inside Zimbabwe.[21] With the majority of ex-combatants hailing from agricultural backgrounds, the government could not have encouraged reintegration through the establishment of sustainable, income-generating agricultural activities when the government did not have the freedom to redistribute land. The problem is that the ex-combatants and the landless have been waiting for more than twenty years to have their entitlement to their motherland restored. The return of the ex-combatants and other displaced populations resulted in the overcrowding of the semi-arid areas left available for indigenous population settlements. Twenty years after independence, the land problem resurfaced, haunting the liberation struggle leadership. Whenever he addressed gatherings, Joshua Nkomo, the late vice president, always reminded the government on what would happen to the land of the people. The inclusion of the clause on freedom from deprivation of property in the Lancaster House Constitution was nonnegotiable.[22]

The Lancaster House Agreement clause on freedom from deprivation of property was the most critical to Zimbabwe and was a modern version of the Rudd Concession, which was the most critical concession to Zimbabwe. The Royal Charter was granted, in spite of King Lobengula's assertions he had been deceived. King Lobengula repudiated the Rudd Concession, stating that he would "not recognize the paper, as it contains neither my words nor the words of those who got it." Her Majesty Queen Victoria Advisor responded to King Lobengula's assertion to this development, "[It] would be unwise to exclude white men."[23] In 1893, the BSAC declared war against King Lobengula for sending troops to punish alleged cattle thieves in Mashonaland. As a result, the pledges made at the signing of the Rudd Concession were suspended. 110 years later, based on land acquisition pledges the British and American governments made, which were never fully honored, Robert Mugabe and Joshua Nkomo also claimed to have been deceived into signing the Lancaster House Agreement. The British government did begin honoring the Lancaster House pledges, but it suspended further funding after discovering the land redistribution program was not benefiting the bona fide landless beneficiaries.[24]

---

21. *Ibid.*
22. *Ibid.*
23. *Letter of protest from King Lobengula and reply from Queen Victoria Advisor to King Lobengula-April 23, 1889*
24. *Ibid.*

4.0 History and Structure of the Zimbabwe African National Union PF

The political party, ZANU-PF, has ruled Zimbabwe since the attainment of political independence from the United Kingdom on April 18, 1980, and the establishment of democratic rule. The governmental system is democratic, holding free and fair elections once every five years. All adults have the right to vote. The economic system has been largely liberalized, and market forces of supply and demand largely determine it. The constitution guarantees the independence of the judiciary, and a vibrant parliamentary system reinforces it.

ZANU-PF was born in the 1960s as a nationalist movement seeking independence and freedom for the indigenous people of Southern Rhodesia (now Zimbabwe). It challenged and finally defeated the completely undemocratic colonial governmental system that was based on racism and minority rule. The local white settlers, who accounted for less than five percent of the total population, ran this oppressive system with the concurrence and full support of successive British governments. As the challenge to white/colonial/racist rule grew and support for the nationalist movement spread in the cities and rural areas, the regime passed draconian legislation in its parliament to suppress the movement by banning the organizations, detaining leaders without trial, and finally killing 50,000 patriots, as well as injuring and maiming many thousands. ZANU-PF performed the historic national duty of mobilizing the broad masses of the people against colonialism, racism, and imperialism, leading the fight for their national independence.

In the process of mobilization, ZANU-PF sought to unite the people into one nation. In 1976, it formed an alliance between the two parties fighting for independence—ZAPU and ZANU—and called it the Patriotic Front. In 1979, when the British government convened the Lancaster House conference to develop a new constitution for Zimbabwe, the Patriotic Front emerged as the authentic voice of the Zimbabwean people. In February 1980, the PF won the first general elections the British government organized. The two parties finally merged in December 1987 when their leaders, Comrade Robert G. Mugabe and Comrade Joshua M. N. Nkomo, signed the historic unity accord. The accord and the policy of national reconciliation ZANU-PF adopted, created the social conditions of peace and security, which the country has enjoyed since its independence.

ZANU-PF is an open, Democratic Party with transparent structures as follows: a four-man presidency or presidium composed of the president, two vice presidents and the national chairman. These four men regularly exchange views on current affairs.

The first organ is the Politburo, a standing committee of the Central Committee. The Presidium appoints the Politburo. It is charged with the responsibility of the day-to-day implementation of the party policy and programs as well as prepares the agenda for the meetings of the Central Committee. It also presents special provincial and/or national reports to the Central Committee. The Politburo consists of secretaries of the ten departments, their deputies, and four committee members. Its twenty-four members hold regular meetings once a month.

The second organ is the Central Committee, a decision-making body between congresses. Its 150 members meet once every three months. The Central Committee is the standing committee of the National People's Congress if the need should arise and is chaired by the National Chairman.

The third organ is the National Consultative Council, a gathering of the aged leaders and retired veterans who meet semiannually to render advice to the Central Committee on matters of importance.

The fourth organs are the Women's League and the Youth League, national organizations that elect their own national executives once every four years.

The fifth organs are the ten Provincial Councils, which are elected at provincial congresses held once every three years. The Provincial Councils wield significant power and influence in the provinces and make decisions with far-reaching consequences. Each Provincial Council has seventy-one members representing the men's wing, the women's wing, and the youth wing. District Councils, consisting of at least 5,000 members in each, are underneath the Provincial Councils. Branches with 500 members and cells (or village committees) with 100 members follow.

ZANU-PF have a nationwide network of members who are regularly consulted on all topics of importance. It is not a dictatorship—far from it. In fact, to the contrary, it is ultra democratic. The vicious campaign launched in the international press, which characterized President Mugabe as a dictator, was both wrong and mischievous. Given the structures of ZANU-PF, it is impossible for any one man to set up a dictatorship. It is ironic that the same people who practiced racism and minority rule before independence as well as killed and brutalized our indigenous people by the thousands, should accuse a party that campaigned for and brought democracy to this land of dictatorship. ZANU-PF members call each other "comrades" as a practice that was developed during the liberation war of independence (1964–1980), but it does not have any other significance. They are not Communists. They are simply Zimbabwe nationalists.

The system of the Politburo was a hold over from the former Soviet Union and Chinese Communist party, although with a different meaning in present-day

Zimbabwe. Party members still address one another as comrades despite the transformation of the party from socialism to capitalism. The Politburo and the Central Committee were enlarged at the Special People's Congress held in Harare on December 2000. An additional fifty female members were included. The Politburo now consists of the presidency with four members, eighteen secretaries heading departments, eighteen deputy secretaries, and eight committee members, accounting for a total of forty-eight members.[25]

Analysis of the Political Evolution of ZANU-PF and Its Structures

The history of ZANU-PF dates back to the early 1960s when a group of nationalists under the leadership of the Reverend Ndabaningi Sithole as well as Leopold Takawira, Herbert Chitepo, Robert Mugabe, Enos Nkala, Edgar Tekere, and others left ZAPU, led by Joshua Nkomo, to form ZANU. The split was due to differences in policy on the adoption of the armed struggle. ZAPU believed in independence through negotiations with the British government and the Rhodesia Front government under Ian Smith. Alternatively, ZANU believed in the attainment of independence through negotiations and armed struggle. Immediately after the Unilateral Declaration of Independence by the minority white-dominated Rhodesia Front, ZANU, under the leadership of Reverend Ndabaningi Sithole, was formed in Highfield, Harare. Both ZANU and ZAPU were soon banned in Rhodesia, and they returned to internal politics beneath the umbrella of the United African National Congress (UANC) under the leadership of Bishop Abel Muzorewa. The UANC vigorously campaigned and registered a majority *No* vote to independence before majority African rule during the Pierce Commission Referendum on independence before majority rule.

While ZANU leadership—Reverend Ndabaningi Sithole, Robert Mugabe, Edgar Tekere, Enos Nkala, Morris Nyagumbo, and others—were being held in Zimbabwe detention centers, the party appointed Herbert Chitepo to the post of chairman of the war council, which was responsible for the planning and execution of the armed struggle. At the ZANU Review Conference of September 1973, the following were elected to the Dare—War Council:

- Herbert Chitepo, chairman (Manyika)

- Mukudzei Mudzi, administrative secretary (Karanga)

- Noel Mukono, secretary for external affairs (Manyika)

25. Zimbabwe African National Union—Patriotic Front political structure 1990.

- Kumbirai Kangai, secretary for labor, social services, and welfare (Karanga)

- Rugare Gumbo, secretary for information and publicity (Karanga)

- John Mataure, political commissar (Manyika)

- Henry Hamadziripi, secretary for finance (Karanga)

- Josiah Tongogara, chief of defense (Karanga)

Apart from being an astute politician, Chitepo made history when he became the first black advocate in southern Africa. Tribalism influenced decision making during the armed struggle in Zambia after the Nhari rebellion when the High Command executed rebel leader Thomas Nhari; John Mataure, a member of the Dare War Council; and others. Before the tribunal, Noel Mukono and other alleged senior party collaborators were sentenced to death in absentia. Chitepo was named as a suspect, even though there was no evidence at the time. The Zambia government intervened, but it was told the clique died at the hands of the party.

The same group of the Dare War Council was implicated in the assassination of Herbert Chitepo. Commenting on the Chitepo assassination on Zambia national radio on March 31, 1975, President Kaunda of Zambia said:

> We are shocked. We are still grieved and angered. We remain bitter against the murderous act, bitter against the murderers—the enemies of Zambia and Africa. Many Zambians are, to say the least, very dismayed and justifiably irritated by statements made by some Zimbabwe nationals. Some, even nationalist leaders, have shown no concern whatsoever for the assassination of Mr Chitepo. To them, Mr Chitepo has been assassinated and that must be the end. Instead of calling upon the party and government to track down the killers of this gallant fighter, they are either completely silent, while others virtually demand that we stop the investigation altogether and thereby shelter the assassins.[26]

Herbert Chitepo was killed in Zambia in a car bomb, later established to have been planted by a faction within the party. Without tangible evidence, ZANU representatives quickly concluded the car bomb was the work of agents of the Rhodesian government. The Zambia government strongly suspected the assassi-

---

26. *President of Zambia Kenneth Kaunda speech on Zambia Broadcasting Cooperation Narch 31, 1975.*

nation was executed from within ZANU. The Zambia government detained most of the party leadership and called for a United Nations Commission of Inquiry, including terms of reference to establish the circumstances surrounding the death of the nationalist leader. The Chitepo Commission identified those responsible for planning and planting the bomb that killed Herbert Chitepo. The Zambia government released the suspects in the interest of the continuation of the armed struggle. After the conclusion of the Chitepo Commission, ZANU moved its headquarters from Zambia to Mozambique. Twenty-fours years later, after visiting the grave of the late vice president, Joshua Nkomo, former president of Zambia, Kenneth Kaunda was still bitter in an interview with the *Standard* newspaper in 1999:

> Chitepo was a committed leader. And some day, we will talk about how he died. It is one blot in the history, a sad reflection of the whole liberation of this region. Some of the ZANLA leadership left Zambia soon after the burial. I didn't expect them to leave immediately…this was their death. It was our death too, and it required all of us to work together on it.[27]

After the assassination of Herbert Chitepo, the subsequent detention of the ZANU leadership in Zambia, and the continued detention of part of the leadership in Rhodesian prisons, the combatants under General Rex Nhongo continued executing the armed struggle. The combatants had lost confidence in the political leadership and only saw some hope when Robert Mugabe and Edgar Tekere joined them after their release from Rhodesian prisons. At a Peoples' Congress held at Mugagau in Mozambique, the Reverend Ndabaningi Sithole was deposed from the ZANU leadership. Robert Mugabe replaced him, and Edgar Tekere assumed Mugabe's post of secretary-general. Under the leadership of Robert Mugabe, ZANU-PF separated from UANC because of Bishop Muzorewa's support for an internal settlement with the illegal Rhodesian government. Naturally, the new ZANU leadership of Robert Mugabe and Edgar Tekere was not comfortable with the senior party members, who were allegedly involved in the Herbert Chitepo assassination. As such, they were likely to keep the group under close surveillance. The group led by Henry Hamadziripi, Mukudzei Mudzi, Rugare Gumbo, Joseph Chimurenga, and others were detained, disgraced, and expelled from the party while they were in Mozambique because of their involvement in an alleged coup to remove President Mugabe.

---

27.   The Standard interview with Former Zambia President Kaunda in Harare n 1999

After realizing the internal settlement was not going to bring about genuine independence, ZAPU also pulled out of the internal settlement, leaving behind ZANU Ndonga, a faction of ZANU, which remained loyal to the deposed leader, Reverend Ndabaningi Sithole. This renegade faction disrupted the armed struggle after it joined forces with the Rhodesians. With the support of the ZANU Ndonga, ex-Zimbabwe African National Liberation Army (ZANLA) commanders, Felix Santana, Nkosana Zimuto, and others, the faction recruited captured guerrillas and party militias who masqueraded as freedom fighters and penetrated the liberation movement fighting forces, thereby confusing genuine combatants and the rural sympathizers of the armed struggle. This group became recognized as the enemy within. Through the support of the Rhodesian government, the internal settlement partners of the UANC of Bishop Muzorewa established militia forces whose membership was drawn from members of the political party. These party militias were mostly deployed to guard government-protected villages and the provision of information to the security forces on guerrilla movements in their areas of deployment. The militias were not trained in civilian law and human rights. These defectors from the armed struggle and the party militias did not have any alternative except joining with the Rhodesian regime to hopefully defeat the Patriotic Front in order to protect themselves. Likewise, the postindependence Zimbabwean government also established militia groups to perform duties outside police and military areas of jurisdiction.

The present Politiburo, Central Committee, and other structures were reinforced after transformation from a war to a political party. The present-day ZANU-PF has a wealth of seasoned politicians from all Zimbabwe political persuasions, ranging from PF-ZAPU, ZANU, UANC, Peoples Movement (PM), FROLIZI, Zimbabwe Unity Movement (ZUM), and so forth. The fact that the present-day ZANU-PF is a democratic party cannot be disputed because its various bodies represent youth, women, leadership, and presidency. However, a further analysis of the party organs shows the party does not have any representatives from the workers. The workers' voice remained with the Zimbabwe Congress of Trade Unions (ZCTU) ever since independence. This can be one of the reasons why the all-powerful trade union decided to form an alliance with the Movement for Democratic Change (MDC). It would be interesting to know why ZANU-PF did not include the workers in its structures. The party was once called ZANU-PF workers' party during the liberation struggle and pre-independence times. The MDC president, the former secretary-general of ZCTU, succeeded veteran trade unionist Albert Mugabe, who died in a swimming pool accident immediately after independence. Based on his own personal contribution to the emanci-

pation of the workers in Zimbabwe, there is no reason why Albert Mugabe was
not granted national hero status and burial at the national heroes' acre.

Zimbabwe political analysts find it is very hard to understand why a leader can
remain at the helm of a vibrant political party and government for more than
twenty years. The reason behind perpetual leadership might be that the party is
composed of leaders who are not capable or are not ready to assume leadership.
The international community and the intellectuals in Zimbabwe accuse President
Mugabe of not identifying a successor, which is untrue. President Mugabe has
two vice presidents of the party in addition to government and a chairman of the
party who are all members of the presidency. In the event of a president who is
incapable of performing his duties due to health or other reasons, the speaker of
parliament will assume the role of president until such time as and when a president is elected and inaugurated. Presidential candidates can be from the ruling
party, opposition parties, and independents. Any one of the vice presidents can
act as the president in the temporary absence of the incumbent president. Given
the situation, the question of President Mugabe nominating a successor does not
hold water. If President Mugabe nominates a successor, his critics will have the
grounds to accuse him of dictatorship. In a democratic state, the president does
not have the mandate to nominate his own successor.

Under normal circumstances, the party secretary-general replaces the president. Unfortunately, in the case of ZANU, President Mugabe assumed the post
of secretary-general after the incumbent, Edgar Tekere, was removed from the
post for his involvement in a gunfight, which resulted in the death of a Mr. Gerald Adams on August 14, 1980 immediately after independence. The government and the party provided Edgar Tekere with all financial and moral support
during the trial. Edgar Tekere was found guilty of murder but was acquitted
under the notorious Rhodesian promulgated anti-terrorism act. He won the
court case, but he lost his post of minister of public services. He later resigned
from the party and parliament in protest. Out of all those who left the government and ruling party, Edgar Tekere was the only one who could publicly challenge government policy. Feeling betrayed, Edgar Tekere alleged one of his main
reasons for resigning from the party was that democracy was in intensive care and
that he opposed the one party-state concept. Edgar Tekere formed the Zimbabwe
Unity Movement opposition party and challenged President Mugabe for the
presidency.

Following allegations that senior government and party officials were using
their positions to procure new vehicles from Willowvale Motor Company, the
government set up a commission to investigate the allegations under the chair-

manship of Justice Sandura. The commission's findings resulted in veteran nationalists, Morris Nyagumbo and Enos Nkala, falling out of favor because of their involvement in the scandal. Instead of being brought before the courts to answer criminal charges, Morris Nyagumbo committed suicide. Enos Nkala opted to resign from the party, which was formed at his house in Highfield, Harare. Minister Frederick Shava was brought to the courts. He was sentenced to a prison term but was granted an eleventh hour presidential reprieve just before he was imprisoned. He returned to the party and became chairman of the Midlands province. Education Minister Dzingai Mutumbuka resigned from government and joined the United Nations Educational Scientific and Cultural Organization (UNESCO). Reverend Canaan Banana, the Zimbabwe postindependence ceremonial president and a convicted homosexual, retired when Robert Mugabe, then prime minister, became executive president. Reverend Canaan Banana was brought before the courts to answer charges of sodomy and homosexual allegations after his bodyguard shot and killed a policeman, who was calling him Banana's wife. In mitigation during the murder trial, the bodyguard told the court how the president used to rape him and other staff working at the statehouse. Before the commencement of the trial, Canaan Banana escaped to South Africa. President Nelson Mandela advised him to return to Zimbabwe and face trial. Canaan Banana was found guilty of sodomy, a crime in Zimbabwe and was eventually sentenced to ten years imprisonment. However, he only served six months in a newly constructed "open prison," which allowed him shopping trips to Harare. The exposure of Banana's crimes against young men gravely embarrassed the government of Zimbabwe as it came within months of President Mugabe's denunciation of homosexuals and encouragement of Zimbabweans to arrest any they saw. Reverend Canaan Banana died a disgraced man and was denied a national shrine hero burial due to his imprisonment for homosexuality and sodomy.

The death of vice president Muzenda created a power vacuum, as well as heightened the need to identify a successor for President Mugabe. The presidential aspirant, Dr. Eddison Zvobgo, died after a brain tumor operation. After losing the new constitution referendum, Professor Jonathan Moyo, an ardent critic of the ZANU-PF government, who participated in the preparation of the new constitution, surprisingly joined the ruling party and was immediately appointed cabinet minister and member of the ZANU-PF Central Committee and Politburo. Professor Moyo, a constitutional lawyer by profession, was of strategic importance to ZANU-PF due to his capacity to advise and strategize the party and government in the information and publicity areas. Vice-President Dr.

Joshua Nkomo died in office and was replaced by Joseph Msika. Vice-President Simon Muzenda also died in office after a long illness and was replaced by Joyce Mujuru, the wife of General Solomon Mujuru, a retired army commander.

The democratic governance of Zimbabwe is exercised through political party and independent legislators elected by the people. The president nominates an additional thirty legislators from all walks of life. The majority of those nominated is from the ruling party and those who have lost an election. The presidential nominees have an equal right to participate in debates and vote in parliamentary decisions. In most cases, they vote with the ruling party legislators. This system has caused confusion regarding election results and the achievement of electorate representative decisions. In the case of Zimbabwe, the ruling party has a mandatory thirty seats ahead of the opposition before the start of the elections. The presidential-nominated seats will not impact political decisions if they are reserved for technocrats with a ceremonial president who is not politically aligned. With a two-thirds majority, all major decisions are made at the ruling party Politiburo while parliament becomes a forum for decision ratification and law enactment.[28]

Zimbabwe has a multiracial and multiethnic population of approximately 12.5 million people. Generally, the individual members of each racial or ethnic group live happily with others. A justifiable bill of rights guarantees the rights of each individual. The policy of national reconciliation the government announced at independence has remained the guiding principle in the day-to-day relations of people as well as within the national culture of Zimbabweans. In addition to the efforts of the government, several human rights organizations formed by concerned citizens keep a keen eye on any allegations or violations of human rights. ZANU-PF strongly supports the continuing efforts of the government to maintain law and order as well as uphold the rule of law. Furthermore, the rights of all Zimbabweans to private property are upheld at all times. Our people value private property such as their huts in the villages and their livestock, even if they are few. The party wants to ensure all Zimbabweans can do their daily business in peace and the governmental system guarantees their property rights as well as protects them against any arbitrary action. We condemned the violence that occurred before the general elections of last June, and we urge all political parties and individuals with both money and ambitions to seek political power by peaceful means and dialogue.[29]

---

28. Ibid.
29. *Zimbabwe African National Union—Patriotic Front Party Manifesto.*

5.0 ZANU-PF Democracy and United States Initiatives to Promote Democracy

The people of Zimbabwe, drawn as they are from different sectors of the economy as well as diverse social and cultural backgrounds, drive the policy and program of the party. The constitution states the highest policymaking organ is the National People's Congress. Meeting once every five years, it elects the leadership, namely the president, vice presidents, and the Central Committee. It is also that body with the power to amend the constitution and pronounce new policies. More than 10,000 delegates from all the organs of the party and all provinces attend. It is genuinely a peoples' congress convened to deliberate on matters of policy, elect new leaders, and review the running of the organization. The Central Committee meets once every three months (four times a year) to deliberate on policy issues. The standing committee of the National Peoples' Congress is empowered to act on behalf of Congress in the five-year period. It forms the direct link between the people and their wishes and the leadership in that period.

In addition to the structures mentioned earlier, the constitution provides for the annual holding of a national conference to broaden and deepen the processes of consultation between the people and the leaders. After the president and first secretary, Comrade Mugabe, have opened the conference, delegates are free to raise issues concerning the people in their respective areas and suggest ways to resolve the problems. Delegates gather to hear proposed policies from the leaders, but they also propose new policies and amend areas of existing policy. For two years, the party has been engaged in a restructuring process that established new village committees, branches, and districts. This exercise culminated in the election of new leaders for the District Development Committees and the Provincial Councils. What has been described briefly is the democracy of ZANU-PF at work. It is a peoples' party that fully expresses the aspirations and wishes of the people, identifies their problems, and finds solutions to serve the best interests of the people. Consultation of the people, identifying their wishes (*zvido zve vanhu*), and transforming them into governmental policy is the heart of the program and work of the party. Contrary to what the international newspapers propagate, Zimbabwe is not a dictatorship. It is a working democracy.[30]

---

30. *Zimbabwe African National Union—Patriotic Front, the annual National People's Conference.*

Promoting Democracy in Zimbabwe

On June 20, 2001, Thomas Carothers and Marina Ottaway, codirectors of the Democracy and Rule of Law Project of the Carnegie Endowment for International Peace, hosted a roundtable meeting on democracy promotion in Zimbabwe. Participants from the State Department, United States Agency for International Development (USAID), nongovernmental organizations (NGOs), and think tanks discussed current conditions in Zimbabwe, prospects for democratization, and possible roles for the international community. A synopsis of the discussion follows:

- President Mugabe is leading Zimbabwe on a downward spiral. He has launched the war veterans' invasions of white farms, killing dozens and injuring hundreds. The invasions have now spread to the factories. He has mounted a concerted and sometimes vicious attack on the independent judiciary, the free press, and the burgeoning opposition. He has lashed out at homosexuals, the West, global capitalists, and white Zimbabweans. He has sometimes united the whole lot of them. All the while, the economy has disintegrated. More than half the workforce is now unemployed. The vast majority of the population has been reduced to poverty, and the gross domestic product (GDP) has shrunk rapidly. (It may shrink as much as ten percent this year). Despite record low support levels (according to some surveys, three out of every four Zimbabweans want President Mugabe to step down), President Mugabe and ZANU-PF still cling to power.

- President Mugabe, by all accounts, is past the point of persuasion. The only retreat he has made came in the wake of the war veterans' attacks on international business and their threats against embassies and the international furor that followed. Otherwise, President Mugabe has been impervious to international pressure. President Mugabe appears to genuinely believe he is the object of an international, imperialist conspiracy. Above all, he will not allow himself to be removed from power, no matter the cost to Zimbabwe.

- ZANU-PF is key to President Mugabe's power. The president has lost some key allies recently. The head of the war veterans, Chenjerai "Hitler" Hunzvi, died of an AIDS-related illness. The ministers of employment and defense, Border Gezi and Moven Mahachi, two of President Mugabe's closest allies, died in mysterious car accidents. Yet, he still appears to maintain strong control of ZANU-PF and, thus, the country. At one point, there was quiet talk by ZANU-PF officials of President Mugabe stepping down, but this has long ceased. President Mugabe has acted decisively to root out dissidents, and his bands of thugs have cowed the rest of ZANU-PF. When the trade minister, Nkosana Moyo, resigned in May, he left the country with his family before faxing his resignation. The moderates who remain in the party are clearly fearful of straying from the party line. It is simply unclear whether moderates within ZANU-PF will be a resource.

• President Mugabe's power also depends on his capacity to control the military. The position of the military is unclear. High-ranking officers have been enriching themselves in the Congo. Therefore, they have an incentive to stick by President Mugabe. However, only a few have benefited from that intervention. There is significant discontent, both with the Congo adventurism and the appalling conditions in Zimbabwe in general. The military will certainly play a critical role in any transition, whether by instigating a coup d'état (of which there have been credible rumors of late) or refusing to act against opposition protests. No one seems to know how the military is lining up, and how it will act in the near future.

• Despite President Mugabe's ruthless measures to maintain power, a credible opposition has emerged in Zimbabwe. The powerful Zimbabwe Congress of Trade Unions (ZCTU) led demonstrations and strikes from 1998. Soon after, it launched the MDC. The MDC was able to form a broad opposition coalition that not only includes only urban workers. Church groups, women's groups, human rights organizations, students, pro-business groups, whites, and rural workers are represented as well. This coalition scored its greatest success when it mobilized the public to defeat the government's draft constitution in a February 2000 referendum. This was President Mugabe's first defeat at the polls since 1980. The MDC rode the momentum into the June 2000 parliamentary elections, where it won fifty-seven of one hundred and twenty available seats. This happened despite significant, widespread intimidation and chicanery. (The International Republican Institute called it "the worst we have ever seen.") President Mugabe's response was to remove judges who found fault with the conduct of the elections and simply increase the repression of opposition actors. The opposition has eschewed real confrontation with the regime so far, fearing President Mugabe would declare a state of emergency and unleash even greater forces of repression.[31]

The international community is anxious to see a peaceful but quick resolution of the Zimbabwe problem. It fears a prolonged economic and political crisis would permanently damage state institutions and undermine Zimbabwe in ways

---

31. Democracy and Rule of Law Project of the Carnegie Endowment for International Peace—On June 20, 2001, T. Carothers and M. Ottaway

that are difficult to remedy. The problem the international community faces is that the moderate steps it has taken to facilitate the transition have not worked, and more radical steps raise many questions.

Participants discussed the two approaches for the United States and other external actors to promote democracy in Zimbabwe: a moderate activist strategy and a heightened activist strategy. The moderate strategy—already being attempted for the most part—is to support progressive actors within Zimbabwe. This involves providing technical assistance to the opposition, assisting civil society at large, and aiding the independent press. The purpose of this strategy is to promote the political prospects of the opposition as well as provide the tools for free and fair elections. This is the strategy that was employed so successfully in Serbia to facilitate Milosevic's exit from power. This strategy faces increasing obstacles. The Zimbabwean government recently passed a bill prohibiting foreign assistance to political parties, and a similar bill concerning civil society organizations is being readied. The party bill explicitly bans financial assistance, but there is some concern the ban even extends to technical assistance. This international assistance is nominally nonpartisan, that is, it is aimed at bolstering democratic conditions in general, not the fortunes of the MDC in particular. These legal measures may partially or substantially block it.

A more radical activist strategy would entail both external and internal components. Externally, the international community would exert various pressures, including freeze the assets of key ZANU-PF officials, impose travel restrictions on them, investigate capital flight from Zimbabwe and external holdings of top officials, further isolate Zimbabwe in international Assemblies, withhold balance of payment support, and restrict the sale of military and "dual use" equipment. The international community might also create a transitional assistance package, which could be held up as a reward to Zimbabwe if it took the appropriate democratization steps. Nobody believes this promise of increased aid would sway President Mugabe, but it might convince moderates in ZANU-PF to break with him. Internally, this strategy would consist of providing direct funding to the MDC, setting up a rival radio station (for example, "Radio Free Zimbabwe") to combat the government's information monopoly in the rural areas, and supporting areas currently under the control and administration of the MDC.

Participants raised various criticisms of these strategies, particularly the heightened activist strategy.

First, concerns were raised about the feasibility of specific measures. If the international community prevents ZANU-PF officials from traveling outside the country, it might cut itself off from allies of reform, who are afraid to talk within

Zimbabwe. No country in the region would likely allow the presence of a radio transmitter on its territory. Direct funding to the opposition would run afoul of American laws and international obligations to Zimbabwe's laws. Realistically, only the United States and a handful of western actors—no genuine, multilateral alliance—would adopt the more radical strategy.

Second, some participants argued technical assistance to the MDC, which would help it hone its message and organize its political base, has dubious utility. The MDC already has widespread political support and would win handsomely in any free and fair elections. In the view of some participants, assistance should therefore be focused not on strengthening the MDC for electioneering, but on bolstering the electoral process itself.

Third, some disagreed with the very premise of the activist strategies. It is possible to peaceably push President Mugabe from power, either via an electoral process or increasing the pressure to induce his resignation. In this view, if one recognizes President Mugabe will not concede power, then these efforts only serve to alienate regional leaders already weary of western imperialism, play into the hands of President Mugabe's conspiracy theory, provide a pretext for further repression and a state of emergency, and make eventual resolution of the problem even more difficult. Those participants who were dubious of the activist strategies advocated a broader international focus on "supporting Zimbabwe," rather than on "getting rid of Mugabe."

Fourth (and in many ways following from the previous argument), some proposed the focus of international efforts should be on the long-term, post-Mugabe democratization of Zimbabwe, rather than on his short-term overthrow. According to some participants, the international community should work to help prepare the opposition to eventually govern Zimbabwe and foster links with moderate members of ZANU-PF. Some participants also tried reconciling the two positions, arguing it was possible to take measures—within and outside Zimbabwe—that would contribute to the downfall of President Mugabe and long-term democratization.

Finally, where does the regional community fit in? A general consensus stated regional pressure, especially from South Africa, would be very productive, and the international community would do well to solicit it. However, regional leaders have done very little to this point and seem unprepared to do much in the future. Various explanations are available, including they are weak governments facing their own domestic problems, they are uncomfortable with helping unseat a neighboring leader, they do not sense they have the stature to have any influence on President Mugabe, and the land reform issue has touched raw nerves across the region, especially in Namibia and South Africa. But the primary problem is the regional suspicion and skepticism of the West. British and American involvement in Zimbabwe is viewed with suspicion of imperialism, and regional leaders are very reluctant to be seen to carry out the mandate of the West and be cast as western lackeys. President Mugabe, of course, is exceedingly adroit at the political game of using suspicions of the West to his advantage.

Some participants argued the international community has been soliciting regional support in the wrong way. Rather than emphasizing the terrible nature of Zimbabwe's internal affairs, the international community should perhaps point to the devastating impact of Zimbabwe on the entire region. For example, development efforts there are being undermined. It is causing pain for the workers and trade unions in the region. By casting the problem as one of regional self-interest, the international community may be able to mobilize more regional support. Still, significant intervention on the part of regional leaders appears unlikely. Moreover, the international community will have to grapple with Zimbabwe's problems by using the tools of external pressure and internal support.[32]

The United States Democracy and Economic Recovery Act 2001—Zimbabwe

The United States Senate subcommittee on African Affairs approved the Zimbabwe Democracy and Economic Recovery Act 2001, which slaps travel restrictions on President Mugabe, his ministers, service chiefs, and their families.

The bill, which was first introduced into the Senate last year in 2000, went through two readings in the Senate before being referred to the foreign relations committee. The committee approved the bill on Thursday, paving way for the proposed law to sail unopposed through the House of Representatives. The bill will restrict President Mugabe, his immediate family, his cabinet ministers, government officials, and the ZANU-PF henchman implicated in political violence from traveling to the United States.

The American government and all institutions with American links will also be barred from dealing with the Zimbabwean government. It will also stop aid and bilateral trade worth millions of United States dollars, dealing a body blow to the already ailing Zimbabwean economy. There are some prerequisites needed for restoring normal relations:

---

32. *Synopsis prepared by Gideon Maltz, junior fellow in the Democracy and Rule of Law Project at the Carnegie Endowment.*

The restoration of the rule of law, respect for ownership and title to property, freedom of speech and association, an end to lawlessness, violence, and intimidation which is sponsored, condoned, or tolerated by the government of Zimbabwe, the ruling party, and their supporters or entities.

The bill also reads:

It is the policy of the United States to support the people of Zimbabwe in their struggle to effect peaceful, democratic change, achieve broad-based and equitable economic growth, and restore the rule of law.

It is the sense of Congress that the (American) President should begin immediate consultation with the governments of European Union member states, Canada, and other appropriate foreign countries on ways in which to identify and share information regarding individuals responsible for the deliberate breakdown of the rule of law, politically motivated violence, and intimidation in Zimbabwe; to identify the assets of those individuals which are held outside Zimbabwe; implement travel and economic restrictions against those individuals and their associates and families and provide for the eventual removal or amendment of those sanctions.

Senator Bill Frist, who introduced the bill, told the *Standard* in Washington that the bill sought to restore economic prosperity and good governance in Zimbabwe:

The crisis in Zimbabwe raises the possibility of a complete collapse of economic and social cohesion in a country, which has historically served as a stable and promising anchor on a troubled continent. If we allow Zimbabwe to continue down its current path, we risk further instability in Southern Africa. This legislation represents an immediate, positive response that the United States can take to improve stability and economic growth for the entire region.

Senator Russ Feingold, who seconded the bill, said the following:

I am pleased to join Senator Frist in offering the Zimbabwe Democracy Act, and I hope that it will win support in the full Senate. The Senate subcommittee on African Affairs recently held a hearing on the situation in Zimbabwe, and much of the testimony given at that hearing was truly distressing. Over the past year-a-and-a-half, conditions in Zimbabwe have deteriorated dramatically. This downward spiral of lawlessness and economic collapse is tragic as it is occurring in a remarkable country, one that is rich in human capital, had a sophisticated economy, and boasts a vibrant civil society.

This bill imposes no sanctions and cuts off no sources of assistance that have not already been suspended. It does lay out reasonable conditions for the resumption of assistance and authorizes meaningful conditions for assistance to Zimbabwe's economic recovery, including support for rule-governed land reform once conditions have improved.

The bill notes the Zimbabwean people are suffering because of the government's mismanagement of the economy:

> Through economic mismanagement, undemocratic practices, and the costly deployment of troops to the DRC, the government of Zimbabwe has rendered itself ineligible to participate in the International Bank for Reconstruction and Development and the International Monetary Fund programs, which would otherwise be providing substantial resources to assist in the recovery and modernization of Zimbabwe's economy. The people of Zimbabwe have been denied the economic and democratic benefits envisioned by the donors of such programs, including the United States.

The proposed law sets a number of measures to be taken by the American government should Zimbabwe meet certain conditions, including holding free and fair presidential elections; an equitable, transparent, and legal land reform; restoration of the rule of law; a fulfillment of the Lusaka Peace Accord to end the Democratic Republic of Congo (DRC) war; and a commitment that the police and army be subordinate to a civilian government.

Once these conditions are met, the bill states:

The (American) secretary of the treasury shall:

- Undertake a review of the feasibility of restructuring, rescheduling, or eliminating the sovereign debt of Zimbabwe held by any agency of the United States of America.

- Direct the United States director of each international financial institution to which the United States is a member to propose to undertake financial and technical support for Zimbabwe, especially support that is intended to promote Zimbabwe's economic recovery and development, the stabilization of the Zimbabwe dollar, and the viability of Zimbabwe's democratic institutions.

- The (American) president should direct the establishment of a Southern Africa Finance Center located in Zimbabwe that will include regional offices of the Overseas Private Corporation, the Export-Import Bank of the United States, and the Trade and Development Agency for the purpose of facilitating the development of commercial projects in Zimbabwe and the southern Africa region.

The bill also states the United States government's commitment to supporting Zimbabwe's land reform program in the context of the International Donors' Conference held in Harare in 1998.

At the conference, Zimbabwe undertook to carry out land reform in a transparent, legal manner. However, after last year's general election, which ZANU-PF narrowly won, government reneged on its promise when it unleashed war veterans onto farms. The invasions set the tone for a chaotic land reform program that has reduced Zimbabwe to Africa's basket case.[33]

Zimbabwe Response to U.S. Democracy and Economic Recovery Act 2001

The opposition MDC has succeeded in its campaign for the imposition of economic sanctions on Zimbabwe following the passing of the Zimbabwe Democracy and Economic Recovery Bill in the American Congress on December 5, 2001, by an overwhelming majority. The secretary-general of the MDC, Professor Welshman Ncube, and the secretary for legal affairs, Mr. David Coltart, drafted the first such bill three years ago at the request of right-wing members of Congress, such as Jesse Helms from North Carolina. The first thing to underline is that the bill will and is intended to impose economic sanctions on Zimbabwe by denying it the financial support it needs for its fledging industries. American representatives will be instructed to oppose measures or proposals that may give Zimbabwe monies from international organizations such as the International Monetary Fund (IMF), the World Bank, the African Development Bank, and others. The clear intention of the sponsors of the bill is to increase economic hardships on the ordinary people of Zimbabwe and cause as much suffering as possible. As for the MDC, a political leadership that campaigns for a policy that brings suffering and hardship to its own people could be charged for treason. It is quite clear they want political power at any cost, even if it brings economic hardships and suffering to their own people. The campaign for this bill in the United States has brought together right-wing elements that supported apartheid in South Africa and Ian Smith's racism in Rhodesia. These right-wing elements are now concentrated in South Africa, the United Kingdom, America, Australia, New Zealand, and Canada, and they fight any measures or policies that are aimed at improving the social condition and political sovereignty of the black people in the third world, especially in Africa. It is a great pity that some of our black brothers in America join hands with these elements on certain issues.

The major reason for the legislative action taken by Congress is to counter the land resettlement policy of the Zimbabwe government. That fact is quite clear, in spite of the denials from these right-wing groups that they are not opposed to

---

33. Zimbabwe Democracy and Economic Recovery Act 200—December 5, 2001.

land distribution and reform. The major thrust of the land reform policy of Zimbabwe is to redistribute the land in such a way that the large landholdings of the
white commercial farmers will be reduced, multiple ownership of commercial
farms will come to an end, absentee land ownership will be terminated, and those
indigenous people who have no land or eke out an existence on small, barren
plots will be settled on reasonable and viable plots. That is the major reason for
their opposition to President Mugabe and his government. All the other reasons
they give—such as the return to the rule of law, access to a free press, holding free
and fair elections, allowing monitors and election observers from Europe,
appointing an independent electoral commission and so forth—are ancillary to
the main question of land ownership, and land distribution. The government is
addressing most of these issues, and more rapid progress could be made if the
opposition party was cooperating in the process. Instead, the MDC is taking the
lead in promoting and propagating violence in order to disrupt the elections in
the knowledge the overseas, biased press will blame ZANU-PF for any bad thing
that happens.

In the past twenty-one years, the ZANU-PF administration has conducted
four parliamentary elections, two presidential elections, and one international referendum in an admirable way that satisfied all opposition parties. Before the
arrival of the MDC on the scene, there were no complaints and no violence organized by the opposition parties. Furthermore, the ZANU-PF government
accepted defeat in the results of the referendum and abandoned the proposals of
the new constitution. Any fair-minded person and objective observer will admit
ZANU-PF is a democratic party and has introduced a functional and working
democratic system in Zimbabwe. There was no democracy at all when ZANU-
PF came to power in 1980. It introduced the Zimbabwean democracy that has
accommodated a vociferous opposition party; unpatriotic, white judges who are
opposed to the system (such as Antony Gubbay, former chief justice who is now
campaigning against Zimbabwe in England); a recalcitrant and stubborn white
minority community with the commercial farmers as the fountainhead of antigovernment feelings; and an irresponsible, so-called independent press that is
highly critical of government. It takes much tolerance and commitment to certain principles to run a democratic system in such a hostile environment. There
are few governments in Africa that can produce a track record of democratic practice that can compare favorably with Zimbabwe's record.[34]

---

34. *ZANU-PF response to Zimbabwe Democracy and Economic Recovery Act 2001.*

6.0 Zimbabwe's Demobilization and Reintegration Programs (1980–2000)

Not only has the absence of a dedicated policy toward demilitarization, demobilization, and civil reintegration by government since 1980 pushed the country to the brink of economic collapse, it has also engendered social and political strife. The source of the present-day, internal, near-breakdown of law and order that has embroiled former combatants is the failure of the government to demobilize and reintegrate 19,163 former combatants by 1983.

Around this plight of destitution and impoverishment grew the present-day Zimbabwe National Liberation War Veterans Association (ZNLWVA). While elements among the war veterans have taken up a political position in support of the ruling party, as is their constitutional right, it is unfortunate that some have publicly stated they will not support the emergence of any opposition political party. Not surprisingly, these comments have created social and political tensions as the country approaches what has turned out to be an uncharacteristically bruising election to be held in June this year. This development is not entirely unexpected however. A World Bank Report called *Demobilization and Reintegration of Military Personnel in Africa: The Evidence from Seven Country Case Studies* released in 1992[35] warned as follows:

> The mixed record of success with demobilization and social reintegration programs (some aborted, others delayed, others carried out successfully in the initial stages) underlines the fact that their success or failure is intertwined to the political backdrop against which they take place. The more ambiguous the conflict and its termination, the more susceptible the demobilization and reintegration program seems to be embroiled in factional disputes. In mobilizing for war, a society politically motivates the armed forces and harnesses the economy in order to bring about the defeat of the adversary. These facets are organized and coordinated to inflict maximum injury to the opposing elements of the armed forces, its economy and society in general.
>
> Demobilization is therefore the reverse process of mobilization. Once peace is secured, the human, material and abstract facets have to be demilitarized in order that they fit into the new peaceful order. Demobilization of manpower after a war is but one of the aspects that a country undertakes within the broad range of demilitarization and the general reversal of elements that would have been placed on a war footing. Rocky Williams has also provided a working

---

35. Demobilization and Reintegration of Military Personnel in Africa: World Bank released in 1992

definition of demobilization when he asserts that demobilization programs are often organizationally complex and politically contentious by nature. A wide range of factors has to be considered if the ultimate success of these programs is to be ensured including preparation for demobilization, organizing, planning, and ensuring the provision of effective education and training for former military personnel.[4]

Different strategies are employed. In the case of the economy, restrictive blockades and sanctions, for example, are lifted while new lines of trade and exchange are established according to the reigning political philosophy. For example, take the experience of World War II and the Cold War when the world was split between east and west. As a consequence of competing ideological philosophies that informed economic conduct, no uniform practices were in either camp in the area of demobilization and civil reintegration. In regards to the society, policies of coexistence and reconciliation are normally put forward. However, it is within the area of transforming the armed forces that we find complexities requiring both direct and indirect policies to make a favorable impact. As a result, while much can be said about the overarching framework to this debate that is demilitarization, we will focus on the policy and operational levels of demobilization. This paper only seeks to confine itself to the aspect of assessing the state's inability to carry out demobilization and civil reintegration between 1980 to the present and suggest the way forward. Because proper demobilization and civil reintegration has not been carried out, this national problem will not go away and will need to be confronted directly as part of a general demilitarization of the Zimbabwean society that must come at some point in the future. Furthermore, some elements of the war veterans have aligned themselves with the ruling party. However, they have also vowed to take up arms if their party is defeated at the polls. This is unfortunate, and it heralds political and social strife for the country. Therefore, it is very important we offer policy alternatives for practitioners who will be faced with the task of addressing the demobilization problem in the future.

Demobilization and Reintegration in Zimbabwe, 1980–1987

Since 1980, the Zimbabwean government has undertaken at least two distinct demobilization initiatives. Sadly, both have failed and have since mired the country into economic, political, and military-related problems. The initial formal and comprehensive demobilization and civil reintegration policy was launched on October 5, 1981, and was terminated with the closure of the Demobilization Directorate in 1983.[5] Several distinguishing features of the exercise could be isolated once peace had been attained through the political process of elections held in February and March 1980. Within the demilitarization framework, based on shifting the allocation of resources from security to education and other social welfare sectors, emphasis was to be put on development.

Soon afterward, an agreement was made to form a core force of approximately 33,000 men and women from between 80,000 to 100,000 available.[6] A majority was former ZANLA and Zimbabwe Peoples' Revolutionary Army (ZIPRA)[7] combatants with several thousand African troops from the former Rhodesian Security Forces. The ratios emerging would influence aspects of force design and the desired political orientation of the force. The latter aspects also considered the colonial inheritance as well as military aid through the British Military Aid Training Team (BMATT) that was extended toward the remaining core force.

In order to cater to those away from the armed forces, a demobilization agency, the Demobilization Directorate, which operated under the ministry of labor and social welfare, was established to supervise the human transition from war to peace. The agency was allocated an average of just over Z$50 million equivalent USD 10 million a year for the three fiscal years of 1981–1982, 1982–1983, and 1983–1984. The resources allocated were also targeted to benefit the small-scale enterprises as well as establish a skills training center at Msasa for members entering this category.[9] However, as it later turned out, the socialist philosophy informing government policies at this time did not favor private enterprise. This route did not make a serious dent in providing a solution to the demobilization problem.

Donor support augmented the state's efforts, including more than 3,400 scholarships from the Canadian government that targeted critical areas in the economy. These were to run from the mid-1980s until 1988. Meanwhile, the economy, which would be evident by 1988–1989, was already experiencing a slowdown in growth as no jobs were being created. Given the impact of the resources at the individual level, which was set at Z$185,00 equivalent of USD 3 at that time per month over twenty-four months, the sums were generally far short of what was required to adequately assist former combatants to ease themselves back into the capitalist economy inherited from Rhodesia. Many lacked the necessary skills. Alternatively, those in command of the economy spurned the new entrants. Furthermore, serious government corruption was later unearthed in the selection and allocation of scholarships. As a result, these did not really benefit the intended beneficiaries, the ex-combatants.

However, the most important development to undermine the first policy of demobilization in this country was the political fallout occurring soon after independence with the coalition government and, secondly, the apartheid South Africa policy of destabilization. For a start, the political attempts to establish a coalition government between the ZANU led by Robert Mugabe and the ZAPU led by Joshua Nkomo collapsed in late 1982. Joshua Nkomo was forced into exile in March 1983. At the military level, units being integrated fell under the vicious faction fighting of units comprised of former liberation war fighters. This trend characterized problems surrounding attempts to establish a core force. Many businesses and properties acquired by ZAPU and its armed wing, ZIPRA, were confiscated, including farms, transport companies, and other enterprises acquired by demobilized, former ZIPRA combatants who had invested their severance payments. In undertaking this line of action, government—almost without realizing it—was undermining one of its own policies, that is, demobilizing combatants with a severance package.[14] Furthermore, the early political and military conflict between elements of the Patriotic Front as well as the external factor as presented by South Africa's destabilization efforts at this time had effectively forced government to abandon demilitarization and demobilization.

Barely two years into independence, the overarching framework of demilitarization was abandoned as the threatened state and people undertook rapid militarization to deploy forces on two fronts. This was on the external front in Mozambique along the Beira, Limpopo, and Nyamapanda corridors and inside the country. In the latter case, troop deployment was concentrated in and around Matebeleland.[15] New, "politically correct units" were established from 1981 and 1982, giving birth to the Korean-trained Presidential Guards, the Artillery Regiment, the Fifth Brigade, and the now-defunct People's Militia. Overall, the armed forces rose to nearly 52,000 and have stayed at this level since.

Basically, from the above practice, demobilization and civil reintegration had been formally abandoned when the Demobilization Directorate presented its final report after closing down in June 1983. On hand were 19,163 former combatants, now expected to reintegrate into society with the assistance of the severance payments spread over two years, as described previously. Many of the former ZIPRA combatants had taken up arms during this "dissident era," and the government deployed soldiers against them and the general population in the western part of the country. A full political, economic, and military offensive was ongoing against ZAPU and former ZIPRA cadres.

Furthermore, those from ZANLA or in full employment began finding it difficult to make ends meet. Consequently, many gathered around the debilitating plight of the "Class of '83." Against this background, we will seek to isolate some of the pitfalls that led to the failure of the first demobilization and civil reintegration initiative. The exercise began against a background of intrigue and mistrust—both internally and externally—as real or suspected plans by the Rhodesians supported by South Africa and ZAPU to challenge the new and perceptively weak state of Zimbabwe. This influenced the politics of the country in the first few years. Subsequent policies adopted had little to do with demilitarization and the orderly demobilization and reintegration of former combatants. As a result, no comprehensive policy of demobilization existed after the cursory passage of the one in 1981. That is, this policy was not annually evaluated and finetuned to respond to developments that would negate its success.

Much more importantly, the state did not undertake any postexercise evaluation of demobilization after 1983. Decisions based on questions of security by government therefore dominated. In the decreasing military, capacity was the last thing being contemplated. On the basis of the perceived insecurity, the government needed support and began vigorously recruiting and establishing new units, which included the mobilization of its party cadres as militia. In addition, an inadequate amount of resources[16] and political attention was paid to demobilization during this period.

The management of the economy to encourage growth and a careful watch on inflation was not the primary concern of the socialist government policies in the first decade of independence. At this time, the state was grappling to turn a capitalist economy into an egalitarian and more equitable structure. Thus, it tended to emphasize distribution, not production. Consequently, the framework the demobilized members was expected to enter became a highly contested territory where individual members became early victims. In the confrontation, the only place where comrades could be welcomed was the public sector.

By the end of the first ten years, the capitalist economy began faltering, and the jobless market kept expanding. The initial policy had placed too much responsibility on the demobilized members with minimal state responsibility. Almost no role was created for the private sector to play toward resolving a national problem. Unsurprisingly, many of the comrades attempting to enter into the private sector met hostile reception that tended to perpetuate philosophical differences, attitudes, and approaches to business and profit. Given all these negatives are fundamental to successful demobilization—lack of political will, no carefully considered demobilization plan, inadequate resources, a hostile economic environment that soon registered lack of growth, unemployment, and rising inflation—the initial effort soon collapsed. Former combatants thrown into society without skills or further material assistance soon began agitating for basic requirements, such as accommodation and welfare support.

The circumstances of the former ZIPRA cadres eventually returned to the government agenda after the signing of the Unity Accord between ZANU and ZAPU on December 22, 1987, thereby establishing a joint, former liberation movement war veterans' association as a foregone conclusion. This occurred in 1989 in spite of the state's vigorous efforts via successive ministers of labor and social welfare. Ministers Nathan Shamuyarira, Florence Chitauro, and John Nkomo all acknowledged government dereliction had led to the destitution of the 19,163 ex-combatants. However, while they agreed to the further support of the "Class of '83," they were not prepared to create a privileged class by making grants to a wider body of war veterans available.

In 1992, the parliament passed legislation formally recognizing the war veterans' association and making provisions for government to offer limited benefits. A narrow definition was adopted. As will be shown subsequently, this has led to serious problems of exclusion during the era of the second initiative. The definition of beneficiary ex-combatants holds that only those who had undergone military training and participated consistently and persistently in the liberation struggle that occurred in Zimbabwe and in neighboring countries between January 1, 1962, and February 29, 1980.

Given the adverse background, both ZANLA and ZIPRA cadres made concentrated efforts to influence government to pay attention to their deteriorating plight. Even those in full employment found it difficult to make ends meet and congregated around the sorry plight of the "Class of '83."[21] Basically, this was an indication the initial attempts to demobilize had failed. In 1988, the government admitted in parliament that its "demobilization policy had failed to achieve the intended targets."[22] During the same debate, "it was estimated that 35,709 ex-combatants had been demobilized by 1988, and between 15,000 to 25,000 were without employment."[23] This admission should have been an early warning as well as an indication that future efforts to solve the demobilization problem would need to focus on employment creation. But this obvious route was never pursued.[36]

---

36. *Journal of Peace, Conflict and Military Studies Vol.1, March 2000, ISSN 1563-4019 Gerald Mazarire* and Martin R. Rupiya***Teaching Assistant, Department of History, University of Zimbabwe**Lt. Col. (Rtd.), Senior Lecturer, Department of History and Executive Director, Centre for Defence Studies, University of Zimbabwe*

Second Policy on Demobilization and Reintegration, August 1997 to the Present

Following a marathon meeting with the war veterans, President Mugabe launched the second policy on the grounds of the statehouse in August 1997. The appointed minister in the president's office was responsible for war veterans later reiterated this policy before the third War Veterans' Congress held at Umzingwane in 1998. This policy has continued to be viewed with mixed reactions.

Grants made by presidential decree defied all arguments his cabinet colleagues, especially the ministers responsible for labor and social welfare, had advanced. In a single action, the president's action not only reversed government policy, but it went to accord further privileges and grants to serving members in government and elsewhere, as long as they had been ex-combatants and qualified according to the criteria above. As a direct result of the policy, the government paid out more than Z$4.5 billion equivalent USD 90 million at Z$50,000 equivalent USD 1,000 apiece to more than 52,000 claimants with little or no consultation with the taxpayers or officials expected to implement the policy. Average economic growth between 1991 and 1997 had been a disappointing 1.5 percent and had not created a major surplus for disbursement.

While the principle of extending government assistance may be right, considerations need to be made about national economic affordability and sustainability. Furthermore, the level of disbursements made must take into account the primary aim of demobilization, that is, of reintegrating demobilized soldiers permanently into society. Consequently, the departure point for any credible policy is the maintenance of economic stability for the rest of society into which the demobilized soldiers wish to enter. If the former is destabilized, then benefits extended to the demobilized soldiers put them in a special class. This observation concerning the balancing act that policymakers must attempt to ultimately achieve in undertaking demobilization contains the seeds that will determine the success or failure of the program.

The economy needed prudence and moderate expenditure policies to reverse the stunted growth. Furthermore, each war veteran, whether employed or not, was to receive a pension worth Z$2,000 equivalent USD 40 tax-free per month. An unrealistic number stepped forward. The treasury was not only faced with demands to finance the lump sum grants, but it also had to contend with unexpected long-term expenditure. By January 1998, the state paid Z$106 million equivalent USD 6 million as monthly pensions to war veterans. The figure increasingly rose as more and more came forward to make claims. In February,

$109 million equivalent USD 2 million was paid.[25] Because the criteria used was loosely worded, more than 4,000 claimants were soon discovered as frauds. The only recourse shown following this revelation was, "War veterans were to vet themselves and submit names including those of fakes to their patron—the President." Unfortunately, some of the monies paid out in haste have been irretrievably lost. Clearly, as shown by the process and disbursement undertaken, national resources continue to be wasted. Exactly who are the ex-combatants? How many are there that need to be compensated? As it stands, the ruling party and policies handed down from the presidential decrees do not exactly lend themselves to these searching questions that are critical for establishing a means test and marshaling sufficient resources. Before continuing to see exactly what errors of judgement were made in the second policy, a review is needed on its impact on the wider Zimbabwean society.

Because the grants and pensions had not been included in the budget, funding the second demobilization initiative became problematic for the minister of finance. First, he tried introducing special taxation before the end of 1997. Workers and the public, who went on the streets to express their displeasure, met this plan with stiff resistance. When these were arbitrarily paid out in November, the dollar fell against other currencies, losing more than seventy-three percent of its value. By January 1998, the events had caused price rises, resulting in serious riots in the townships as well as the outlying regions. People in Mutare, Gweru, Murewa, Bulawayo, and Harare experienced running battles with the police who could not contain the very robust and spontaneous response to the economic hardships. Order was grudgingly restored after armed troops had been brought out. Clearly, the funding of the lavish, all-embracing grants and pensions of ex-combatants had ignited the uneasy, existing relationship. The downward trend continued with alarming speed. By the end of 1999 and early into 2000, inflation had reached seventy-four percent before easing, but it was set to rise. Domestic debt was more than $93 billion equivalent USD 2 million compared with zero in 1980. More than half the adult population was unemployed.

Given the political, social, and economic upheavals partly resulting from the second policy, an interrogation of the factors reveals that at least four elements appear to have been missed out when the policy was announced.

The first is lack of focus on the "Class of '83." That is, handing out exactly the same levels of grants and pensions to war veterans who had been unemployed since 1980 and those in the cabinet or the top leadership of the armed forces creates a gap. This action does not narrow or close the chasm. In fact, because of the currency then collapsing by losing nearly three-quarters of its value, the "Class of

'83" could not weather the economic hardships in the same way as the other employed colleagues.

Second, disbursing large sums of cash to previously unemployed and homeless privates who did not have any preparation for the windfall and without any strings attached was an ill-conceived idea. Many simply squandered the proceeds. Within weeks, they lined up outside government doors for further assistance. A possible suggestion would have been to provide partially assisted housing in the various towns funded by the grant and the balance being paid by the individual over a period of time. As it stands, even after the grants were distributed, many have become worse off as the economy soon nose-dived afterwards, a situation from which it has never recovered.

Third, the numbers of people being supported have placed an extra burden on a small economy with less than two million workers who are formally employed and providing the regular tax revenue.

However, even as the new policy was being launched, several interest groups—including former political prisoners, former war collaborators, past and present widows of former war combatants, children of former combatants, and, curiously, former Rhodesian African soldiers—emerged and began organizing themselves to champion their particular position in a bid to secure government assistance that, in their perception, had been unfairly extended to the war veterans. The various groups challenged the criteria that had been hastily set up by the war veterans.

The first to emerge—and appears to have already won state and national support for its cause—is the Zimbabwe Political Detainees and Restrictees Association (ZIPDRA). Numbering more than 7,000 members, this group has argued, not only were they the first to organize cadres to go for training outside the country, they themselves could not physically leave the cells and homes around which they were surviving under armed guards. In their defense, many were executed for recruiting youths for military training.

Because of the solid nature of their case, the government backtracked on the exclusive criteria and instituted legal action to cater to ZIPDRA members. This change of heart also resulted from the prodding action of ZIPDRA members who have occupied known farms owned by senior government officials and cabinet ministers in order to precipitate favorable action from the government.

The second group to emerge and robustly challenge the war veteran benefits linked to the problem of demobilization is the Zimbabwe Liberation War Collaborators (ZILIWACO). Formed at the time of the disbursement of the benefits in late 1997, Ranjinos Kawara, a recently deposed, former lance corporal leads

ZILIWACO. With a membership of 35,000, it is comprised of Mujibhas and Chimbwidos. (These groups claim to have provided intelligence and served as aides and runners to the guerrilla movements). Some were eventually trained locally to lay the odd mine or place explosives onto rail lines, roads, or near some vulnerable point in then-Rhodesia. Consequently, many refer to themselves as "trained at the front." In order to press their point home, ZILIWACO members engaged in the "decampaigning" of the ruling party in the rural areas by rounding up all villagers who were ZANU-PF supporters and demanding party cards, T-shirts, and other insignia. These were then publicly burned or destroyed. Not only were the methods ZILIWACO employed a rerun of the liberation struggle practices, but this level of anomic violence alarmed the ruling party. It hastily agreed to a meeting held at the Catholic Centre, Silveira House, just outside the capital. Second, the agreement to meet with ZILIWACO also reveals the government acknowledged it has partly erred in arriving at the exclusive criteria that created a privileged class.

A third group to challenge the presidential policy on demobilization and benefits emerged around the widows of deceased former combatants. It is unclear if these were from members of the "Class of '83" or from the wider body, but surviving wives also stepped forward, claiming they also deserved benefits. The widows' faction soon split into two. Without any formal announcement, an urban section numbering about 3,000 to 4,000 led by Mrs. Pamela Tungwarara was soon discovered to have been authorized to receive benefits, which riled the other group of 12,000 mostly rural-based women under Agnes Rusike who were not accorded similar privileges.

A fifth group, if we accept the two distinct divisions of the widows, also stepped forward and expected to be included. Former Rhodesian African members comprised this group. This forced the Zimbabwe National Army, an institution being employed to vouch for the credibility of war fighters, to issue a statement disowning the former Askaris' perceived right of compensation. The former Rhodesian organizers then approached the British Embassy and the former prime minister, Ian Smith, for support, which was also spurned.

Finally, a children's organization, comprised of kids born to deceased former combatants and had been left destitute, also sought to convince the government of their right to be supported through the second demobilization policy. As yet, following their establishment at the beginning of 2000, the state has not given a meaningful response. Given the policy on demobilization and the criteria put forward, a number of well-deserving categories have come forward to challenge the exclusive nature of that policy.[37]

Recommended Way Forward and Conclusions

Two wrongs do not make a right. The two attempts by Zimbabwe at demobilization since 1980 have both failed dismally so far. The plight of the "Class of '83" in requiring basic support in the form of being accorded opportunities for skills training in order to fit them for a new role in society must still be addressed. Not only must they be equipped with useful skills, but employment opportunities must be created for them as well. Secondly, while this is taking place, enough resources in the form of basic accommodation and minimum survival and welfare must be made available to the core impacted group. It was illustrative how each of the categories spent their grants when the Z$50,000 equivalent to USD 1,000, popularly known as the "50kg," handouts were paid. Many cabinet ministers and their entourages, senior armed forces personnel, police, and other government department officials simply used the sums to extend their urban houses, purchase another vehicle, or simply clear outstanding mortgages. Others pooled their resources in the commercial undertakings established by the ZNLWVA that have since been mired in financial controversies, whereas many members of the "Class of '83" desperately tried feeding, clothing, paying school fees, and securing accommodation with the dollar that, from November 14, 1997, lost its purchasing power on a daily basis. This trend has continued ever since. The result has been a widening of the gap of the haves and have-nots among the former combatants.

What lessons can we draw from the conduct of government on the two initiatives on demobilization and civil reintegration since 1980? The point of departure in undertaking effective demobilization is to define the problem. That is, demobilization must be part of demilitarization, and this government has not undertaken any serious demilitarization since 1980. Decisions have been made from a political and security point of view, sacrificing any rationale input. Demobilization is a national problem and requires the involvement of all concerned in order to address it. The exercise so far has been provincialized as a preserve of government, shutting out the business, the private sector, churches, and other support.

Meanwhile, key issues constituting the background to the elections reflect an appalling situation in which a faction of the war veterans has become involved.

---

37. *Journal of Peace, Conflict and Military Studies Vol.1,March 2000, ISSN 1563-4019 Gerald Mazarire* and Martin R. Rupiya Teaching Assistant, Department of History, University of Zimbabwe Lt. Col. (Rtd.), Senior Lecturer Centre for Defence Studies, University of Zimbabwe*

More than fourteen people have already been killed. As a result, the international community and the Commonwealth to which Zimbabwe belongs has strongly censured the country's political leadership. The nation is also experiencing unprecedented economic pressure. Domestic debt stands at over Z$93 billion equivalent USD 19 million and is rising. Inflation, hovering at more than sixty percent, is also set to increase. More than half the adult, working population is unemployed. Financial relations with the International Monetary Fund (IMF), the World Bank, and the European Union (EU) have been suspended. Related bilateral relations with Sweden and Denmark have also been put on hold as the world urges the Zimbabwean government to respect court rulings from its judiciary system and desist from politically stirring violence, anarchy, and chaos. While a section of the war veterans has been involved, it still is the duty of the government emerging after the June elections to provide a permanent solution to the "Class of '83."

Past experience has shown that countries that have succeeded in the exercise attribute their success to macroeconomic policies, within which demobilization is a small part. Generally, two important control points have had their impact cascade to positively influence peaceful, permanent reintegration. These are the state encouraging a growing economy through creating employment opportunities by encouraging business and managing inflation. In this macroframework, issues of demobilization are tasked to a triumvirate committee of the ministries of finance, education, and industry and commerce and occasionally supported by of the ministries of housing and local government. The idea would be to harness both public and private support for the national problem as its resolution goes beyond the capacity of the state. Once the policy framework is established at the highest level, the second stage is to establish an agency or directorate that is charged with the coordination of the demobilization of the personnel as well as judiciously manage the resources allocated to the project. Although resources are generally always in short supply as they are finite, consideration must be made to muster adequate amounts, even going out to seek donor support for the successful completion of the project. Its successful conclusion has direct implications on peace building.

Finally, a time limit must be set, and the implications of the exercise must be disseminated to all key players. In other words, the exercise should place a burden of responsibility on the policymakers, the implementers, the demobilized members, and the society.[38]

Independent Commentary on the Reintegration of Ex-combatants

Peace agreements, accords, and protocols with conditions for demobilization and reintegration of ex-combatants were signed and implemented worldwide with the majority resulting in sustainable peace and economic development in countries, including Mozambique, Haiti, Angola, Mali, Guatemala, Philippines, Kosovo, East Timor, Cambodia, Congo, Guinea Bissau, Bosnia-Herzegovina, Uganda, and Sierra Leone. In addition, there were some disarmament and demobilization with no political will to disarm and demobilize and without guided reintegration into civilian life. These included Liberia (1995), South Africa, Namibia, Ethiopia and Somalia, Zimbabwe and Angola. In the case of Zimbabwe, the absence of a dedicated policy toward demilitarization, demobilization, and civil reintegration by the government since 1980 has not only pushed the country to the brink of economic collapse, but it has also engendered social as well as political strife. The source of the present-day, internal, near-breakdown of law and order that has embroiled former combatants is the failure by the government and international community to transform the identified 19,163 former combatants from military to civilian life by 1983 through sustainable, income-generating reintegration assistance.

For disarmament, demobilization, and reintegration of ex-combatants to occur, an authentic desire between the belligerent parties concerned to lay down their weapons must exist. This may be manifested through the formal signature of a peace agreement or an informal agreement in which the concerned parties agree to negotiate a process of surrender or national reconciliation. Once the above has been achieved, it is possible to establish a political agenda for the coordinated process of disarmament, demobilization, and reintegration, which signals the process of returning home and reintegration of ex-combatants and their dependents. Downsizing the national army after conflict sends a confidence-building message to the at-large population and reduces the financial burden on the transitional government, which needs to reduce defense costs and consolidate financial expenditures for the country's socioeconomic reconstruction. In the case of lengthy conflicts, support from the international community is sought to ensure successful transition from war to peace and economic reconstruction via the monitoring of compliance of activities related to the quartering, disarma-

---

38. *Journal of Peace, Conflict and Military Studies Vol.1,March 2000, ISSN 1563-4019 Gerald Mazarire and Martin R. Rupiya Teaching Assistant, Department of History, University of Zimbabwe Lt. Col. (Rtd.), Senior Lecturer Centre for Defence Studies, University of Zimbabwe*

ment, demobilization, return, and reintegration of ex-combatants and their dependents to their areas of origin.

In cases in which ex-combatants do not undergo a rapid process of reintegration into the national army, other state security institutions and reintegration into civilian life through sustainable, income-generating initiatives, such peace agreements have little chance of achieving sustainable peace and economic development. In the case of Zimbabwe, the ex-combatants underwent a rapid process of reintegration into the national army and other state security institutions. Unfortunately, they were not afforded the opportunity of rapid reintegration into civilian life. Despite the fact the majority hailed from agricultural economy-based societies, they were deliberately denied the choice to reintegrate through sustainable commercial agriculture. Resettlement land could not be made available for ex-combatant reintegration due to the Lancaster House Constitution clause on freedom from deprivation of property. Instead, they were redirected toward reintegration through cash grants and trade training courses conducted at specified vocational training schools located at government established centers far away from their areas of resettlement. The vocational training was infiltrated with non ex-combatants benefiting from the bona fide ex-combatants. It is also a truism that, instead of prioritizing on demobilization and reintegration of ex-combatants, the Zimbabwean government was forced to start mobilization of ex-combatants to protect export routes through Mozambique and contain the increasing South African cross border raids against Pan African Congress (PAC) and African National Congress (ANC) activists. This saw the emergence of the Korean-trained Fifth Brigade to protect the trade routes through Mozambique and assist the FRELIMO government fight against the RENAMO rebels while the Peoples' Militia was created to protect the rural population against insurgents from South Africa and Mozambique. Given the situation, the Zimbabwean government was correct in prioritizing national defense over demobilization of ex-combatants at a time when they were required to protect the independence they fought for with their lives.

The Mozambican government signed the Italian government-sponsored Rome Peace Agreement with the RENAMO rebels in 1994. Among other things, the following was agreed: quartering, disarmament, demobilization, and reintegration of the RENAMO ex-combatants. Simultaneously, the government agreed to downsize the national army and reintegrate qualified RENAMO ex-combatants into the new national army and state security institutions. The remainder of RENAMO and the deinducted government soldiers were reintegrated into civilian life through vocational, apprenticeship, on-the-job training, and sustainable, income-generating microprojects. The United Nations Mission to Mozambique (UNOMOZ) closely monitored the implementation of the peace process and democratic elections. As of this date, Mozambique continues to progress in economic recovery and development under sustainable peace.

In 1994, the Angolan government and the National Union for the Total Independence of Angola (UNITA) signed a peace agreement in Lusaka, Zambia, known as the Lusaka Protocol. They agreed to form a government of national unity, disarmament, demobilization, and reintegration of UNITA ex-combatants. The United Nations mission to Angola monitored the implementation of the peace agreement. In 1998, due to lack of political will, fighting resumed in Angola after UNITA refused to fully comply with the terms of the Lusaka Protocol. Immediately after the death of the UNITA leader in 2002, the government suspended military operations and entered into peace talks with the remaining UNITA leadership. A Memorandum of Understanding was signed inside Angola between the government and UNITA military commanders, pledging to work together on the disarmament, quartering, and reintegration of UNITA ex-combatants into the national army and other state security institutions. The remainder were to be reintegrated into civilian life through sustainable, income-generating microprojects as well as vocational, apprenticeship, and on-the-job training. The government did not invite the United Nations to monitor the disarmament, demobilization, and reintegration process because the circumstances, which brought the peace, were tantamount to an act of surrender by the battlefield-defeated UNITA movement.

In October 1995, the Council of State of the Liberia National Transitional Government (LNTG) invited the international community to participate in the reintegration of ex-combatants in Liberia. Unfortunately, the process could not be started due to the outbreak of hostilities in April 1996. After the 1997 elections, which brought the NPFL into power, the international observers reported the election was free and fair while the political opposition indicated the election was conducted under intimidation and was essentially rigged. Some opposition leaders left the country. Some ex-combatants from opposition factions were reintegrated into the national army and the antiterrorist unit. The demobilization and reintegration program could not be restarted due to the war against the Liberians United for the Restoration of Democracy (LURD) rebels, which started in 1999, calling for the conscription of all legal ex-combatants back into the fighting ranks. The demobilization of ex-combatants was automatically suspended with the nation remobilizing and rearming for the protracted war against insurgents.

In Sierra Leone, the disarmament, demobilization, and reintegration of the
Armed Forces Revolutionary Council/Revolutionary United Front (AFRC/RUF)
ex-combatants started in July 1999, but it was disrupted in May 2000 when RUF
pulled out of the Lome Peace Agreement, destroyed the demobilization centers,
rearmed, and took United Nations peacekeepers hostage. However, the disarmament, demobilization, and reintegration process was restarted in May 2001 after
the signing of a cease-fire agreement between the Civil Defense Forces and RUF.
The United Nations mission in Sierra Leone ensured both sides comply with the
terms of the agreement. As of this date, out of a total of 56,000 ex-combatants
who registered for the reintegration program, 35,000 have completed training or
are in ongoing reintegration programs into the national armed forces and civilian
life through vocational, apprenticeship, and on-the-job training and income-generating microprojects. A total caseload of 21,000 remains outstanding. The Sierra
Leonean government decided to downsize the national army to reduce the financial burden on the government, which needs to reduce defense costs and consolidate financial expenditures for the socioeconomic reconstruction of the national
economy.

Experience has proved that ex-combatants and their dependents need to be
categorized as a special group in need of assistance. There is a distinct difference
between ex-combatants and other war-related vulnerable categories. During a
conflict, Internally Displaced Persons (IDPs) and refugees abandon their homes
to escape from the fighting, whereas militias, soldiers, or irregular combatants
abandon their homes because they are sent to fight. Refugees survive the conflict
as civilians that escape to safe areas under United Nations High Commission for
Refugees (UNHCR) protection, whereas combatants and soldiers remain in areas
of combat through the law of the gun—defending, attacking, and killing in the
process. In many cases, peace signifies abandoning their identity and previous
survival strategies. Typical of protracted wars, the majority will have spent more
than ten years in the military and do not have any marketable skills. The ex-combatants need to be methodically transformed from military to civilian life as soon
as possible after the signing of a peace agreement through guided reintegration
initiatives.[39]

The Demobilization Directorate and international peacekeeping mission must
conduct a registration exercise and socioeconomic demographic survey of all
quartered ex-combatants with a view to establish a comprehensive database on
their needs in the camp, return transport requirements, and their perceived rein-

---

39. *Ibid.*

tegration livelihood needs on returning to their areas of origin. Based on the report, humanitarian assistance agencies will be in a position to access the database. They can formulate and design intervention initiatives to benefit the ex-combatants, their dependents, and their communities of reintegration. The database will assist other agencies with updated data on the ex-combatant profiles for present and after returning to areas of origin needs in the areas of health, food and non-food items procurement, water and sanitation, shelter, education, vocational training, and transport Assistance. The database will also assist the peacekeeping force and the government in the selection of suitably qualified ex-combatants for reintegration into the national army and other state security agencies. The profiling of the ex-combatants was conducted by government officials and Commonwealth peacekeepers who were not specialists in postconflict registration and reintegration of guerrilla war ex-combatants.

Based on the database's individual ex-combatant profiles, the resettlement agency will prepare movement and resource plans for the return of ex-combatants and their dependents to their areas of origin. Before transporting ex-combatants and their dependents to their areas of origin, the transporting organization must undertake a road assessment mission, noting the road conditions, bridges, fuel stations, vehicle maintenance garages, health centers, police stations, and permanent security road blocks. Visits must be conducted to the areas of resettlement where the population of resettlement will be advised of the return of the ex-combatants and their dependents. The village reception of returning ex-combatants is normally conducted at the nearest church or place of worship. Choice of the mode of transport depends on the route, distance, availability, and cost. The organized return concept is very important because it breaks the ex-combatants' chains of command. Because the Zimbabwean ex-combatants were from the perceived winning side, the need to officially hand them over to local community leaders was not important. The understanding one is now free from the rigid command structure initially brings fear of the unknown. Thereafter, there is a sense of liberty and freedom, which generates a strategy of survival within the framework of sustainable, transparent, income-generating activities. The concept of local government, democracy, and human rights the ex-combatants learned from the assembly areas should become the principles guarding their reintegration.

Facilitation of reintegration assistance, which is delivered to the communities of absorption via the resettlement of ex-combatants, includes the issuance of comprehensive emergency resettlement kits, rehabilitation of infrastructures, the creation of income-generating microprojects, and the implementation of capacity-building initiatives, which cushion the impact of returns. Therefore, the possibility of competition for scarce resources is reduced at the grassroots level. Wars result in significant damage to the physical infrastructures of the country. Furthermore, the majority of the ex-combatants who constituted the various fighting forces have been alienated from education, skills training, civil behavior, civic education, and gainful employment that foster their intellectual growth. In the case of Zimbabwe, the majority of the ex-combatants had formal education acquired before joining the armed struggle or inside the refugee and military training camps.

United Nations agencies and other international organizations normally prepare and implement the disarmament, demobilization, and reintegration strategy on behalf of the government-established disarmament, demobilization, and reintegration commission headed by a commissioner reporting directly to the head of state. In the case of Zimbabwe, the Demobilization Directorate was under the ministry of labor and social welfare. The reintegration project will be designed to facilitate outlets for vocational, apprenticeship, and on-the-job training for ex-combatants in trades such as agriculture, carpentry and joinery, auto mechanics, welding, gara and tyre dying, soap making, electrical repair, masonry, blacksmithing, bakery, hairdressing, tailoring, metalwork, and so forth. This component targets ex-combatants who will be placed in institutions located in their areas of resettlement specializing in the various trades mentioned previously. Once the combatants acquire marketable skills, they will be assisted toward self-employment by attempting to link them with institutions providing microcredit. Ex-combatants seeking paid employment will be assisted with job search and placement initiatives. The majority of ex-combatants who participated in the Zimbabwean liberation war hailed from the rural, agricultural-based economies. They should have been given the opportunity to train as commercial farmers under the supervision of the commercial farmers before they could be allocated state land for their successful reintegration through agriculture. The awarding of cash grants was only a temporary solution to the ex-combatant reintegration problem, which later resurfaced in the form of farm invasions. Most of the ex-combatants are now more than forty years old and need to be assisted with setting up productive, sustainable, income-generating projects, training in commercial farming and government support in securing agricultural inputs in the new resettlements.

The veterans of the Zimbabwean independence war believed only the liberation war government will be in a position to sympathize with their deteriorating conditions of survival. They also strongly believe a new government will ignore their problem, terminate their pensions, and even prosecute them for the land invasions. This is why they have vouched to support the ZANU-PF government and fight for its reinstatement, even if it loses the elections. Their loyalty to ZANU-PF is based on the fact they managed to gain concessions in the form of pensions from the government after a few public demonstrations. They subsequently came to the assistance of the landless and the government when they spearheaded the land invasions. The war veterans, supported by the armed forces whose leadership hails from the liberation war, will continue harassing and blaming the government for their failure to reintegrate into civilian life. Should the government have intervened against the land invaders and ex-combatants there was a possibility of confrontation incited by Chenjerai "Hitler" Hundzwi, the late chairman of the war veterans association. Who was to blame for this explosive situation? What was and is needed to put the issue to rest?[40]

---

40. Ibid.

7.0 Harare International Land Reform Donor Conference

At the opening of the three-day International Donors Conference in September 1998, donors and the Zimbabwean government exchanged views on how to create a land reform program to begin alleviating poverty and benefiting a wide section of Zimbabwe's population. A representative for the EU said, although the draft program Zimbabwe prepared presented an ambitious framework for land reform and resettlement, a number of issues need to be further addressed. Peter Leitenbauer, the Austrian ambassador to Zimbabwe, told the conference:

> In our opinion, the implementation of a land reform program of the proposed scale would have to be spread over a longer period of time.[41]

The government intended to acquire five million hectares from the large-scale commercial farming sector over a period of five years. On which, it plans to resettle 150,000 households.

> Leitenbauer continued:
> Land acquisition, selection of beneficiaries and project implementation should be part of a transparent, integrated and consultative process which increases production and alleviates poverty.[42]

Forty-five out of the more than sixty invited local and international donors attended the conference, which sought to raise Z$40 billion equivalent USD 800 million. About Z$25.5 billion equivalent USD 500 million—or sixty percent of the amount required for the exercise—was sought from the international community. The government provided Z$15 billion equivalent USD 300 million (or 35.8 percent) while other beneficiaries met approximately 1.5 percent. The conference had initially been scheduled for June 24 and 25, 1998 but it was postponed amid speculation that very few donors were willing to subsidize the land reform. The World Bank, often at variance with the government over its lavish spending, said it supported the reform exercise because it is "incontestable on

---

41. *Frank exchange begins on Land—Development Bulletin, Lewis Machipisa September 9, 1998*
42. *Frank exchange begins on Land—Development Bulletin, Lewis Machipisa September 9,1998*

equity, efficiency and poverty reduction grounds."[43] Barbara Kafka, the World Bank country director, said the following:

> We are delighted that the government has called this conference as a key step in our working together to make sure that Zimbabwe reaps the results it deserves from its land reform program.
>
> Kafka then cautioned as follows:
>
> Nevertheless, we must not be naive. The downside risks are high. There is abundant international experience to show that poorly executed land reform can carry high social and economic costs. For instance, a program that does not respect property rights or does not provide sufficient support to new settlers is underfunded or is excessively bureaucratic and costly, or simply results in large numbers of displaced farm workers, can have very negative outcomes in terms of investment, production, jobs and social stability.[44]

The World Bank immediately said it would offer technical and financial support and would be willing to cooperate with other development partners in completing the design and initiating the implementation of a successful land reform program in Zimbabwe.

Eighteen years after independence, prime, arable land remains a privilege of Zimbabwe's white minority. In the few cases where it has been redistributed, it has not been done fairly. Alternatively, where people were resettled, infrastructure was not made available. In November, 1997 the government designated 1,503 mostly white-owned commercial farms for takeover. Whites constitute two percent of the population, yet they still own half of all the prime land. At the same time, a million black families are still settled on barren land after being forced to vacate their original fertile areas by the colonial rulers.

> President Mugabe told the conference:
>
> The victims of expropriation have suffered humiliation and impoverishment throughout several decades to the present day…The average population density in the communal areas is thirty-five people per square kilometer and rising to fifty per square kilometer in the most congested districts.[45]
>
> President Mugabe continued:

43. *Frank exchange begins on Land—Development Bulletin, Lewis Machipisa September 9,1998*

44. *Frank exchange begins on Land—Development Bulletin, Lewis Machipisa September 9,1998*

45. *Zimbabwe Financial Gazette President Openning Speech Land Reform Donor Conference September 1998.*

The recent spate of occupations of large-scale commercial farms by communal commercial farmers desperate for land, reflects heir deep-seated anger and mounting frustration with the present pattern of unequal distribution of land ownership, and the pace at which resettlement has been conducted since independence (in 1980). Government cannot afford to betray the faith and trust reposed in it by the people to deliver land to the landless.

President Mugabe, noting his government remained committed to orderly resettlement and would not tolerate people taking over white commercial farms by force, stressed:

If we delay in resolving the land needs of our people, they will resettle themselves. It has happened before and it may happen again. Such anarchy will not be helpful to anyone. We, therefore, trust that the government's efforts for orderly resettlement will receive the necessary support.[46]

Leitenbauer stated, to a considerable extent, the success of the land reform program depended on a macroeconomic environment conducive for investment, including the energetic pursuit of the second phase of the country's economic reform program.

Land reform should also be part of a general reorganization of Zimbabwe's agriculture through a revised national land policy with a view to promoting greater efficiency of landholdings in the communal as well as in resettlement areas. A land reform program should also aim to enhance agricultural production and efficiency and thus generate rates of return necessary to justify the investment required. For this reason, training programs of prospective commercial farmers will be an essential element of a support package focusing on poverty alleviation. We are confident that a land reform program meeting the points I have raised will command wide support.[47]

Political, Social, and Economic Justification for the Harare Donor Conference

The Harare International Donor Conference participants were not interested in the political justification of the proposed land redistribution program. They were

---

46. *Zimbabwe Financial Gazette President Openning Speech Land Reform Donor Conference September 1998.*

47. *Frank exchange begins on Land—Development Bulletin, Lewis Machipisa September 9, 1998*

more interested in funding an economically justifiable program, which should include a reasonable return on capital investment, the participation of the commercial farmers in the capacity building and training of the newly resettled commercial farmers, and guaranteeing sustained, agricultural contribution toward national economic development. Addressing the conference, President Mugabe justified the landless social need for land as demonstrated by the increasing population densities per square kilometer. He cited the recent spate of invasions on commercial farms as a reflection of the landless deep-seated political anger over the slow government land distribution system. The president reminded the donors that his government could not afford to betray the trust bestowed on it by the people to deliver land to the landless. The landless and ex-combatants had waited patiently for ten years after the expiration of the Lancaster House Constitution. They even waited again for a further ten years of fruitless land redistribution negotiations.

The donors should have been reminded the donor conference was called to respond to the British suspension of honoring the pledges made at the Lancaster House conference instead of presenting a new project proposal. There was no reason to rejustify the need for land with convincing congestion figures and fear of the people taking the law into their own hands. The president advised the donor conference that his government remained committed to orderly resettlement and would not tolerate people taking over white commercial farms by force. However, he reminded the donors that delays in resolving the land needs of the people would result in the people resettling themselves by force. It happened before, and it could happen again. The commercial farmers would lose. The landless would repossess the land at the expense of the national economy with its resulting shortages in foreign exchange and inputs to sustain farming operations. The president basically pleaded with the donors to generously contribute toward the acquisition of white commercial farms for the benefit of the black landless. The program was designed to acquire five million hectares from the minority white commercial farmers for the resettlement of 150,000 landless households. To achieve this noble objective, the Zimbabwean government requested the international community contribute Z$25.5 billion equivalent USD 510 million. The Zimbabwean government was in a position to contribute $15 billion equivalent USD 300 million.

According to the donor community, the program was ambitious. As such, it needed to be implemented over a period longer than the proposed five years. The extension of the program implementation period was not going to be accepted by the ex-combatants who had been waiting for the past twenty years. The donors also wanted the program to include the training of resettled commercial farmers to ensure sustainability of farming activities. The government should also realize an acceptable rate of return to justify such a large investment. According to the donors, the success of the land reform program would depend on the establishment of a political environment conducive for macroeconomic development, including the energetic pursuit of the second phase of the country's economic reform program. The donors reminded the government that a program that does not respect property rights or does not provide sufficient support to new commercial farmers is underfunded or is excessively bureaucratic and costly. Simply stated, it results in large numbers of displaced farm workers, which can have very negative outcomes in terms of investment, production, jobs, and social stability. This statement represented the donors' view of the Zimbabwe Land Reform Project, which was being implemented under the same stated negative conditions, a recipe of donor underfunding and failure. In conclusion, international donors said they understood and supported Zimbabwe's land reform program subject to its being revisited to meet the transparency, efficiency, return on investment, and the establishment of a political situation conducive for investment and the resumption of economic activities.

The donors were not interested in the political objective of acquiring land from the commercial farmers for the resettlement of the untrained landless majority. It is common knowledge the commercial farmers were making a major contribution to Zimbabwe's economic development. There was no way to prove the newly resettled landless would have the capacity to sustain the commercial farm production levels. The donors were also stakeholders in the program and would only subscribe to programs whose objectives were supported by their respective countries. Realizing these conditions were not prevailing at that time, the donors did not immediately back their statements with money. The donors developed preconditions before considering funding the Zimbabwean government's land reform program, making it clear the Zimbabwe Land Program was a stand-alone and had nothing to do with the political Lancaster House Agreement. Donors who had made pledges withdrew them without conditions. The World Bank represented the international finance houses, while the Austrian ambassador represented the EU, whose views included those of the United Kingdom. The result of the Harare International Donor Conference was that the donors were quite frank and to the point in advising the Zimbabwean government on prerequisite conditions required for them to consider funding the land reform program. The Zimbabwean government should have thanked the donors, returned back to the drawing board with lessons learned, addressed the political and economic situation, and called for another donor conference.

The British and the American governments were the only countries who could have supported a land redistribution program based on a political need for land acquisition as promised in their out dated historic Lancaster House pledges.[48] The Zimbabwean government should have requested the British and American governments to convene the donor conference on their behalf. The donor negative response to the Harare International Donor Conference fueled the already mounting ex-combatant anger against the government over its failure to redistribute land to the landless. The ex-combatants realized the government did not have any power to redistribute land. As such, they decided to take over commercial farms by force. The government decided to become oblivious to the farm invasions instead of being seen to be supporting the commercial farmers. At the same time, it did not want to be seen to be publicly supporting the illegal farm invasions. The government land acquisition amendment acts and commercial farm invasions led to the formation of the opposition MDC, an alliance of disgruntled intellectuals, socialists, workers, and agricultural and industrial employers.[49]

---

48. *Ibid.*
49. *Ibid.*

8.0 Movement for Democratic Change (MDC) May 1999 Declaration

The National Working Peoples Convention held in Harare on February 1999 gathered working people from all corners of Zimbabwe, rural and urban, and all economic sectors. The Convention noted:

- The disempowerment of the people and breach of rule of law through state-sponsored violence and abuse of human rights

- The inability of the economy to address the basic needs of the majority of Zimbabweans

- The severe decline in incomes, employment, health, food security, and well-being of people

- The unfair burden borne by working women and persistence of gender discrimination in practice

- The decline and, in some cases, collapse of public services

- The lack of progress in resolving land hunger and rural investment needs

- The weak growth in industry and marginalization of the vast majority of the nation's entrepreneurs

- The absence of a national constitution framed by and for the people\

- The persistence of regionalism, racism, and other divisions undermining national integration

- Widespread corruption and lack of public accountability in political and economic institutions

Accordingly, the Convention resolved:

1. The right to a minimum standard of health inputs (food, water, shelter) and health care be defined and entrenched in the constitution, guaranteed and funded on an equitable basis by the state through its mobilization of national resources. Greater priority should be given to prevention of ill health. Community mobilization of resource inputs for health should be complemented by the equitable allocation of health resources (drugs, staff, and so forth) to

the district level. Public participation and accountability in health should be entrenched through stakeholder health development structures from village to national level that are adequately supported to plan, mobilize, and monitor agreed health standards and interventions.

2. Mechanisms should be put in place to equitably and efficiently distribute public, private, and household resources for education to enhance the quality of education and to review the nature of the education curriculum and the support services provided to better prepare children with the skills and orientation needed to tap the economic and employment opportunities in the next millennium. Education and learning should be treated as an ongoing process with facilities for decentralized vocational training in service training and incentive systems to encourage and reward such training. The changes in education should be driven by intersectional planning to ensure education is oriented toward and supports areas of economic and social development and by mechanisms for participation of key stakeholders, including parents.

3. The right of equality of opportunity and treatment for men and women should be recognized and entrenched in the Constitution with appropriate measures to implement this in law and practice in the domestic, educational, health, economic, employment, and political spheres, where gender discrimination is still found.

4. A housing policy should be developed that integrates housing development across the country; matches community efforts and resources with state, employer, and institutional resources; develops new possibilities for building materials and for procurement and distribution of materials; decentralizes the organization of housing delivery and ensures, through joint state/stakeholder mechanisms and public reporting, public accountability in the management of finances for and delivery of land and other inputs to housing.

5. Media freedom should be enshrined in the constitution, supported by an independent media commission and by laws providing for public rights of access to information and for curtailment of government control over and interference in the media. Media and public information should respect the diverse cultures and religious groups.

The National Working People's Convention noted these resolutions—and the more detailed agenda for action arising from them—would not be realized without a strong, democratic, popularly driven and organized movement of the people. Such a movement should recognize and protect the discrete, independent role and mandates of the various organizations of working people, including the labor movement, informal traders organizations, and peasant commercial farmers associations. The Convention thus resolved to take these issues to the people across the country, to mobilize them toward the working peoples' agenda, and to implement a vigorous, democratic political movement for change.

Identity

The mass movement is a united front of Zimbabwe representing various interests and organizations who have come together with common objectives and common principles that are nonnegotiable, that is, to seek political change so as to ensure that the interests of working people, the unemployed, and the rural people are advanced. The movement allows flexible tactics and strategies. The movement shall be called Movement for Democratic Change (MDC).

Objectives

1. To unite organizations of working people, as currently set out in the Working People's Agenda and Declaration

2. To ensure that there is a government, which makes decisions on national policies that are in the interests of the people who are the source of sovereignty

3. To ensure the conditions for and from the base/foundation upon which a political party can be built that is able to contest the 2000 elections. To create, mandate, and own the political party formed and to monitor its performance in relation to the aims of working people

4. To build nation integration so that all Zimbabweans work together without barriers of race, color, tribe, ethnicity, status, and political or religious affiliation

5. To embark on voter education for change

6. To democratize all political processes in the country

Principles

In line with the resolution of the National Working People's Convention held in February, a strong and vigorous political movement for change in Zimbabwe be formed. A postconvention meeting was held in Harare on May 7–9, and this meeting saw the birth of the Movement for Democratic Change (MDC).

The MDC is a united front of Zimbabweans representing various interests and constituent organizations coming together to pursue common objectives and principles that advance the interests of all people in Zimbabwe (workers, professionals, women, peasants, the disabled, and the unemployed, to name but a few).

The MDC stands for the supremacy of the nation and its people and rejects systems that prioritizes the defense of leadership interests at the expense of the defense of people's interests.

The MDC will aim to ensure that government and national policies will be in the interest of all Zimbabweans. The MDC will vigorously campaign for the democratization of political processes and institutions in order to create an environment in which the electorate can make meaningful and informed choices.

The MDC stands for social democratic, human-centered development policies, pursued in an environment of political pluralism, participatory democracy, accountable and transparent governance. The development will take place in a manner that recognizes equality of opportunity and treatment of all people in the building of a united, nonracial, nonethnic democratic society.

The MDC stands for a real people's constitution, written in a democratic, broad-based, and participatory process involving all stakeholders and accountable to a conference of elected representatives, civil and other social groups.

The MDC will advance the participation of citizens and civil society in nation building through organs of participatory democracy that complement the existing forms of representative democracy, Parliament and the Executive.

The MDC will advance development policies that invest in and develop the capabilities and opportunities of Zimbabweans, their national resources, and infrastructure toward real, sustainable, long-term growth.[50]

---

50. *Movement For Democratic Change (MDC) May 1999 Declaration.*

The Shona-language Slogan of the Popular New Political Party, the Movement for Democratic Change (MDC), Spreads Far and Wide throughout the Countryside

Change is urgently needed in Zimbabwe. The country is bedeviled by a fuel shortage. The army is overcommitted in a hopeless war in the Democratic Republic of Congo, and Zimbabweans grieve for lost family and friends in the horrific AIDS pandemic. The economy suffers from forty-nine percent inflation and soaring interest rates and is losing businesses and shedding jobs at a rapid rate. (Unemployment hit fifty percent in 1999). Income inequality has risen to among the world's worst, especially with respect to control of good farming land. Rife with corruption, the ZANU-PF government, led by President Mugabe, seems to have finally reached its death throes. The country's twelve million people appear restless and often furious.

The MDC, led by Morgan Tsvangirai, the popular trade union leader, may be on the verge of winning a majority in the national parliamentary election scheduled for late April. 2000 The results of an opinion poll conducted by Gallup International, released on March 10, 2000 found that sixty-three percent of respondents thought it was "time for a change" while thirty-six percent felt President Mugabe's ruling party should continue in power.[51] A February 2000 referendum on a new constitution promoted by President Mugabe revealed both the impressive mobilization capability of the MDC and the apathy of the peasantry that has normally championed ZANU-PF. The referendum was defeated with fifty-five percent against. It was President Mugabe's first electoral defeat.

While the next presidential election was not until 2002, seventy-six-year-old President Mugabe announced he will not stand again. There is no obvious successor within President Mugabe's fractious, crisis-ridden party. The forty-eight-year-old former mineworker Tsvangirai visited Johannesburg in early March to seek support from the huge Zimbabwean expatriate community. In two well-attended meetings, he also eased the fears of South Africa's business elite. The conservative *Business Day* newspaper recently condemned the MDC as "unproven."

The apparent president-in-waiting has argued for the need to quickly build a broad coalition, drawing support from beyond the trade union movement he has headed since 1989. Some fear, by bringing Zimbabwean, South African, and international capital on board in advisory positions (including a top Confedera-

---

51. *Uneven Zimbabwe: A Study of Finance, Development and Underdevelopment—Patrick Bond's 1998 book*

tion of Zimbabwe Industry dealmaker, Eddie Cross) and also as donors, Tsvangirai will repeat the wretched experience of Zambia. Zambian trade union leader Frederick Chiluba's multiclass alliance won the 1991 election against veteran nationalist Kenneth Kaunda and quickly applied neoliberal economic policies with even worse results than those of his predecessor.

Zimbabwe's other two significant opposition movements line up far to the right of the MDC. In February, a collection of octogenarian, 1960s/1970s nationalists—Ndabaningi Sithole, Abel Muzorewa, and even Rhodesia's last, white minority rule leader Ian Smith, back from political retirement—launched a united democratic front. The other is the democratic union of charismatic former ZANU-PF activist, now self-described liberal, Margaret Dongo (one of just three non-ZANU-PF MPs), whose supporters are quickly shifting to the MDC. For President Mugabe, the MDC's popularity has occasioned a renewed round of bashing the few thousand white commercial farmers and the IMF. Tsvangirai accurately derides this as hollow political posturing.[52]

Tsvangirai Opposed Mugabe's Road to Capitalism

Two decades ago, Zimbabwe's liberation from 200,000 white, colonial, settler Rhodesians was won after a brutal war (with 40,000 black casualties) waged by guerrillas with mass support from peasants. President Mugabe and his on-again, off-again ally, Joshua Nkomo, who died in July 1999, established a nationalist ideology with socialist overtones. However, ZANU-PF's status quo development strategy failed to raise living standards, aside initially from a few rural clinics and schools and the growth of a 200,000-strong, lower middle-class state bureaucracy.

The adoption of a structural adjustment program authored by the IMF and World Bank during the 1990s, compounded by two severe droughts, set the country on a raw and often chaotic capitalist road. Zimbabwe became disastrously dependent upon World Bank and IMF loans and neoliberal policy advice. From 1991, living standards plummeted, and the deindustrialization of Zimbabwe's once-strong manufacturing sector caused huge job cuts.

Between 1989 and 1992, Tsvangirai opposed the structural adjustment from a classical leftist position. (He spent two weeks in jail in 1989 for defending student protests. In 1992, a peaceful protest was broken up and organizers arrested.) When the state reacted with brute force, Tsvangirai shifted into conciliatory gear.

---

52. *Uneven Zimbabwe: A Study of Finance, Development and Underdevelopment—Patrick Bond's 1998 book*

In an alternative economic plan issued by the unions in 1996, Tsvangirai argued
the government's free market economic program was "necessary but insufficient."

After 1992, Tsvangirai advocated tripartite bargaining forum with big government and big business, which also proved fruitless. When a deep economic crisis
began in late 1997, amplified by President Mugabe's political gaffes, the ZCTU
pursued a more sustained attack on ZANU-PF's political power. Meanwhile,
Zimbabwe's middle-class intelligentsia, which, in Zambia, had helped shift Chiluba's Movement for Multiparty Democracy from political liberalism to economic neoliberalism, began self-destructing. One reflection of this was the ease
with which, during the course of the debate over constitutional reform in 1999,
President Mugabe was able to pick off several key academic opponents, who were
once left-leaning critics, and turn them around to become into ZANU-PF boost-
ers. With the weakness of this layer and the strength of its backing from the
ZCTU, over the past two years the MDC has come together as Zimbabwe's
"Workers' Party," its colloquial name. The prime electoral challenge will be to
overcome the rural and liberation movement loyalties to President Mugabe and
patriarchal/ethnic traditions. Moreover, the MDC must get permission from
white commercial farmers to gain access to the two million farm workers
employed on Zimbabwe's 3,000 large plantations. This may result in pressure for
the MDC to soft-pedal land redistribution demands. (A good sign is the appointment of Tendai Biti as head of the MDC's land policy desk. Biti is a left-wing
lawyer, formerly of the small but influential International Socialists movement.)
Likewise, the movement has a desperate need for funds to run a national electoral
campaign, which may make concessions to business interests seem an attractive
thing to do. What degree of ideological flexibility will be required to add peasant
votes and capitalist bucks to the MDC's core union and social movement networks? Given the party's lack of skilled politicians and relatively short, undeveloped program, the MDC's social democratic line depends largely on Tsvangirai's
enormous personal influence.[53]

The Movement for Democratic Change against Land Redistribution Program

The MDC suddenly attracted membership from the ZCTU, disgruntled intellectuals, socialists, owners of industry and commerce, commercial farmers, and their
workers. ZANU-PF was aware that such a movement should not be underesti-
mated due to its grassroots base. Each one of these disgruntled stakeholders had a

---

53.   *Frank exchange begins on Land—Development Bulletin, Lewis Machipisa September 9*

specific reason to wish the success of the MDC and the failure of the ZANU-PF government. Unfortunately, notable ZANU-PF leadership did not defect to join the MDC, which they continue to view as a neocolonialist puppet party sponsored by revolutionary reactionaries and foreign governments. The MDC leadership is composed of young intellectuals who are familiar with textbook politics. Yet, they still need to be exposed to politics in real-life situations. The young cadre of leaders' credibility becomes doubtful, especially when the MDC information and publicity secretary Learnmore Jongwe murdered his wife on suspicion she was involved in an extramarital affair. The government took advantage of this murder case to demonstrate to the nation that the opposition legislators were socially and politically immature to administer their domestic affairs, let alone the country. Those who took part in the armed struggle perceived the union between the commercial farmers, industrialists, workers, and intellectuals as a true front of political malcontents whose agenda was to return the country back to the former colonial masters. The majority of MDC supporters were born after independence. As such, they did not value the contributions made by those who lost their lives during the armed struggle for independence. The majority of the electorate is now composed of the born-free groups, who were born after independence and have been to the same schools with the descendents of the former colonial masters. They do not see the difference between black and white.

The farm invasions were perceived as a violent socialist revolution whose objective was to forcibly acquire developed farms and redistribute them to the landless who did not have any contribution to their development. Most of those who took over the developed farms did not have experience and training to sustain the level of development and production already achieved at these farms. Without training in appropriate technology, the newly resettled farm invaders will only run down big farm management and production activities to small-scale communal farming levels. It should be considered that Zimbabwe was rated among the most outstanding international agricultural production nations. The complex equipment on the farms need operation experience, administration and technical capabilities to repair the machines, electricity maintenance, schoolteachers, finance, and skilled workers. However, it can be argued the initial capital to acquire all these expensive commercial farming agricultural equipment and materials came from forcibly acquired land, forced labor, and the use of the same land as collateral for securing loans from the agricultural development bank. The farm workers, some second-generation workers on the same farms, were convinced that only the MDC government would be able to save their income-generating employment at the farms under their time-tested and capable employers.

The trade unionists were aware the demise of the commercial farmers would result in loss of employment in the agricultural sector. Most intellectuals supported the MDC as the only genuine vehicle for change after witnessing the downfall of the once-vibrant economy in the subregion under the stewardship of the ZANU-PF government. The population was now prepared to ensure that ZANU-PF policies would be prevented from further ruining the economy with fresh memories from the effects of the economic structural adjustment program, which rendered thousands unemployed as well as created and encouraged such vices as prostitution, armed robbery and corruption. The United Kingdom and the international community supported political change with the hope a new government in Zimbabwe would suspend the land reforms and revert to the Lancaster House type of land redistribution. This is why it was cheaper to support the aspirations of a political party that respects the interests of the IMF and whose winning the elections would result in having the land dispute resolved at the advantage of the minority white commercial farmers.

The recently resettled peasants are scared this type of victory will result in their eviction and return to the status quo in which the white commercial farmers would be able to regain the farms. More than seventy-five percent of Zimbabweans are found in the agricultural industry and believe in the importance of land ownership. Some people might say the MDC is a group of puppets supporting the minority white commercial farmers. It can be true, but the white commercial farmers are actually part of a greater coalition of groups with the common objective of changing the government that has served the nation diligently but whose usefulness has now expired. The problem with ZANU-PF is that the old leadership is reluctant to hand over power to the young generation party stalwarts who are now politically mature to take over leadership. Those who joined the MDC have grievances and have identified inefficiencies and corruption within the ZANU-PF government. They would prefer a change from within or outside the ruling party. Even Gwisayi of the Zimbabwe International Socialist Party joined the MDC and became one of its legislators, but he was dismissed later due to his political utterances and after his support for the land reforms became incompatible with the policies of the MDC, which supported the commercial farmers and international new order.

After signing the Lancaster House Agreement, ZANU-PF contested the elections under a socialist manifesto guaranteeing the landless masses eternal life on earth during the life of their government. After winning the elections, the ZANU-PF government could not implement the much-publicized free education and health scheme due to the costs involved. ZANU-PF gradually dropped all socialist-related policies and moved toward capitalism. The Lancaster House Constitution is a road map toward capitalism. The MDC lost the June 2000 parliamentary elections because of alleged government intimidation of the electorate. Before the presidential elections, the MDC leader was accused of planning to have the president of Zimbabwe assassinated through the assistance of a Canadian-based consultancy company. The 2002 presidential election results were contested in the High Court of Zimbabwe. After a fair trial, the opposition leader was finally acquitted of the alleged assassination attempt. At the same time, the opposition leader's treason trial continued in the High Court of Zimbabwe two years after the presidential elections.

The Zimbabwean people were tired of fighting over previous elections, treason trials, and reconciliation meetings, and so forth. They wanted the politicians to bury their differences and pull together for the development of their country. Massive grassroots defections happened from the ruling ZANU-PF to the MDC opposition party as insignificant veteran nationalists crossed the line from ZANU-PF to the MDC. The MDC had a chance to form the next government in a free and fair election. ZANU-PF was never accused of election rigging until the last presidential and parliamentary elections, which were held when the national economy was on the demise. ZANU-PF is slowly waking up from its sleep and is slowly realizing the need for a leadership succession plan. The popular musicians, Thomas Mapfumo and Oliver Mutukudzi, sang about the economy being in tatters and the president accepting retirement due to old age. Maybe the ZANU-PF leadership is forcing President Mugabe to continue at the helm until the land issue is resolved because he was a participant to the Lancaster House Agreement, which plunged the country into the land and economic crisis. The problem might be that whoever takes over from President Mugabe will inherit the problems facing the party and government today. The leadership needs President Mugabe to continue at the helm so they also continue to enjoy the benefits of power seating under the presidential umbrella. The cabinet ministers know the economy continues in the downward direction due to mismanagement and corruption. The former minister of local government, Honorable Tonny Gara, publicly compared President Mugabe with Jesus Christ. This type of misguided appeasement from politically drunk and blind leaders contributes to the misinformation of the executive on the actual situation in the country. Should these sentiments have been inconsistent with party policy, the president or the party could have publicly dissociated the party and government from such fanatic sentiments. These types of exaggerated hero-worshipping sentiments are not made out of respect. Instead, the intent is to impress a leader who extends special favors to his personality cult supporters.

The party does not have any room for policy critics. Those with different ideas have been branded reactionaries and saboteurs. The ZANU-PF axe does not hesitate to descend on the necks of those who criticize government and party policies, for example, Edgar Tekere, who publicly criticized the one party-state. He was then excommunicated from the party. Simba Makoni, former minister of finance who recommended the devaluation of the Zimbabwean dollar against major currencies, was accused of economic sabotage and removed from the post. The MDC guiding principles are based on the reestablishment of a democratic state and the creation of a political atmosphere conducive for economic development in Zimbabwe. It becomes apparent the demise of the modern state named after the ancient Great Zimbabwe was due to overcompromise on the land issue at the Lancaster House conference, economic mismanagement, corruption, resistance to political change, and dictatorship, culminating into the post–Lancaster House Constitution land redistribution and economic crisis. To gain support from the electorate, a democratic state can employ socialist principles by inciting and supporting the electorate in the transferring of wealth generated by the wealthy minority for the benefit of the less privileged majority in exchange for popular support.

Will the MDC government be able to stop the democratic decay, redress the land redistribution issue, and develop an acceptable formula to reasonably compensate those who lost the physical ownership of their farms to unorganized farm invaders and constitutional amendments? The MDC government will find itself in a difficult position to unilaterally reverse the land redistribution implemented by the ZANU-PF government due to possible resistance from those who benefited from the scheme. The MDC government must develop policies ensuring the newly resettled commercial farmers become productive and contribute to the economic development of Zimbabwe. A bold decision needs to be made on the present government policy of hanging onto power through undemocratic means of appeasing ex-combatants and the landless at the expense of national economic development. The Zimbabwean government and the international community need to contribute toward the economic development of those voluntarily displaced from the overcrowded rural areas to the commercial farming areas. Will the majority MDC government reverse the forced land acquisition outside the Lancaster House Agreement through constitutional means with the involvement of the international donor community? Fear of the unknown is very likely to influence ex-combatants and the resettled landless to vote in favor of ZANU-PF for the foreseeable future. The ex-combatants who failed to be reintegrated through custom-made reintegration projects after demobilization are now at the mercy of the government social services. As such, they are no longer a force to be reckoned in the politics of Zimbabwe today.[54]

---

54. *Ibid.*

9.0 Zimbabwe's Twentieth Anniversary Presidential Address

Congratulations and happy anniversary to you all!

It would have been my wish and that of government to mark this very special day in an equally special way. After all, twenty years is a significant marker in the life of any young nation, more so ours, which, phoenix-like, emerged from the cauldron of war into the relative peace we have enjoyed over the two decades gone by. Our twentieth anniversary coincides with the dawn of a new millennium, itself yet another significant marker of the passage of time. It also coincides with our general elections that vital exercise through which we reaffirm our democratic right to choose those we deem fit to lead us. By all counts therefore, this is a date rich in meaning and thus one deserving very special recognition indeed. Regrettably, we mark our twentieth anniversary against the pall of a devastating cyclone, which hit at least three of our eight provinces, causing some deaths and extensive destruction to property and vital infrastructure. As I speak to you, some of our countrymen still reel from the devastating aftereffects of that cyclone.

They are short of food. They are short of clothing. Their homes were destroyed, and they are, in some cases, still exposed to the elements. Their promising harvests were ruined. And, for them, what should have been a good cropping season carries emptiness. Our heart goes out to them. These our people, our citizens, our parents, brothers, sisters, uncles, aunts, neighbors, so unhappily circumstanced, look up to and depend on the rest of us for support and assistance. Happily, many have risen to the challenge, and support in various forms has been mobilized to help families in distress by way of money, clothing, food, shelter, medicines, and even prayers. For all this, we in government are truly grateful.

Yet, a lot more remains to be done by way of rebuilding these broken lives: putting in place new and secure homes; food relief for not just a day, a week, a month, but until the next season; by way of infrastructure—roads, bridges, telecommunications, energy systems, schools, health institutions, facilities and other service centers, dams, and other water points. The children need food so their nutritional standards are maintained. The affected communities need medicines, more so now when the ground is so soft with the chances of waterborne diseases so great. The need remains compelling, and resources will have to be mobilized both from government and from all well-wishers within and outside the borders. Accordingly, government decided that all the resources originally earmarked for celebrating our independence at national level this year be marshaled and redirected toward lightening the severity of the disaster on our people and toward restoring broken infrastructure.

I remind you today that our independence followed over ninety years of oppressive settler colonial rule imposed on us in 1890 when the British occupied our country. Our independence followed years of bitter and protracted struggle. Ask yourselves how many had to die for this great day to come. Apart from our well-known national heroes of the struggle such as Comrades Leopold Takawira, Herbert Chitepo, Jason Ziyapapa Moyo, Nikita Mangena, Josiah Magama Tongogara, we recall on this day our freedom fighters who perished inside and outside the country. We also cannot forget the refugees and others—men, women, and the children who were cut down in cold blood, often tattered book in hand, at Nyadzonya, Chimoio, Tembue, Mkushi, Luangwa, Solwezi, where to this day, they lie buried in mass graves. Even in their death, we could not grant them the dignity of a grave each. How could we, given their severed limbs, their bodies burnt and charred beyond recognition?

The twenty years we have lived as an independent people have, by and large, been years of security and harmony, itself a foremost achievement of our independence. Against dire predictions, we managed to integrate the hitherto three hostile armies from the war into one cohesive, professional, national defense force, which is a source of national pride at home and a dependable player in global stabilization, peacemaking and peacekeeping missions: Mozambique, Somalia, Angola, and currently in the Democratic Republic of the Congo. The 1987 Unity Accord, which ushered in the peace and sense of national cohesion and belonging, which abide in our nation, overcame the conflict, which marred the early part of our independence. Today, there is no sense of alienation among Zimbabweans who feel free to go and even settle in any part of the country. This is truly remarkable given the history of failed, imploding nations on our continent, and, of course, given the sad turn of events in the early part of our independence. This is an achievement we dare not let slip, now and in the eternal future.

The bitterness of our colonial experience could have so easily driven us into a pogrom against the white community, most of whom diligently served and sustained UDI. Yet, our high level of political consciousness soared above bitterness and had long made us see the Rhodesian problem, as inheriting a system of racial injustice and not in the color of the skin of those who manned that system. Except, of course, for those who did not know our politics, and its non racial character for which Zimbabwe has been applauded. What we reject is the persistence of vestigial attitudes from the Rhodesian yesteryears, attitudes of a master race, master color, master owner, and master employer. Our whole struggle was a rejection of such imperious attitudes and claims to privilege. That is why we launched the policy of national transformation alongside that of national reconciliation. We saw the two operating hand in hand in, achieving our goal of reconciling and transforming attitudes for a new nation. We remain sworn to that goal.

The sacrifices we have made for our country and independence simply mean that, as Zimbabweans, we cannot settle for nominal sovereignty. It is not sufficient to have a national flag, a national anthem, and a black president. These are mere signifiers and symbolic accoutrements of our independence and sovereignty as a people. They need content, and content is what we have been struggling to give in the past twenty years. We successfully consolidated people's political power by gaining control and transforming instruments of governance. We also ensured that the majority of our people who had been disenfranchised by colonialism got back and exercised their vote in choosing who governs them. We had free and fair parliamentary elections in 1985, 1990, and 1995. We had presidential elections in 1990 and in 1996. We are set to have both parliamentary and presidential elections next month and in 200 and 2002, respectively. The elective principle has also been entrenched in local government politics and even in internal party politics. The democratic ethic has thus been deepened and consolidated, and we congratulate none but Zimbabweans for that achievement. All these developments gave political content to our independence and sovereignty.

The past twenty years have also seen enormous developmental changes that have touched practically every life. Dramatic and unmatched strides have been made in education at all levels. We have universal education, and our children go to school. In sharp contrast to the 2,401 segregated primary schools with a combined enrolment of 81,958 pupils in 1979, now we have over 4,500 with a combined enrollment in excess of 2,274,178 pupils. The mere 177 secondary schools with 66,215 pupils we had at independence have grown to 1,548 schools with a combined student population of nearly 700,000. Overall, compared to 1979, there are now three times as many children in primary schools and twelve times as many in secondary schools.

Teacher training colleges, which, at independence, were a mere four with a combined intake of 1,000 trainees, have now risen to fifteen with an intake of 17,000. Technical colleges have risen from two with an intake of 2,000 to the current fifteen with an intake of 20,000. The sole university we had in 1980 with 2,000 students is now sharing the load with seven others, all carrying a student population of over 30,000. Our professionals—doctors, teachers, nurses, managers, engineers, academics, and so forth—are respected and in great demand throughout the region and in Europe. The sixty-two percent literacy level we had at independence has risen to eighty-two percent, the best on the continent and among the best in the world. We are leaders in education and skills development, and we continue to introduce changes to our educational system to ensure we remain among the best and broad enough to meet our manpower and skills requirements. Again, this is a resounding achievement for which we make no apologies.

In the past twenty years, we have constructed or upgraded 456 health centers, 612 rural hospitals, twenty-five district hospitals, as well as one provincial hospital in each of the country's eight provinces. I am happy that as I address you today, over eighty-five percent of our population is now within eight kilometers of a health facility. The twenty-five percent coverage of immunization at independence has now been boosted to ninety-two percent, while antenatal coverage rose from twenty percent at independence to the present eighty-nine percent. Regrettably, the enormous progress we have been making over the years has been reversed by the growing menace of the HIV/AIDS pandemic, which is raising infant mortality and reducing life expectancy. However, a lot is happening by way of raising awareness of the AIDS menace, And, in December last year, I launched the National AIDS Policy, which should provide a framework for our anti-AIDS initiatives. We continue to review the national health budget to ensure that the health infrastructure we have put in place can begin to deliver more meaningful services to our people. This we do in the context of the recommendations of the Ten-Year National Health Strategy, which emerged from the Commission of Inquiry into National Health.

But, of course, our focus has always been on the preventive primary health care, which is a lot better than an approach with an emphasis on curative measures. We have done remarkably well in respect of rural food security, building a general awareness of nutritional food intakes at household level as well as ensuring clean rural water supplies. Whereas the country had a mere 1,226 boreholes, currently we have 34,538 boreholes, 10,536 deep wells, and 520 piped water schemes, up from a mere twenty-six at independence.

In terms of infrastructure, the investment has been extraordinarily heavy. At independence, we only had 121 dams, most of which serviced the commercial farming and urban sectors. Today, the country boasts of 2,438 dams, most of them linked to thriving irrigation schemes. We achieved this by pursuing a policy of one major dam per district. And, as I speak to you today, work is underway at Wenimbi, Biri, Dande, Dotito, Mundi, Mataga, Mutawatawa, and Mpudzi dams. Having completed the Pungwe Water Project, which I commissioned a few weeks ago, focus is now on major water projects for Matebeleland in general and Bulawayo in particular. Many roads were also either built or upgraded in the past twenty years. I also recognize the enormous strides done by our power utility, ZESA, in bringing electricity to many rural centers through its laudable rural electrification program.

Another area, which is a source of national pride, is that of agriculture. I have already referred to infrastructure-related developments, as well as the vital area of skills development. These gains have a direct bearing on agriculture. Early on in our independence, we recognized agriculture as the engine of growth and deliberately directed resources toward its boost. The number of agriculture training institutions has risen from four to seven, and the coverage of extension work has greatly improved with the ratio of extension worker to commercial farmers improving from one per 1,200 at independence to one per 800 currently. This growth has shown by way of increased output in practically every crop yielding the current position of surplus which we enjoy and which has made us chair the Southern African Development Community (SADC) region's food security portfolio. Phenomenal growth has been registered in the crops of maize, cotton, tobacco, and horticulture, as well as in beef production.

More needs to be done especially in the area of the economy where gains have been both lean and erratic. Growth has been marginal, and unemployment has risen, accounting for current hardships. The resources available to sustain the high level of development we have achieved since independence are diminishing. Some businesses are faced with closure, although some, especially in the financial sector, are doing remarkably well. Interest rates are high, as is also inflation, making life quite difficult for many people, especially our workers. Our export performance has been dismal, made worse by the depressed nature of prices of those commodities we trade in on the international market. Government is concerned about this negative turn in the economy and hence its new Millennium Recovery Program, which seeks, among other things to consolidate fiscal reforms, accelerate public enterprise reforms, stabilize prices at lower levels, stabilize the value of the Zimbabwe dollar as well as resolve the foreign currency shortages, and stimulate the growth of the productive sector. We think this program, which has already come under examination in the National Economic Consultative Forum, should form the basis of our economic recovery. The issue of land remains both emotive and vexed. It has always been so, and many will recall that negotiations for independence almost got bogged down over this matter. Between 1980 and 1995, we were able to resettle 71,000 families on about 3.3 million hectares excised from the commercial sector. This was a far cry from the 162,000 families we had hoped to settle on eight million hectares of land. We resumed land reforms under what we have termed the Second Phase, and, to this day, over 2,422 households have been resettled on sixty-six farms. The Second Phase of Land Reforms envisaged the excision of about five million hectares of land from the commercial sector, with a million hectares set to be delivered for resettlement every year. We had hoped that this would start with nearly a thousand farms we had designated for acquisition. Sadly, this was not to be as the commercial farmers contested the matter in the courts, forcing government to abandon the acquisition process.

The process of land delivery has been both slow and frustrating. Between 1980 and 1990, we were slowed down by the "willing-seller, willing-buyer" clause in the Lancaster House Constitution. Equally, the resources, which the British and the American governments had pledged to make available at Lancaster House, either stopped or were reduced to a trickle. Even after removing the constitutional barriers, we were still faced with the issue of diminishing resources against ever-rising prices. After 1997, we also had to content with the reluctance of the new Labor government, which did not want to honor commitments made by previous British governments on the land issue. We also faced greater commercial farmer resistance, whose manifestations included not just the legal challenges I have already referred to, but also resistance to the land clause we had introduced in the rejected draft constitution.

Naturally, this created frustration leading to the current spate of farm occupations by the war veterans and sporadic clashes in which two lives have regrettably been lost. We can understand the frustrations of the war veterans just as we appreciate the pressures faced by the commercial farmers. Yesterday and today, I have been meeting with the leadership of the commercial farmers and the war veterans so we can reach some understanding. Two weeks ago, I met with the British foreign secretary, Robin Cook, who suggested Zimbabwe send a delegation to the United Kingdom to reopen negotiations on land reforms. We should be able to find a way forward, but one that recognizes the urgent need for land reforms. It is the last colonial question heavily qualifying our sovereignty. We are determined to resolve it once and for all.

Let us continue to cherish our independence, as well as uphold the principles of our sovereignty. Let us defend our freedom and deliver the benefits of independence to our people. Happy Anniversary.[55]

---

55. *President Robert Mugabe, address on the occasion of Zimbabwe's twentieth independence anniversary, 18 April 2000.*

Indirect Election Campaign in the Presidential Speech

The president informed the nation about the retrogressive impacts of the HIV/AIDS pandemic and how government was involved in attempting to stop its spread. Going back to politics, he reminded the nation about how the independence came after more than ninety years of oppressive settler colonial rule imposed on Zimbabweans in 1890 when the BSAC occupied the country. Under the conditions of the Rudd Concession, the BSAC came to Zimbabwe at the invitation of King Lobengula of Matebeleland. Stressing ZANU-PF contribution toward the independence of Zimbabwe, he justly paid tribute to liberation war heroes in the likes of Leopold Takawira, Herbert Chitepo, Jason Ziyapapa Moyo, Nikita Mangena, and Josiah Magama Tongogara, who are all former PF-ZAPU and ZANU-PF political and military leaders. The president did not mention the first Chumurenga heroes—Nehanda, Kaguvi, Mukwati, Mashayamombe, and others—probably because the names of these heroes, whose gallant actions inspired the second Chimurenga, which brought about the Lancaster House Agreement negotiations leading to independence, are now long forgotten and now belong to the political achieves of Zimbabwean history. For the same reason, the ruling party must remember the second Chimurenga war heroes' contributions toward the achievement of independence are also gradually fading out of peoples' lives. In addition, the president further reminded the nation of the sacrifices made by those who died at the hands of the Rhodesian forces in refugee camps in Zambia and Mozambique. The majority of the Zimbabwean electorate was born after independence, and some do not even understand the reason why Zimbabweans resorted to the armed struggle instead of dialogue, which finally brought about independence through the Lancaster House Agreement.

The president reminded the nation of the success in the integration of the three former hostile armies from the war into one cohesive, professional, national defense force twenty years ago, which is a source of national pride at home and a dependable player in global stabilization as well as peacemaking and peacekeeping missions, including Mozambique, Somalia, Angola, and currently the Democratic Republic of the Congo. In Mozambique and the Democratic Republic of the Congo, the governments of those countries invited the Zimbabwean government, whereas, in Somalia and Angola, the United Nations invited the Zimbabwean government. The nation was reminded the 1987 Unity Accord ushered in the peace and sense of national belonging, which abide in our nation, as well as overcame the conflict marring the early part of our independence. The former ZAPU party was serious in the Patriotic Front alliance to the extent that Joshua

Nkomo returned to Zimbabwe under the banner of the Patriotic Front. Nkomo received a national hero welcome at the Zimbabwean grounds from both ZANU and ZAPU members who were now under the banner of the Patriotic Front. The next week, President Mugabe returned to Zimbabwe and was welcomed by a bigger crowd, which was now less the PF-ZAPU component because it was apparent that ZANU-PF had decided to stand the elections separate from PF-ZAPU.

After the elections, the two Patriotic Front parties combined to form the cabinet of an independent Zimbabwe. This alliance was short-lived when arms of war were discovered in PF-ZAPU ex-combatant-owned farms. The government annexed the farms, detained the PF-ZAPU leadership, tortured some of them, and released terminally ill survivors who later died out of custody, the most popular being Vote Moyo, Major General Lookout Masuku, and Brigadier Charles Grey. We must also remember the unity agreement followed disgruntled elements of the reintegrated Zimbabwe National Army, former ZIPRA forces who had deserted the army and started dissident activities in Matebeleland and the Midlands areas under the leadership of renegade ex-ZIPRA field commanders, Morgan Gayigusu, Tennison Tambolenyoka, Richard Gwesela, and Fidel Castro. The government unleashed the North Korean-trained Fifth Brigade into Matebeleland and the Midlands to counter the dissidents causing untold fatalities on the civilian population. This dissident activity occupied most of the Zimbabwe National Army, resulting in the government accepting the dissident war could not be won in the battlefield. Zimbabweans should also thank Canaan Banana, the first president of independent Zimbabwe, for his efforts in the unification of ZANU-PF and PF-ZAPU, bringing an end to the dissident war and political tribalism in Zimbabwe.

The failures in the management of the economy marred the successes in education, agriculture, and domestic and international politics. The president accepted that more needed to be done, especially in the area of the economy where gains were both lean and erratic. The nation was advised that economic growth had been marginal and unemployment had risen, accounting for current hardships. The resources available to sustain the development achieved since independence were diminishing. Some businesses were faced with closure, although some, especially in the financial sector, were doing remarkably well. Interest rates are high, as well as inflation, making life quite difficult for many people, especially the workers. Our export performance has been dismal, worsened by the depressed nature of prices of those commodities we trade on the international market. Basically, the president officially announced the economy was sliding in the downward direction and very little could be done to avoid total collapse. The actual causes of economic failure were related to the externalization of funds and institutional corruption.

President Mugabe accepted the fact the process of land delivery had been slow and frustrating. Sitting that between 1980 and 1990, land acquisition was slowed down by the "willing-seller, willing-buyer" clause in the Lancaster House Constitution. Equally, the resources, which the British and the American governments had pledged to make available at Lancaster House, either stopped or were reduced to a trickle. On this issue, it will be very unfair to blame anybody for the slowness of the land acquisition process except the Zimbabwean nationalists who signed the Lancaster House Agreement. "Willing-seller, willing-buyer" depends on supply and demand. During the life of the Lancaster House Agreement Constitution, the commercial farmers did not have any incentive to sell their properties. Even after the removal of the constitutional barriers, Zimbabwe found itself confronted with the issue of diminishing resources against ever-rising prices and the reluctance of the new Labor government, which did not want to honor commitments made by previous British governments on the land issue. In addition, the government faced greater commercial farmer resistance, whose manifestations included not just the legal challenges but also resistance to the land clause introduced in the rejected draft constitution. Resistance to the land acquisition amendment might have been due to the fact the clause was part of the proposed new constitution, which was rejected, in a national referendum.

The delay in land acquisition created landless and ex-combatant frustration, leading to the spate of commercial farm invasions and occupations as well as sporadic clashes in which lives were regrettably lost. The government appreciated the frustrations of the war veterans just as they appreciated the pressures the commercial farmers faced. The president informed the nation he had been meeting with the leadership of the commercial farmers and the war veterans to reach some understanding. Nobody could expect the commercial farmers and the war veterans to reach a compromise when the Zimbabwe and the British governments could not reach a compromise over the land issue. The president informed the nation he recently met with the British foreign secretary, Robin Cook, who suggested Zimbabwe send a delegation to the United Kingdom to reopen negotiations on land reforms. [56] At that point and time, the government was still optimistic the Zimbabwe/British negotiations could produce a miraculous solution to the land issue. The president was skeptical of the outcome of any land-

---

56. *President Robert Mugabe, address on the occasion of Zimbabwe's twentieth independence
     anniversary, 18 April 2000.*

related negotiations with the British government and accepted it was the last colonial question qualifying Zimbabwe sovereignty. There was no reason for a genuinely independent country to continue pestering its former colonial master for financial assistance. The British started honoring the Lancaster House pledges, but it suspended the funding because of corruption in the resettlement program.

The president had exhausted all peaceful means of resolving the land issue, but he failed to secure support and financial assistance from the British and—yet indeed—the international community. The president made it clear to the British government and the international community to anticipate violence over the land issue and the government would not be morally obliged to stop the land invasions. Not only the ex-combatants but also the landless majority were now questioning the government's credibility because, ten years after the expiration of the Lancaster House Agreement, they could still not have access to land. The alternative was for the government to stop farm invasions in support of the minority white commercial farmers. In the making, it would face a violent rebellion, which could lead to the removal of the government by force. The solution was to become oblivious to the invasions and simultaneously secretly support the farm invaders. Historic achievements and past glories cannot be converted into food and services. The people are more interested in the immediate plans to salvage the economy and regain their position of respect in the international community. Successes in military reintegration and national unity are initiatives of the past, which do not need reminding and repeating every year. Through transparent and efficient economic management, the government should have been in a position to buy out the commercial farmers from their own reserves accrued over a period of ten years instead of depending on handouts from donors. We all remember, during the first ten years of independence, government entourages to international conferences were too large to be desired in an efficiently managed economy. As a country, Zimbabwe is not popular with the donors because of government's lavish spending.

The people complained about government overspending, but corrective measures were not implemented in time. These tours cost a lot of money in foreign currency in the form of travel allowances for officers participating in meetings and bodyguards. The allowance was the same for the officers and bodyguards because they were all considered to be equal outside Zimbabwe. These tours became shopping sprees for some unscrupulous officers who felt they were underpaid at home. In order to smuggle non-duty-free goods, some of the officers urged their baggage should not be searched because they were holders of Zimbabwean diplomatic passports and government identification cards. However, due to the scarcity of foreign currency, tours outside of the country have been drastically curtailed. The government implemented a task force to investigate the leakage in export foreign currency remittances. As a result, top government supporters—and not the Western powers—were netted for withholding export revenue remittances outside the country. In addition to the embarrassment, it was revealed the reserve bank foreign currency transaction inspectors were actually soliciting for bribes from the suspected foreign currency remittance evaders. What do we expect from a system that tolerated corruption of the fiscal through the liberalization of tender procedures, whereby government procurements are craftily channeled through indigenous private suppliers at exorbitant markup prices with the profits shared between the tender board officers and the suppliers?

The commercial farmers and industrialists were also losing confidence in the government. As such, agricultural production was reduced, negatively impacting the foreign currency returns from agriculture. Some commercial farmers, industrialists, and entrepreneurs, including indigenous businessmen even deliberately withheld the remittance of export foreign currency due to the continued uncertainty of the future. The major enemy of the country is now the new breed of capitalists who hailed out of corruption and survive on milking the national treasury to the extent of building mansions with helipads in anticipation of owning helicopters in the near future, owning fleets of private cars, and enjoying the pride of having numerous mistresses.[57]

---

57. *Ibid.*

10.0 Anglo-Zimbabwean Land Reform Negotiations Reinitiated

The land question has been and remains the central social, political, and economic issue for Zimbabwe today. It is central to the attainment of social and political stability as well as economic development to the country. The majority of the nation's black population still lives in congested, ecologically marginal regions of the country twenty years after the attainment of independence. Against this background, the primary goal of the land reform program of Zimbabwe is to reaffirm and reassert its sovereign right over its land and natural resources that were extinguished during the period of British colonial rule. Accordingly, Zimbabwean government will acquire the remaining five million hectares of the 8.3 million hectares targeted for redistribution under the resettlement program. The five million hectares will primarily benefit poor, land-hungry peasants currently living in congested rural areas and veterans of Zimbabwe's war of liberation as well as contribute to wealth creation and cost effect ways of land utilization.

My government has embarked on a program of indigenizing medium- to large-scale commercial agriculture through the Commercial Farm Settlement Scheme (CFSS). The government continues promoting the development of an efficient large-scale commercial farming sector as a parallel process to land redistribution under the resettlement program. To this end, the CFSS inherited from the colonial regime is being used as a vehicle to facilitate entry of black, indigenous commercial farmers. This initiative is one of many that successive colonial governments and the present government has used to support individuals with the appropriate potential to pursue commercial farming through providing land to them on specified leasehold terms. The beneficiaries in colonial times were British veterans from the two World Wars, other European immigrants, numerous white government officials and ministers of past regimes, and other members of the public.

The current CFSS selects beneficiaries using similar criteria inherited from past colonial schemes, using leasehold conditions more stringent than those followed in the colonial period. The CFSS initiative is based upon an improved policy. The scheme is not—and will not—benefit from land acquired for redistribution under the resettlement program. Instead, the Zimbabwean government has transferred land from the leasehold and state-farming sector to the CFSS. In fact, the government has also transferred land from the leasehold and state-farming sector to the resettlement program. Whereas, under colonial overlordship, the CFSS empowered the white community, in independent Zimbabwe, the same instrument empowers black indigenous people with potential in agriculture and, in the process, indigenizes large-scale commercial fanning.

Objecting to the purpose and scope of the CFSS now that the beneficiaries are black Zimbabweans and exalt its effectiveness during the colonial period when it benefited whites would be unmistakably racist. Furthermore, less than ten percent of those who have benefited from this scheme are government officials and ministers of the present government. At any rate, those few government officials benefiting from this scheme have qualified openly for the farms and use them adequately. The beneficiaries of the CFSS scheme are also not to be confused with those indigenous persons who have bought their farms using loans and their savings.

Zimbabwe's land acquisition and resettlement program is undertaken within the existing legal framework and policies of the Zimbabwean government. Currently, this framework is expressed in two policy documents: the Land Reform and Resettlement Phase II and the Inception Phase Framework Plan.

Efforts at acquiring land compulsorily have been undertaken through the Land Acquisition Act (1992–1996) while more than ninety-eight percent of all farms so far acquired for redistribution have been acquired through the "willing-seller, willing-buyer" method. The government, within the existing legal framework and following due legal process, has also pursued the 841 farms, which are currently being contested in the courts by large-scale commercial farmers opposed to their compulsory acquisition. The intent of the recent constitutional amendments on the land clauses is to reduce the financial, cumbersome administrative burdens faced by the government in land acquisition. The government is not against the principle of compensating commercial farmers for land acquired if resources by its partners and friends can be made available to enable speedy, efficient land acquisitions.

The government respects the rule of law. However, the government's assessment is that a massive confrontation of the war veterans on farms by the police would not only overstretch their limited capacity so as to make them ineffective, but it would also incite greater violence and conflict on the farms. The government views the current demonstrations as a political phenomenon needing political solution. This is why President Mugabe has taken it upon himself to encourage dialogue among all concerned parties. This method worked before when occupations have occurred. We are already seeing the benefits of such dialogue with the calming of the situation on the farms.

The root cause of the current impasse is the self-evident failure of the main parties to operationalize the agreements reached at the Harare International

Donor Conference. The donors have hardly financed the Inception Phase Framework plan, which was developed and agreed upon by all stakeholders following the conference. Donor support has not been given for land acquisition and infrastructure on resettlement schemes. No progress has been made by non-state actors in delivering land or in support of resettlement through the so-called complimentary approaches.

Nonetheless, the Zimbabwean government hopes the current negotiations between itself and other stakeholders and donors will result in greater support to the land resettlement component of the land reform program. The Zimbabwean objective in the redistribution of acquired land will go beyond the political and moral imperatives to include sound economic management and higher agricultural productivity among, not only the newly settled, but also those remaining in the communal areas who will be reorganize simultaneously with the resettlement program. All internal parties now agree there is a need to intensify the pace of redistribution and resettlement within the framework of the agreed principles of the Harare International Donor Conference. The government is determined to start the land redistribution process starting with 841 farms that were identified in 1997 using the following criteria: derelict land, underutilized land multiple-owned farms, absentee-owned farms, and land adjacent to communal lands.[58]

Resumed Land Reform Funding Negotiations Failed

In early April 2000, President Mugabe met with the British foreign secretary, Robin Cook, who suggested Zimbabwe send a delegation to the United Kingdom to reopen negotiations on land reforms. Minister John Nkomo led a government delegation to London in order to follow up on this suggestion. At the London meeting, Minister John Nkomo restated the position of the government and the people of Zimbabwe over the land issue, which remained the central social, political, and economic issue for Zimbabwe. At the time of the meeting, the majority of the Zimbabwean population still lived in congested regions of the country twenty years after the attainment of political independence.

Against this background, the political justification of the land reform program was to reaffirm and reassert the sovereign right of Zimbabwe over its land and natural resources that were suppressed during the period of British colonial rule and further denied for ten years after independence through the Lancaster House Constitution clause granting commercial farmers freedom from deprivation of property. The British government contributed some funds toward the acquisition

---

58. *Zimbabwe Minister John Nkomo, London Land Negotiations, 27 April 2000.*

of land from willing commercial farmers for the benefit of the landless, but it suspended further contributions because of corruption in the allocation of the acquired land. The British government was informed the intent of the Zimbabwe Land Reform Program was to result in the indigenization of medium- to large-scale commercial agriculture via the CFSS.

The Zimbabwean government delegation assured the British government that it continued promoting the development of an efficient large-scale commercial farming sector as a parallel process to land redistribution under the resettlement program. To this end, the CFSS inherited from the colonial regime was being used as a vehicle to facilitate entry of black, indigenous commercial farmers. These are the very same types of unpopular, class discrimination settlement schemes, which resulted in the armed struggle. Even the British knew the referenced colonial schemes were not designed for the empowerment of the landless natives but to protect the interests of the ruling minority.

The Zimbabwean delegation advised this initiative was one of many that successive colonial governments and the present government had used to support individuals with the appropriate potential to pursue commercial farming by providing land to them on specified leasehold terms. It should be recalled the beneficiaries in colonial times were British veterans from the two World Wars, other European immigrants, numerous white government officials and ministers of past regimes, and other members of the public. The Zimbabwean delegation statement justified the allegations the land acquired through British funds benefited government and party officials instead of the bona fide landless majority was far short from being a satisfactory for the British to consider lifting the funding suspension.

The root cause of the current impasse was the self-evident failure of the main parties to implement the agreements reached at the Harare International Donor Conference. The donors had hardly financed the Inception Phase Framework plan, which was developed and agreed upon by all stakeholders following the conference. Donor support for land and infrastructure acquisition on resettlement schemes had not been given, and non-state actors had not made any progress in delivering land or in support of resettlement through the so-called complimentary approaches. In as much as the British government would have wanted to see the land issue resolved in Zimbabwe, they could not be seen to compromise the well-being of the children of their kith and kin. Minister John Nkomo's self-explanatory speech was intended to herald the government position and planned course of action under the scenario if negotiations failed. Despite the threatening remarks from the Zimbabwean delegation, the British refused to accept responsibility for compensating fast-track or violently displaced landowners.

The John Nkomo delegation should have included representatives from the Commercial Farmers Union (CFU) in order to have a formidable alliance of the impacted stakeholders the Zimbabwean people mandated to negotiate the land redistribution process with the former colonial master. Naturally, the British felt sympathy for their kith and kin, influencing the results of the negotiations in favor of the Zimbabwean government and the commercial farmers. Even if the British government had continued funding the scheme, honoring the pledges made at Lancaster House, the commercial farmers had a right to hold onto their land or inflate the prices beyond market value, as what had happened in Kenya. Donors did not support the land redistribution program because it did not include training to ensure sustainable, income-generating agricultural activities.

The commercial farms should have been allocated to those with agricultural qualifications and experience who could have jointly owned the land with the resettled landless in the concept of cooperatives. The position on the ground is that the landless people now have land through resettlement or invasion. However, land without capital, equipment, and materials for viable agricultural activities become internal displacement, which is worse than being landless. The British government was not interested in any method of land redistribution outside the "willing-seller, willing-buyer" Lancaster House Agreement clause on freedom from deprivation of property. The Zimbabwean government delegation failed to explain the allegations of corruption in the redistribution of land acquired through the British government initial honor of pledges made at the Lancaster House conference.[59]

---

59. Ibid.

11.0 Structural Adjustment Program Social and Economic Disasters

In 1980, the World Bank and IMF intervened in Zimbabwe's economy to disastrous effects. Since then, it has undermined the country, bringing it nearly to the brink of social and economic collapse in the 1990s. The impact of its pressure by the late 1990s caused the Zimbabwean government to begin opposing IMF reforms. These demanded savage public spending cuts to meet loan obligations, which could never be met and were intended to shackle the country to Western interests, especially to enable easier foreign direct investment. As part of the trap, the IMF ordered the state push its privatization program to the limit to supposedly offset those unattainable obligations. Zimbabwe's chief industry is mining, contributing approximately twenty percent of its GDP. Agriculture dominates at sixty percent. The Zimbabwean government, increasingly squeezed in this vice, began shifting from the IMF plan. However, the British government, while attacking Zimbabwe for consequent economic mayhem, does not make any allowance for the fact that, since 1991, the country have been structurally adjusted and going forward with change.

This underlying factor of social and economic destabilization is crucial to the progress of the land reform program and, ultimately, the farm invasions. The IMF has reacted to Zimbabwe's defensive approach by terminating all loans in 1999 for supposedly defaulting on its obligations. It seems there is no debt forgiveness here. Now, the United Kingdom, the United States, and Europe is exerting pressure to impose economic sanctions. In July, 2001 the United States Senate Subcommittee on African Affairs approved the Zimbabwe Democracy and Economic Act, which proposed partial sanctions. It was then passed to the United States House of Representatives. Meanwhile, the United States Senate has approved sanctions action against Zimbabwe. The Brussels-based think tank, the International Crisis Group, simultaneously called for a Yugoslav-style solution to be brought against Zimbabwe if next year's presidential elections prove undemocratic. Europe is expected to take similar sanctions action in October if dialogue fails.[60]

The present-day Zimbabwe is an example of a once-strong African state that has fallen rapidly through weakness to the very edge of the abyss of failure, reminding us of the possible reasons for the demise of the old city of Great Zimbabwe. All Zimbabwe lacks to join the ranks of failed states are widespread inter-

---

60.   *Steve Lawton, Zimbabwe 'structurally adjusted*

nal uprisings directed at the government. But that could come, particularly if the political and economic deterioration of the country continues unchecked. In 2000 and 2001, GDP per capita slid backward by ten percent per year. Inflation galloped from thirty to one hundred sixteen percent and then to two hundred seventy-five percent in 2003. The local currency fell against the American dollar from thirty-eight to one in 2001 to four hundred to one in the first half of 2002 and to seventeen hundred to one in the second half. Foreign and domestic investment ceased. Unemployment rose to eighty percent in a country of twelve million. Health and educational services vanished. HIV infection rates climbed to thirty percent as approximately 3,000 Zimbabweans died every week in 2003.[61] Respect for the rule of law was badly battered and then subverted. Political institutions ceased to fully function. Agents of the state preyed on its real and its supposed opponents, chilling free expression and the alleged shameless stealing of a presidential election in 2002. The government's legitimacy vanished. Corruption flourished meanwhile as the ruling elite pocketed their local and DRC war gains while letting most Zimbabweans go hungry. Real starvation appeared in mid-2002, despite food aid from abroad. All of this misery—and the tendency to fail—resulted (as it did earlier in the DRC under Mobutu Sese Seko and Sierra Leone during the time of Siaka Stevens) from the ruthless designs and vengeances of omnipotent rulers.

At independence, Zimbabwe inherited a viable economy established during the period of the United Nations sanctions against Rhodesia. Some schools of thought allege the intent of the economic structural adjustment program was to weaken the Zimbabwean government's economic capacity to acquire the farms at the willing-seller buyer price. As of this date, most intellectuals in Zimbabwe are yet to be convinced the country needed a structural adjustment program. By the end of 1989, the government realized it could not meet the IMF targets. As usual, it tried shifting the blame to the alleged inefficiencies of executive managers, especially those of semi government institutions, which were benefiting from the IMF loans.

The most interesting case was that of the national railways of Zimbabwe in which the IMF/World Bank recommended the cannibalization of diesel locomotives to create hybrids, which did not have any defined sources for spare parts, instead of procuring new locomotives. In addition, they even recommended the phase out of steam locomotives, alleging they were uneconomic. Considering the fact that Zimbabwe had vast coal reserves and well-positioned watering points

---

61. *Zimbabwe Financial Gazette.*

with the spare parts being manufactured in the country, appropriate metals being available locally, and the manpower and technology available in the country, there was no reason to believe these machines were uneconomic in the Zimbabwean situation at that time. Suggestions and recommendations to improve the railways performance using appropriate technology were being frustrated by senior officers who were guaranteed of receiving their pensions outside the country, according to the Lancaster House Agreement. In the pretext of recommending measures to revamp the economy, the World Bank/IMF were interested in structural adjustment programs that would eventually drag the country into dept and perpetual dependence on loans from these institutions. Some politicians, through their influence in the parliamentary commissions, investigated the operations of semi government institutions taking advantage of the situation and installed their friends to the helms of semi government institutions and management boards.

These so-called commissions investigated the economic performance of the National Railways of Zimbabwe, which resulted in the removal of the top management and the board of directors. Gross mismanagement and privatization of most of the profit-making activities of the railways followed. The same happened with management and the board of directors at Air Zimbabwe, Wankie Colliery, Zimbabwe Electricity Supply Authority, Grain Marketing Board, Zimbabwe Iron and Steel Company, Zimbabwe Minerals Marketing Authority, and so forth. In particular, the semi government institutions commissions, headed by the vice president's office, targeted those semi government organizations, which fell under Herbert Ushewokunze, the late controversial minister, who allegedly catapulted his Zezuru tribesmen to powerful positions. The whole exercise became a tribal vendetta, resulting in the displacement of Zezuru managers in semi government institutions located in the Midlands and Matebeleland with locals from those areas. As a result of appointing unqualified managers, most of the semi government institutions became inefficient until the verge of a grinding halt was nearly reached. The most remarkable example was that of the National Railways of Zimbabwe, which embarked on a massive privatization of services at the expense of revenue-earning operations, resulting in a mass retrenchment of specialized staff to the extent that the organization struggled to pay staff terminal benefits. The inherited semi government institutions economic incompetence was deliberately tolerated during colonial rule because the semi government-owned institutions cross-subsidized other national activities, which could become uneconomic without these service subsidies. The government was justified to subsidize semi government institutions loses instead of directly subsidizing those industries which could be impacted by semi government institutions operating at realistic economic levels. With the assistance of the IMF, semi government institutions service rates were brought to economic levels. Thus, services were now being rendered at full cost, adversely impacting the economic viability of industry and agriculture. Government departments and other state enterprises were required to reduce staff levels in line with recommended budgets.

The structural adjustment program introduced the concept of the indigenous businessman, popularly known as the briefcase businessman. This type of businessman had his business legalized through declared, unproven capital. They survived and thrived on the buyers in government and other public institutions. Through corruption in the national tender procedures, tenders were granted to indigenous businessman who were selected and financed under the government affirmative action, which was intended to promote indigenous businessman. With their limited resources, these mostly retrenched government officers who became businessmen overnight were granted contracts to procure mainly for the government, doubling the prices with the knowledge of the department buyers who received an agreed percentage of the proceeds. Instead of the budgeted funds benefiting the public, part or most of the funds ended up in the hands of the department buyer and the briefcase businessman. The government eventually failed to deliver the commitments made in the national budget. Some of this affirmative action businessman became so prosperous that they used their ill-earned profits to buy voters. They are now members of parliament, representing the ruling party. The system created a new breed of aggressive supercapitalists who openly boast of owning more than five cars and building houses with more than ten bedrooms and four helipads. Due to the organized siphoning of budgeted funds, the indigenous businessman and the buyers became rich at the expense of the toiling masses. The indigenous businessman further progressed into international tenders, whereby he did not remit all their funds back to the national treasury, resulting in the erosion of the national foreign currency reserve. A time came when ministers became involved in the allocation of tenders and received kickbacks as thanks for granting the tender.

On the attainment of independence, the government developed a noble idea of creating the National Economic Conduct (NEC) department to ensure foreign transactions are remitted back to the country and investigate all economic corruption. The government should now support the activities of NEC and discourage tender awards to baseless, indigenous businessmen and make the buyers directly involved in procurement without passing through a third person. The structural adjustment program created untold suffering, especially in the urban areas. As a result of financial hardships, vices, such as prostitution, became prevalent in Zimbabwe, resulting in the HIV/AIDS pandemic.

The payment of lump-sum pensions and monthly allowances to ex-combatants was seen as a regressive move from an economic point of view. It might prove the ex-combatants were not properly demobilized and reintegrated into society with sustainable, income-generating activities, hence the reason why they still wanted government subsidies twenty years after independence. Under normal circumstances, volunteers who are prepared to lose their lives for a genuine cause without remuneration or material reward fight revolutionary wars. Should the government have denied the ex-combatants' demands for pensions, nationwide disturbances could have occurred, with a possibility of these conflicts being supported by the armed forces whose command structures are still occupied by liberation war veterans. Hence, the political decision to honor the ex-combatants' demands for pensions at the expense of economic transparency and accountability. The ordinary man in the street now wants to know what went wrong with the management of the economy, which was vibrant on the attainment of independence.

The people are not receiving a satisfactory answer, hence the encouragement of rumors and misinformation. In the case of the economic negative growth, the population can only blame ZANU-PF, whose policies have resulted in this situation, which is now worse compared to pre-independence. The country was well structurally adjusted to the extent that it eroded its foreign exchange base, making it impossible to compensate willing sellers of the much-needed land. Fearing a repetition of the land acquisition crisis, the industrialists scaled down operations. Some even relocated equipment and operations to politically stable countries within the southern African region. The same exodus of the means of production occurred on the attainment of independence in most African countries, whereas, in Zimbabwe, the same scenario was repeated twenty years after independence.[62]

---

62. Ibid.

12.0 The Demonization and Democratic Subversion of Mugabe and ZANU-PF

The media focus in the United Kingdom on the way the Zimbabwean government has handled the land reform has suggested that President Mugabe is an unhinged, corrupt, cynical tyrant who is out for white settler blood. In conducting the campaign, he is said to be trampling over opposition democratic rights to secure his reelection early in 2002. The British government decided the ZANU-PF war veterans' actions should be stopped. Unsurprisingly, the Zimbabwean government's own analysis and efforts at land reform is ignored. Its formal decisions are not given any credence. The extent of internal legal opposition through the courts has also been a factor in hampering the conduct of real change and the resolution of the farm seizures. The attack on Zimbabwe's leader and its government is a familiar approach that we continue to see in the denigration of political leaders in all countries targeted by American and British imperialism. Whether they be consistent, outright opponents of imperialism or pragmatic leaders who turn and bite the Western hand that initially fed them, the treatment given to such weaker countries that dare defy Western decrees continues being swift and murderous. It is all done under the guise of promoting democracy, the democratic opposition, and safeguarding human rights. But it is no accident that African human rights should suddenly be discovered after so many years. Or, for that matter, those farm invasions, which have resulted in some commercial farmers' deaths, should suddenly appear with chaotic brutality. The forcible transfer began four years ago in 1997. At any given moment in Africa, one country's human rights record is elevated above others to exercise pressure—in this case against Zimbabwe—as part of the strategy to keep Western interests safe and prevent any African state from falling out of line or standing in the way.

It is now said President Mugabe was looked upon as someone the Western powers could do business, an instrument of African stability for Western capitalist interests while allowing certain limited reforms. However, over the latter part of the last twenty or so years, he and the Zimbabwean government have begun asserting an independent role that does not reflect the blueprint of the big business the British government had decided for Zimbabwe.

The whole point of building this now-emerging, increasingly demonic picture of President Mugabe and ZANU-PF is to prepare for and encourage the undermining and wrecking of the Zimbabwean government. This is the barely concealed British concern, not the militant treatment white commercial farmers are receiving from the war veterans. Even the *Sunday Telegraph* (August 26, 2002)

had to admit, while there were "decent, likeable" commercial farmers, there were
those who were not "innocent victims of the Mugabe regime." It pointed out:

> Some are openly racist; some even undisguised fascists with paintings of Mus-
> solini over the fireplace and dogs named after Hitler's generals.[63]

In general, the degree of racism still runs very deep among the approximately
50,000 whites and estimated 4,500 commercial farmers. Many failed to recognize
the negative impact of years of Rhodesian segregation. Because they have persisted in maintaining their exclusive control of prime land, they have remained
separate from the African people. On those big farms, the black farm workers
invariably live in rundown, inadequate conditions.

Meanwhile, the British government is carefully handling white commercial
farmers' compensation (as required in the Lancaster House Agreement) and the
dispute over it with the Zimbabwean government. This is partly because of the
effect the war veterans beyond Zimbabwe's borders, especially in South Africa
and Namibia. Repercussions could also be found from the move by white commercial farmers to other African countries, such as Mozambique. Zimbabwean
government forces are currently a central part of the defense arrangement bolstering the DRC led by President Kabila. The United States, Belgium, France, and
the United Kingdom have spent most of the last century tearing up that country.
The United States backed the Ugandan and Rwandan invasion of DRC. To protect the DRC, an alliance of forces, including Zimbabwe, Angola and others,
went in. Zimbabwean forces have been there for nearly three years at the invitation of Kabila.

This presence and the fact it is a significant power in the southern region of
Africa is a thorn in the side of the United Kingdom's interference in the DRC.
The IMF also objects and has argued its forces should withdraw. So, the combination of the Zimbabwean government's refusal to accept World Bank/IMF constraints and demands, the role of the country's forces in the DRC, and the
militant uprooting of rich commercial farmers adds up to an unpalatable, volatile
cocktail in Whitehall. Yet again, it has upset the transnationals' vision of a pliable
collection of divided states played against each other, according to the requirements of Wall Street and the Stock Exchange. This placed the ZANU-PF government on the hit list for removal.[64]

---

63. *The Sunday Telegraph (August 26, 2002)*
64. *Zimbabwe and British colonialism bran—27.11.2002 03:08 by Steve Lawton*

The threatening Zimbabwean opposition MDC, a free-market, pro-IMF Trojan horse, has been trying in recent years to unseat ZANU-PF. According to *The Guardian* (March 31), MDC is being used and supplied by American and British sources, euphemistically called well-wishers, to undermine ZANU-PF in the countryside. It reported that millions of pounds worth of equipment have been allocated for its campaign. However, the key institution behind this in an advisory role, *The Guardian* said, is the London-based Zimbabwe Democracy Trust (ZDT), whose patrons include former Tory foreign secretaries Douglas Hurd, Malcolm Rifkind, and Geoffrey Howe. Together, they have major business interests linked to Zimbabwe. *The Guardian* said the following:

> The British High Commission in Harare denies that the UK is officially involved in the operation, Mr Whitehead a Zimbabwe retired mining engineer running the show has been in regular contact with one of its members, a man regarded by the diplomatic community as an intelligence officer.[65]

Meanwhile, the United Kingdom has pushed the Commonwealth to interfere. There are an increasingly number of calls for direct American-led intervention. Financial services groups, for example, Abbey National, have launched international anti-Mugabe campaigns aimed at lobbying United States President George Bush and calling for his direct intervention. The United Kingdom retains a strong influence in Zimbabwe via its business connections with industrial conglomerates, the proliferation of NGOs, and the so-called independent press that has regular encounters with the Zimbabwean government. The MDC has found a ready outlet in sections of that press, which ZANU-PF accuses the United Kingdom of fostering.

Zimbabwean government media has suggested that British intelligence has—among other activities—focused on a Kenyan-registered NGO called Global Witness, Environment, and Law. In May, 2001 officials from the United Kingdom, who allegedly had intelligence connections, arrived in Harare, representing this body and apparently carrying out an assessment of the country's forestry commission timber logging activities in the DRC. The forestry commission has had DRC-Zimbabwe agreed concessions in the DRC since March 2002. However, at a time when it was said the British were not involved with the commission, the two arrivals were purportedly showed "unprecedented interest" in Zimbabwe's operations. Their alleged purpose was to develop a strategy to control both sides of timber company activity in the two countries. In the event of

---

65. *Zimbabwe and British colonialism bran—27.11.2002 03:08 by Steve Lawton*

the election of the MDC leader Morgan Tsvangirai against President Mugabe, this would bolster British control to exclude competing interests and provide one of many routes into tapping African resources for the West's profit amid the turmoil. In fact, there is nothing unusual in this, as can be seen with the corporate vultures' agenda unfolding in former Yugoslavia.[66]

It was enacted in the form of the MDC, the intended target, as fears grow a concerted international effort is being mounted to bring down ZANU-PF. These fears were reinforced in November 2001 as hundreds of MDC supporters demonstrated outside the Zimbabwe Embassy in London, demanding the British government support sanctions against President Mugabe. Before the demonstration, MDC supporters appealed for American and British funding for their campaign.[67] They also handed a petition to Prime Minister Tony Blair. Jennings Rukani, MDC's deputy chairman, called upon him to "move into top gear and mobilize the international community and take a leaf from the American government, which has imposed selective sanctions." Given the comments of the Labor government's present foreign secretary, Jack Straw, MDC is growing bolder. Straw told BBC radio that at the September, 2001 meeting in Nigeria with Zimbabwean ministers and six other Commonwealth countries, he hoped "a process to try to put further pressure on Mugabe] and to resolve the issue of land reform…" would be discussed. He said there are "wider issues of the economic state and need for economic reform in Zimbabwe and the issue of the rule of law because they are linked."[68] The imperial tone resonates. It would no doubt harden at the preliminary September 2001 meeting of the London meeting of foreign ministers from the Commonwealth Ministerial Action Group.[69]

At the attainment of the Lancaster House-negotiated independence, President Mugabe was considered one of the best African leaders in the likes of Nelson Mandela because of his policies of forgiveness, national reconciliation, and respect of the IMF and World Bank policies. Because of the policy of reconciliation, which protected the interests of the former colonial power, President Mugabe was always welcome to visit London and other European capitals. For the about-turn from defender of British and other European descendents' interests to defender of the African landless natural inheritance, he is now considered an enemy of democracy and human rights. Zimbabwe was suspended from the Commonwealth for the suppression of democracy in the 2002 presidential elec-

66.   *Zimbabwe and British colonialism bran—27.11.2002 03:08 by Steve Lawton*
67.   *Zimbabwe and British colonialism bran—27.11.2002 03:08 by Steve Lawton*
68.   *Zimbabwe and British colonialism bran—27.11.2002 03:08 by Steve Lawton*
69.   *Zimbabwe and British colonialism bran—27.11.2002 03:08 by Steve Lawton*

tions. Other factors influencing the Commonwealth's decision were amending the Lancaster House Constitution and allowing the landless to invade the commercial farms. The Commonwealth is not just an association of friendly countries. Instead, it is a group of like-minded countries with the same colonial heritage. The constitutions and laws of these countries, including Zimbabwe, are based on English law and custom.

In the history of the Commonwealth, a few countries have been suspended, mostly because of human right violations and lack of good governance. The most notorious violators of human rights and suppression of democracy included South Africa under the apartheid regime, Rhodesia (now Zimbabwe) under the illegal Smith regime, Nigeria under the Sanni Abacha regime, and Zimbabwe again under the ZANU-PF government. The international finance houses accused President Mugabe of interfering in the affairs of the DRC. Not a word was said about the Zimbabwe military intervention in Mozambique against the rebel RENAMO movement. In reality, the following question remains valid: What was Zimbabwe protecting in the DRC? The involvement of Uganda in the DRC was acceptable to the Western world while Zimbabwe was considered an invasion force, even though it went into the DRC at the invitation of the seating government. Not withstanding the fact that DRC was a member of the SADC group of countries, critics argued Zimbabwe had no common borders with the DRC. As such, the war in the DRC did not have a chance of spilling over into Zimbabwe. In addition, they accused Zimbabwe of ignoring its ailing economy and diverting internal problems toward the war in the DRC. Later on during the war, the intervention forces were accused of plundering the minerals of the DRC. Critics of the Zimbabwean government ignored the fact that Zimbabwe was chairman of the SADC defense committee. The very fact a legitimate government of the DRC was being threatened by a rebellion was enough justification for the SADC defense committee, led by Zimbabwe, to intervene. In 1998, the SADC sent Botswana and South African troops to Lesotho to neutralize a coup in that country. Does Botswana have a common border with Lesotho?

The ZANU-PF government was forced to take the last available option to resolve the land issue. They exhausted all available peaceful means, including sending a delegation back to the United Kingdom, hoping the British would honor the promises they made on land acquisition funding. The international community planned to harass the Zimbabwe leadership on the international arena and placed punitive measures against the leadership in place. For repossessing the land that Zimbabweans considered to have been their natural inheritance, they are now being labeled as land grabbers, violators of human rights, and so forth. Most intellectuals, including Zimbabweans, say, in principle, the land redistribution was necessary, but they still blame the way it was done. From the British perspective, the ZANU-PF government supported the land invasions in retaliation to the nonfulfillment of pledges made at the Lancaster House conference. At the same time, if we understand in the same way, a pledge is not a commitment. It is merely an intention to fund. However, dishonoring a pledge is also a breach of trust. Some analysts can argue the government misdirected funds toward the defense of DRC instead of channeling the funds toward the land acquisition program. All these accusations are correct. However, what was the best available method of redistributing land after all peaceful means failed? If the ZANU-PF government had not taken the unpopular decision of ignoring the land invasions, a possibility existed of the leadership being forced out of power by the ex-combatants who enjoyed popular support within the armed forces and the rural population.

Cadres, such as Chenjerai Hundzwi, plundered the war victims' compensation fund and the ex-combatants trust fund, led the demand for the payment of the war veterans' lump-sum and monthly pension allowance, and led the farm invasions. For his gallant role in leading ex-combatants, Chenjerai Hundzwi was declared a national hero and is buried at the national heroes shrine in Harare. The Zimbabwean people blame the government for paying attention to the land issue twenty years after independence and ten years after the expiration of the Lancaster House Agreement. Worldwide supporters of the minority white commercial farmers would like to ensure the downfall and removal of the ZANU-PF government and its replacement by any government prepared to implement the land and other reforms at their dictated pace. Africans and other internationalists support the concept of land redistribution in Zimbabwe, but they do not support the way it was done. Instead, they not recommend or suggest how it could have been best done, given the Zimbabwean situation. At the end of the day, President Mugabe, in his capacity as head of state, was accused for human rights abuse, murdering innocent commercial farmers, and having a lack of respect for law and order.

Although we all know President Mugabe and the government were not directly involved in the farm invasions, the international community can create a justification to drag him before their courts, just like what happened to the first Chimurenga revolutionaries, Nehanda and Kaguvi, who were tried and punished for fighting for their land. President Mugabe will go down in history as one of the greatest sons and daughters of Zimbabwe, delivering the country from British colonial rule, repossessing the motherland, and redistributing land to the landless masses at the expense of being humiliated by the international community with vested interests in Zimbabwe. International capitalism is so powerful to the extent that Zimbabweans can have the land, but they can be denied access to the resources needed to utilize it. Planned economic strangulation will eventually result in disgruntlement, leading to public disobedience. It can lead to a popular uprising against the government. The negotiated Lancaster House Agreement authorized the majority-elected government to take over the administration of the state of Zimbabwe. According to the agreement, funds were to be made available for the Zimbabwean government to assist the landless with the acquisition of land from the willing sellers for the benefit of the landless. The British began honoring the pledges made at Lancaster House, but they suspended the funding due to corruption in the distribution of farms procured for the resettlement of the bona fide landless. The British asked the Zimbabwean government to show cause as to why they should continue funding a program riddled with corruption.[70]

---

70. Ibid.

13.0 The Post-Lancaster House Agreement Draft New Constitution

The proposed constitutional change was President Mugabe's authoritarian response to the crisis facing his regime. ZANU-PF's propaganda declared the new constitution was a final break with colonialism. Invoking President Mugabe's national liberation credentials, they said the no voters were "sell-out Zimbabweans" who wanted to retain a colonial-style constitution. The main provision of the draft constitution was to strengthen President Mugabe's grip on the presidency. Under the present constitution, he should step down in two years when his current term expired. The proposed change would have limited future presidents to two terms. However, because it was not retroactive, President Mugabe could have stood for another two terms. The draft constitution would also have made his government and military officials immune from prosecution for any illegal acts committed while in office. President Mugabe added a clause empowering the government to seize land held by white commercial farmers and demanding the British government pay compensation, a ploy to win the support of the rural masses, whose land was stolen during the colonial era.

However, the voters did not believe him. Since independence and despite the enormous sacrifices made in the struggle against British colonial rule, the land redistribution promised has not materialized. More than six million black Zimbabweans are crowded into barren, communal areas. The few transfers that have occurred have gifted the most fertile land to ZANU-PF officials and their relatives.

The government's constitutional commission presented draft constitutional proposals to President Mugabe at the end of November 1999. However, indicative of the factionalism in ZANU-PF, even this handpicked body proposed President Mugabe should step down and become a ceremonial president. Power would pass to an elected prime minister. A secret meeting held between the presiding judge and ZANU-PF officials deleted the offending clause and inserted one retaining President Mugabe's executive powers. The doctored report, presented to a full meeting of the commission the following day, was pushed through without a vote, leading to protests and threats of resignation by some commissioners.

Two commissioners appealed to the High Court to get the referendum delayed because of the alleged illegality of the alterations to the draft.

The presiding judge declared President Mugabe had powers under the Referendums Act to make "any corrections, clarifications, alterations, or amendments to the draft constitution he so wishes…he could even have discarded it completely and put his own draft before the electorate."

After the production of the draft, the commission was legally required to disband. Instead, President Mugabe kept the commissioners on and transformed them into a campaign team for a yes vote. Angry crowds attended public meetings organized by the commission, jeering and booing the speakers. Some meetings ended in chaos. Justice Godfrey Chidyausiku, the chairman of the commission, tried addressing a public meeting in Harare but large, hostile crowds drove him out. Other meetings could not go ahead due to mass hostility.

In his address to December 1999, ZANU-PF party congress, President Mugabe spoke of machinations and conspiracies occurring behind the scenes. He feared the constitutional reform process, which began as a safeguard against the opposition and a protection of the system of patronage, was taking a different form, a move against him from within his own party. Debates in parliament degenerated into threats between factions. An article entitled "Contenders eye Mugabe's throne" appeared in the *Zimbabwe Independent*. It claimed confrontations between "ZANU-PF heavyweights" were polarizing Politburo meetings. Soon after, a ZANU-PF "mini congress" to reelect the Politburo was postponed to prevent infighting before the April 2000 general election.

These conflicts inside ZANU-PF are not about the path to a democratic Zimbabwe. Instead, it is about what new forms of political rule can maintain the present regime. Some consider President Mugabe to be the only force capable of holding the government together, while others believe he is setting the stage for the party's downfall. During the referendum campaign, President Mugabe utilized the colonial Law and Order Maintenance Act, enacted under Ian Smith's repressive white Rhodesian State, to break up demonstrations, violently intimidate opposition meetings, and arrest journalists and opposition activists without charge.[71]

Referendum Defeat Shakes the ZANU-PF Government

Voters in Zimbabwe rejected the new constitution proposed by President Mugabe and the ZANU-PF. In a result that surprised most commentators, the vote was 578,000 in favor of the new constitution and 697,754 against. At just over twenty percent, turnout was low. Voters in the cities, like Harare and Bulawayo, voted no by three to one. In the rural heartlands that were expected to vote yes, widespread abstentions existed. President Mugabe declared he will "abide by

---

71. *Barbara Slaughter and Stuart Nolan, "The constitution," 22 February 2000.*

the will of the people."[72] In an interview on the BBC, a ZANU-PF spokesman
said of the Mugabe presidency,[73] "He shall rule this country for as long as he
likes."

However, the vote was a huge blow to the party that has ruled Zimbabwe
since independence in 1980. In recent years, widespread opposition has existed to
President Mugabe's authoritarian rule. Taking place in the run-up to parliamentary elections in April, 2000 the no vote in the referendum has been widely interpreted as a plebiscite on the ZANU-PF government and President Mugabe's
leadership.

Zimbabwe faces an unprecedented economic and social crisis. Unemployment
is more than fifty percent and inflation stands at sixty percent. A fuel crisis crip-
ples industry and agriculture. Spending on education and health has been
slashed. In a situation where at least one-quarter of the population is infected
with HIV/AIDS, the cost of medical care nearly doubled in 1999. A report issued
in 1999 by the Central Statistical Office estimated that seventy-six percent of
Zimbabwe's populations live in poverty, which is "widespread and severe, with a
high degree of inequality, even by regional standards."[74] In contrast to the suffering of the vast majority of Zimbabwe's population, President Mugabe recently
awarded massive pay rises of up to 300 percent to MPs and cabinet ministers.
Local headmen and tribal chiefs, on whom his regime relies, were given even
larger awards of between 500 and 750 percent.

However, external factors greatly influenced the referendum's result. Among
Western governments and financial institutions, there is growing hostility to
President Mugabe's rule. Efforts to destabilize his government or—at the very
least—bring it into line. The IMF suspended funding for Zimbabwe in November last year. All the major banks soon followed suit. Only $34 million (Ameri-
can) of the $193 million (American) credit facility from the IMF has been
extended to the country so far. Throughout the 1990s, President Mugabe's government accepted IMF conditions, restructuring the economy and attacking living standards by slashing public spending. In 1999 the South African *Mail and
Guardian* described his fiscal policies as "Thatcherite." The paper said he was taking the "IMF-approved way out."[75] However, the regime's corruption and nepo-

---

72. *President Robert Mugabe, address to the nation on the results of the referendum on the
draft constitution, 15 February 2000.*

73. *Barbara Slaughter and Stuart Nolan—Zimbabwe Referendum defeatfor shakes ZANU
FF-22 February 2000*

74. *Barbara Slaughter and Stuart Nolan, "The constitution," 22 February 2000.*

75. *Black majority government or meritocracy Bulletin 14, no. 4 (1976): 116–136.*

tism impeded the interests of international investors and brought it into increasing conflict with the IMF and Western governments. ZANU-PF continually interfered with the activities of international corporations bidding for contracts in Zimbabwe. In 1998, the *Mail and Guardian* said the government was "usurping the powers of its tender board regarding a huge digital telecomm project for Matebeleland, a move which may have negative repercussions on international donor funding for similar projects." In an article in the February 16 *Financial Times*, Peter Haine, minister of state at the British Foreign Office, demanded a commitment to "sound economic policies of modernization of bloated, inefficient, state-owned enterprises."[76]

The IMF justified its suspension of funding because fiscal targets for the end of September 1999 had not been met, that is, the public expenditure cuts President Mugabe had made were not deep enough. Another reason given for the suspension of IMF funds was the secret financing of Zimbabwe's intervention into the war in the DRC, not declared to the IMF. The IMF tried giving an ethical cover for its punitive actions against the Zimbabwean economy, despite the fact the most recent release of funds contained a clause allowing President Mugabe to spend an agreed amount of his budget on the DRC war. The American and British governments also attacked Zimbabwe's involvement in the war. The war, involving expenditure on 11,000 troops, was a huge logistical operation. President Mugabe intervened on behalf of Zimbabwean business interests, who wanted to control the vast mining operations, including diamonds, copper, and cobalt, in the DRC, and prevent the regional expansion of Ugandan influence. Initial interventions by Rwanda and Uganda into the DRC were supported by the United States. It is likely Zimbabwe was encouraged to intervene on behalf of the Kabila regime by British and French business interests in the region. However, with the danger the war in the DRC could destabilize all of sub-Saharan Africa, Western governments have backed a United Nations peace deal that calls on Zimbabwe and all other countries to withdraw. While official British policy has been increasingly vocal against President Mugabe and sympathetic to his opponents, still powerful British interests are close to his regime. Eighteen British officers are employed in training the Zimbabwean army, and pressure from the British military led to the recent delivery of spare parts for the country's Hawk jets.[77]

---

76. *Barbara Slaughter and Stuart Nolan, "Zimbabwe: Referendum defeat shakes ZANU-PF government." 22 February 2000*

77. *Barbara Slaughter and Stuart Nolan, "Zimbabwe: Referendum defeat shakes ZANU-PF government." 22 February 2000*

Draft Constitution Presidential Address on Referendum Results

Good Evening, Fellow Zimbabweans. On 21 May 1999, I appointed a constitutional commission to look into the issue of a new draft constitution for our country. This decision followed a desire expressed by Zimbabweans to have a homegrown constitution, that is, one fashioned by our own hands and carrying the wishes and aspirations of our people. Although there were other options and methods of writing a new constitution for the country, most, if not all, of them exclusionary to varying degrees, government took a deliberate decision to open up the whole process to interested Zimbabweans so that, what would emerge at the end of it all, would be a draft document bearing the true character of most, if not all, our people. Government also took great care to accommodate all interests and colors in order to make the whole process both truly democratic and representative of the diversity of our nation. Even more significantly, government deliberately decided that the resultant draft document would be subjected to the will of the people if only to ensure that the document was acceptable to the majority in our country. For that reason, government promised to call for a national referendum. Through which, this public scrutiny and judgment of the document would find loud expression.

A referenda bill, which we did not have on our statute books, had to be prepared to provide a legal framework for this first ever, broad-based consultative process since our independence in 1980. Hence the referendum, which you and me participated in on the 12 and 13 of February 2000. As you most probably already know, the vote-counting process is now complete, and the results of the referendum have since been announced. Of over one million Zimbabweans who participated in the process, the majority of them voted against the draft constitutional document. Government accepts the result and respects the will of the people as expressed through the results. What this means in legal and practical terms is that government business and national processes will continue to be conducted under the Lancaster House Constitution as amended, until such time as the country has an acceptable, homegrown constitutional framework.

As we were able to appreciate draft constitutional document submitted to the people was a sum total of ideas that demanded painstaking efforts. It is indeed a rare assemblage of thoughts and views of our generation seeking and searching for a basic law for the development of our nation. I therefore wish to take this opportunity of thanking all the members of the constitutional commission who tirelessly dedicated their time to gathering and collating our people's views. Equally, I thank our drafters for translating the welter of diverse and even contradicting thoughts, views, assertions, and models into a coherent draft that proved so absorbing and engaging to the whole nation. National frameworks and institutions evolve in tortuous and often agonizing ways. Such processes include many fits and starts, and, for less fortunate nations, lots of bloodshed. We continue to escape that cruel fate. With each effort, we make proving a significant step in the direction of nation building and the overall consolidation of a democratic ethos. There may be some in the constitutional commission who may be wont to take the no vote despondently, and, as marking a failure on their part. I urge them to feel the opposite. We had finally to cause their efforts to be presented to the nation for final judgment. That judgment has unfortunately been a no vote by the majority of those of our nation who voted. It is regrettable that the majority of the registered voters refrained from exercising their right of choice.

May I thank all fellow Zimbabweans who participated in the whole process: from the views gathering stage right up to the casting of votes in the referendum. Especially remarkable was the rare sense of order, maturity, and tolerance during the process. The world now knows Zimbabwe as that country where opposing views and opinions can file so singly and so peacefully, both to and from the booth, without incident. Indeed, this is as it should be, and I have every confidence that the forthcoming general elections will be just as orderly, peaceful, and as dignified. I also make special mention of the white part of our community who this time around sloughed off apathy to participate vigorously in the whole poll. I hope this can be extended to other national events and processes so that, wherever we are, we show the rich mosaic that our nation is.

Finally, I extend my most profound gratitude to individuals and organizations who organized, supervised, and conducted the referendum. They had to put together the voting machinery at short notice and against the background of meager resources. Yet, they exhibited high professionalism, honesty, integrity, and impartiality often not repeated in many parts on our continent. Again, this is as it should be. Electoral processes should be managed in a way that engenders public confidence and upholds our reputation as a maturing democracy. Let us all winners and losers accept the referendum verdict and start planning our way forward.[78]

---

78. *President Robert Mugabe, address to the nation on the results of the referendum on the draft constitution, 15 February 2000.*

Independent Analysis of the Draft New Constitution Referendum Results

David Moyo of the University of Zimbabwe Political Philosophy Department argued there is a general, but erroneous tendency, to equate the process of producing a new constitution with bringing in a new leadership in the country. The dangers can best be appreciated by going back and looking at the making of the Lancaster House Constitution and its bearing not only on Zimbabwe's postcolonial legal processes, but also the politics that emerged. Like the rejected draft constitution of 2000, the Lancaster House Constitution was a marathon process. The draft constitution was hurried, mainly because the ruling ZANU-PF wanted a new constitution to be in place before the 2000 parliamentary elections. The stipulation in the draft that land could be acquired compulsorily would have given President Mugabe the reason to heave a sigh of relief and a good excuse to exit as early as that year. But, in the haste, many fundamental considerations were overlooked, leading to the rejection of the document. The government, which gradually patronized the process, to a large extent, ignored people's views and lobbyists, such as the National Consultative Assembly (NCA), pounced on that and particularly pushed the urban electorate to reject the draft. The constitutional commission should have remained neutral and considered all the views of the people. The NCA took advantage of this material weakness and campaigned for a no vote.[79]

The Zimbabwean government's constitutional commission presented a draft constitutional proposal to President Mugabe at the end of November 1999. The draft proposal recommended President Mugabe should step down and become a ceremonial president. Power would pass to an elected prime minister. It is alleged a meeting held between the presiding judge and ZANU-PF officials deleted the clause and inserted one retaining President Mugabe's executive powers. The doctored report, presented to a full meeting of the commission the following day, was pushed through without a vote, leading to protests and threats of resignation by some commissioners. Here again, the constitutional commission was becoming personal. They should not have mentioned the president stepping down. The constitution should have clearly stated it would have a ceremonial president and an elected prime minister. Although most of the constitutional commissioners were respected and educated citizens, they failed to understand the intent of the new constitution was to become the law of the land during and after the lifetime of the present ZANU-PF government. The constitution was not supposed to be

---

79.   *David Moyo, University of Zimbabwe Department of Political Philosophy.*

focused on the present political setup. Its attention was to be on what will be good for the Zimbabwean population. The opposition and the civil society were also correct in their intervention in protecting the at-large population from a constitution doctored to support the ideas of a political party, which had an interest in winning the forthcoming elections. The commercial farmers also played a major role in nullifying the draft constitution by supporting the no vote because a yes vote could have resulted in them losing title to the land they inherited from their colonial fathers. Obviously, the product of the Zimbabwe Constitutional Commission was some document not better than the Lancaster House Constitution. The Lancaster House Agreement is a leaving document capable of directing us on what to do and not to do for the benefit of the country without personifying the actors and stakeholders.

The lack of foresight and strategy at the Lancaster House negotiations easily relates to what happened to the constitutional referendum. By preoccupying themselves on how best to remove President Mugabe, stakeholders and the electorate created another political complexity. The constitution should cast sight into the far future while simultaneously addressing contemporary concerns. The greatest likelihood here is that a new constitution could be implemented, and President Mugabe would go. However, whoever is to come in might want to shift goalposts to sustain his or her own leadership. That would mean having to return to the drawing board and try manufacturing another supreme law. In the absence of the necessary legislative majority for a single party, as is the case now, that would create chaos and throw the country into yet another vicious cycle. Having said this, it becomes imperative to remind all those who will debate the new constitution that the net needs to be cast wider. It is suicidal to pay lip service to other fundamental aspects of a constitution. These aspects include a bill of rights that should be inspired by the Universal Declaration of Human Rights and other conventions on human rights, a democratic electoral system, the land question, separation of powers, and independent commissions. This input is not lost to the fact that, indeed, some attention is being given to them, and the NCA is a ready point of reference. What is only disturbing is that attention is minimal and peripheral. Fuller consideration of these aspects would make a constitution more holistic and more permanent.

Personally, I do not understand why the referendum rejected the draft independence constitution. The constitution was being drafted during the time of President Mugabe, but it was also intended to outlive all the present politicians. The major reason why the constitution was rejected was that it provided for land acquisition and had to be fought through all available means, including the involvement of trade unions, the commercial farmers, and their laborers who depended on proceeds from industry owned and controlled by the same white minority commercial farmers. Under normal circumstances, the ruling party should have replaced the leadership at a time agreed in the constitution. If the constitution does not have provision for leadership change, then the protracted leadership is justified. The commissioners should have spent the taxpayers' money drafting a constitution for Zimbabwe, which is applicable to the Zimbabwean situation today and tomorrow. The absence of an alternative to the rejected constitution was one of reasons why constitutional scientists (e.g., Professor Jonathan Moyo), who were ardent critics of the government, decided to join the government after the rejection of the proposed post–Lancaster House Agreement draft constitution. If the people reject a proposed draft constitution, they must come up with an alternative. The people forgot the ZANU-PF government had a two-thirds majority in parliament, making it possible to amend the constitution as it desires. How do we expect the government to work without a constitution? The no vote for the new constitution can easily be interpreted to mean the people want to continue with the Lancaster House Constitution. Regretfully, it should be noted the majority of the population in Zimbabwe are ignorant of the constitution. However, they registered a no vote in support of the opposition political forces. The majority of the population who voted against the new constitution did not even understand the meaning of the no vote. Through opposition and constitutional assembly propaganda, they were misinformed the intent of the referendum was to decide if President Mugabe should become life president or not. In future, the government of the day should make every endeavor to ensure all citizens are exposed to compulsory basic constitutional studies at secondary school level. The no vote was a clear indicator of what the government should anticipate from the forthcoming presidential elections.

According to the government, selfish politicians seeking personal political gains at the expense of democracy had infiltrated the electorate. In reality, Zimbabweans rejected a homemade constitution, drafted by their national constitutional experts for the establishment of their own law of the land to replace the Lancaster House Constitution, which was allegedly neocolonialist and fell short of total independence. The government did not have any alternative except developing measures to suppress what was perceived as a counterrevolutionary movement, whose objective was to misguide the electorate through democratic rights manipulation and takeover power, which was quickly slipping into the hands of the opposition. This was the first time the ZANU-PF government was defeated in a postindependence public opinion poll. The ZANU-PF government did not take the referendum defeat lightly. Instead, they started preparing contingency plans to counter the opposition threat through the disruption of the commercial farmers' financial power base. The government perceived the referendum defeat as an opposition and commercial farmers victory against the progressive revolutionary people's party.[80]

---

80. Ibid.

14.0 Government and Commercial Farmers Locked in Land Reform Dispute

For decades, land possession has been a major area of dispute for whites and blacks in Zimbabwe. In 1965, following independence from the United Kingdom, white Rhodesians seized control of the majority of fertile land within the country and forced blacks to use the poorer, arid, and unproductive ground. After minority rule ended in 1980, upon the election of President Mugabe and the implementation of the Lancaster House Agreement, white landowners were granted ten years of protection from land distribution policies and reform. In addition, this agreement provided that land would not be seized without compensation.

In 1990, after the provisions of the Lancaster Agreement no longer constrained the government, the constitution was amended to provide for the redistribution of land within the country. Throughout this time, various amendments have been instituted to provide for an adequate redistribution of the land, while allowing for the fair compensation of landowners. In addition, various governments, including the United Kingdom, have provided land assistance grants to facilitate the process of land redistribution and compensation. However, by 1997, much of the more fertile land remained under the control of a few thousand white commercial farmers. Moreover, much of the land that had been distributed remained in the hands of the black elites and was not accessible for lower-class Zimbabweans. Throughout this period, the population of lower-class laborers within the tribal reserves increased. In 1998, international donor governments that had contributed to financing land reforms held a conference on increased government-enforced acquisition of land. These governments adopted a set of principles to guide Phase II of land reform in Zimbabwe, including respect for the legal process, transparency, poverty reduction, consistency, and ensuring affordability for acquisition and allocation of land grants. However, subsequent to these proceedings, the relationship between the Zimbabwean government and donor governments faced instability, and Zimbabwe accused these governments of attempting to maintain the colonial distribution of wealth.

Over the last five years, political and social tension has increased in Zimbabwe over land distribution and compensation. In July 2000, President Mugabe stated he would adopt a fast-tracts land reform process in Zimbabwe in which a national committee, the National Land Identification Committee, would identify tracts of land for redistribution. This fast-tracts model consisted of two approaches:

- Model A1 to benefit 160,000 of the poor from the general landless population

- Model A2 to create 51,000 black commercial farmers

This process, however, has been noted as an inefficient, inconsistent method of allocating land. Moreover, there were increasing concerns the judicial system was not monitoring these methods.

In December 2000, the Commercial Farmer's Union (CFU) filed a suit in the Zimbabwe Supreme Court, challenging the legality of the current fast-tract land reform system. The CFU succeeded in obtaining an order from the court, barring land distribution under the fast-tract method because the method was held to be unconstitutional. One year later, this interdict was overturned after the government allegedly reformed its policies and procedures. During November 2001, CFU created the Zimbabwe Joint Resettlement Initiative (ZJRI) and proposed redistribution of land with assistance for newly resettled commercial farmers. Since then, there have been reports that the fast-tract land measures continue and the overall level of distribution and compensation remains ineffective.[81]

Even the promises made at the 1998 Land Conference did not give any new life to the resettlement program. Between October 1998 and June 2000, no land was acquired for resettlement due to resource constraints and an unfavorable international perception about the effects the resettlement program would have upon the huge investments the remaining 4,500 white commercial farmers had made on their farms. The land issue could not be solved peacefully because efforts to negotiate with the British government had failed, pressure from the landless and demobilized ex-combatants who failed to reintegrate into civilian life was mounting on the government, and the commercial farmers were fighting the government through the judiciary under the protection of the constitution.

The Zimbabwean government had no alternative except to legally amend the constitution in favor of the landless majority. The judiciary system only interpreted the constitution and, in this case, the Lancaster House Constitution as amended by parliament. In the Zimbabwe land issue, the judiciary system did not have any need to consider the historical facts surrounding the land issue.

Populations can be moved from the barren lands to fertile lands, but this does not mean the resettled landless will immediately acquire the farming skills of the displaced commercial farmers and equally contribute to the development of the national economy. The indiscriminate resettlement of the landless will only result

---

81. *Zimbabwean Government and Commercial farmers Locked in Land Reform Dispute Human constitutional rights.*

in land degradation and deterioration from commercial to subsistence farming, thereby negatively impacting the national economy. As a result of the land redistribution policy (and, to a certain extent, the drought, which should have been planned for under normal contingency planning), Zimbabwe imported food from neighboring countries, which were also drought victims. At the end of the day, failure is attributed to mismanagement of natural resources, including land. Despite the negative impacts on the economy because of the national agricultural disaster, the resettled landless and ex-combatants thank the government for resettling them on the commercial farms at the expense of national economic development.

Political considerations sometimes supersede national economic development policies. For example, in the case of Sierra Leone, President Siaka Stevens hosted the Organization of African Unity (OAU) summit despite being advised the country did not have the economic capacity to host the summit. Due to justification via political prestige, the bank governor was replaced. The summit was held, causing Sierra Leone to become a failed economy state. It will be a pity to see Zimbabwe degenerate into a failed state after only twenty-four years of independence and management by one political party and one leader.[82]

---

82. *CFU.*

15.0 Anglo-Zimbabwean Relations Deteriorate over Diplomatic Cargo

Two events bearing negatively on Zimbabwe-United Kingdom relations took place: the unprecedented refusal by the British High Commission in Harare to cooperate with the Zimbabwe customs authorities to identify the contents of an unusually large, diplomatic consignment nearly seven tons in weight and the recall of the British high commissioner to London following the decision by the Zimbabwe customs authorities to physically verify the contents of the unusually large, diplomatic consignment to ensure it complied with Zimbabwe law.

The Vienna Convention is very clear on these matters. In Article 27, Paragraph 3, it refers to "diplomatic bags" which "shall not be opened or detained."[83] It does deal with what is known as "diplomatic cargo" in diplomatic parlance, which international practice leaves to the receiving state to clear through its domestic regulations. In Article 36, Paragraph 1, where among other things, it states, in the case of "articles for the official use of the mission":

> The receiving state shall, in accordance with such laws and regulations as it may adopt, permit entry of and grant exemption from all customs duties, taxes, and related charges[84].

For twenty years since Zimbabwe's independence, all missions, including the British High Commission in Harare, have fully complied with Zimbabwe's laws and regulations covering diplomatic cargo. However, on this occasion, the British High Commission decided to describe a seven-ton consignment not as "diplomatic cargo" but as "diplomatic bags." The Zimbabwe customs authorities correctly disagreed and treated it as "diplomatic cargo." The contents of the consignment proved—beyond a doubt—the Zimbabwe customs authorities had been correct in their stance. There was no "mail" in the consignment. Instead, it contained various objects and devices for construction, including what the customs officials described as "sensitive communication gadgets." These were clearly "articles for official use of the mission" as understood in Article 36 of the Vienna Convention.

---

83. *Minister of Foreign Affairs I.S.G. Mudenge, Zimbabwe-United Kingdom Relations, 15 March 2000.*
84. *Minister of Foreign Affairs I.S.G. Mudenge, Zimbabwe-United Kingdom Relations, 15 March 2000.*

The developments should normally have been handled through firm, frank exchange of diplomatic notes stating each party's position, but what happened was rather melodramatic. London recalled its High Commissioner for "consultations," a euphemism signifying possible further souring of relations. Peter Hain, the junior minister at the foreign office, came out in full force, describing Zimbabwe as not civilized, paranoiac, and so forth. Normally, the British reaction on this occasion—so uncharacteristic with the famed British phlegmatic nature—would have been cause for concern. But it is not. It was expected. It is very much in line with a pattern of developments in present-day Zimbabwe-United Kingdom relations.

In recent months, Peter Hain has been on an unprecedented anti-Zimbabwe crusade. On many occasions during visits to Africa, in the British media, and the House of Commons, he engaged in a relentless verbal onslaught against the Zimbabwean government and its leadership. Up until now, I have chosen to ignore these unprovoked utterances as the excesses and overzealous nature of a junior minister keen to making a name for himself. Indeed, while at the recent United Nations Security Council meeting on the DRC, I had the opportunity to advise Mr. Hain we were rather concerned by his many anti-Zimbabwe utterances. He told me he was under pressure from the anti-Zimbabwe media lobby in the United Kingdom, which wanted him to say something occasionally. I cautioned I was also under pressure in Zimbabwe to respond to his growing negative comments. In my desire to improve relations with the United Kingdom, I not only continued to restrain myself from responding to the provocation, but I started quietly appealing to some countries known to enjoy good relations with both the United Kingdom and Zimbabwe to advise Mr. Hain to desist from his chosen course as I saw nothing good coming from his chosen one-man mission of vilification. In addition, I facilitated every opportunity for Mr. Hain to have access to the head of state, even when the latter's program was tight. I even invited Mr. Hain to visit Zimbabwe at his convenience. These initiatives have obviously been badly misread in London.

It has now become abundantly clear that Mr. Hain has a preconceived, premeditated agenda of demonizing and ostracizing Zimbabwe and its leadership. He has taken every opportunity to denigrate our sovereignty by attacking our democratic institutions and processes, discouraging investment, and trying to generally influence the IMF, African Development Bank, as well as the donor community to not disburse funds for Zimbabwe. He has attacked our presence in the DRC. In short, he has appointed himself as the prophet of Doom where Zimbabwe is concerned.

Only a month ago, Mr. Hain launched an unprovoked attack on our national constitutional referendum process even before it was held. But, as the world now knows, the conduct and outcome of that referendum has now been hailed internationally as having been free and fair. Yet, this has not silenced Mr. Hain. Instead, he has already dismissed the outcome of our forthcoming elections as undemocratic before we have actually held them. To him, Zimbabwe must be assumed to be guilty until proved innocent. The strange behavior of a foreign government's minister interfering in the internal affairs of another foreign and sovereign state is extraordinary, to put it mildly. Mr. Hein seems to suffer from an unusual overdose of postcolonial hangover. He is oblivious of the fact we are a sovereign, independent state—not a British colonial dependency anymore.

Mr. Hein accused Zimbabwe of paranoia when, in fact, it is only being prudent. It is not a secret that, from 1998 to 1999, the British interests have been in the forefront of a smear campaign aimed at undermining Zimbabwe and its ZANU-PF government. It is established that meetings were convened at Chatham House in London, Brussels, and other capitals and venues to discuss ways and means of toppling President Mugabe and his government by inciting political and economic instability, including sponsoring new political formations in this country. The documents and minutes of these meetings are known. Some we have previously publicly exposed, whereas others have been subjects of diplomatic intercourse between Zimbabwe and the countries concerned. In my discussion during the Commonwealth Heads of Government and Ministers (CHOGM) in Durban with Robin Cook, we agreed to close the above chapter and cooperate to rebuild our relations. Hein obviously had other ideas, as recent developments have shown.

The anti-Zimbabwe crusade originally started when the Zimbabwean government embarked on land redistribution program, a program seeking to redistribute indigenous land the British colonial authorities forcibly seized distributed, without any compensation to the indigenous Zimbabweans, to the British settlers early last century. Zimbabwe and the United Kingdom have fundamental differences regarding the land reform program in the country. These primarily emanate from the United Kingdom's refusal to assume its historical, moral responsibility to help Zimbabweans resolve this British-created injustice sensibly. Rather than supporting efforts to redress the glaring injustices in the current land tenure system, the British government has sought to manipulate international opinion by mischievously suggesting Zimbabwe is grabbing white land. This is racist nonsense. The British colonial authorities grabbed our land. We are engaging in a rational restoration process. We do not intend to acquire all the land the

British originally seized—only about half of the good agricultural land in the hands of nearly 4,000 British settlers. We have said—and repeat here—we will pay full compensation for all the improvements the settlers have made to the land we intend to acquire for resettlement.

It is false and mischievous for the British media to spread lies that we do not intend to pay any compensation to the white commercial farmers. However, unless the British government is prepared to assist us with funds, we are unable to pay for the land itself because the British colonial authorities never paid us when they seized it from us. We take this stand on moral, historic, as well as economic grounds. No amount of vilification and propaganda against us will move us from this just stand. The United Kingdom's responsibility to the descendants of the settlers it brought to this country is to pay for the land it seized and distributed to the settlers on the pretense that it owned our land. The settlers were given what amounted to stolen property. The British colonial authorities misled the settlers, asserting they were being given land in perpetuity as if we, the rightful owners, would never come to reclaim our patrimony. We are now in charge of our country and are not prepared to insult our people by paying for the land that was not initially paid for.

It is this issue, which lies at the core of the anti-Zimbabwe propaganda in white liberal media in South Africa and the United Kingdom. It is also this issue that Mr. Hein and the United Kingdom are trying to launch shameful, anti-Zimbabwe tirades in the media, thereby hoping to turn the victim, Zimbabwe, into the villain. To describe Zimbabwe's action with regard to the diplomatic cargo as paranoia, uncivilized, and so forth is deceitful. The recent incident involving the abnormal diplomatic consignment is just an aspect of these strained relations. Ever since 1980, diplomatic missions based in Harare, including the British High Commission, have been very cooperative in facilitating the clearance of their diplomatic cargoes, normal or abnormal, by dutifully complying with the requirements of our customs regulations, just as Zimbabwe complies with those of host countries where our missions are based. What happened recently is most unusual as the British High Commission took the unprecedented decision to refuse to cooperate with our customs authorities, which was contrary to local regulations and established international diplomatic practice. Recalling the High Commissioner, even for consultations, for such an incident is to render drama where different approaches could have yielded better results.

In view of the twenty-year history of compliance by the British High Commission with these import regulations, one wonders why, on this occasion, the High Commission decided to behave in this uncharacteristic manner. Could it be that this incident was deliberately orchestrated to present Zimbabwe as an uncivilized state? It must be stressed the Vienna Convection does not license the sending state or its agents to flout, contravene, or otherwise disrespect the laws, rules, and regulations of the receiving state. On the contrary, a fundamental precept of that venerable convention is the full respect of and compliance with the laws, rules, and regulations of the receiving country by diplomatic missions and their agents. Observance of that important requirement lies at the core of internationally recognized and accepted diplomatic behavior. The Zimbabwean government will remain steadfast in the assertion of its sovereignty and protection of its security. It will continue, in this regard, to fully observe and uphold international conventions and principles along with practices of international law pertaining to the respect of diplomatic bags and diplomatic cargoes as it has done during the last twenty years.

The British government cannot wish away historical realities of our longstanding relationship with them. It can neither run away from its obligations by creating such incidents. Clearly, our relationship can only benefit from the observance of such basic international principles as noninterference, sovereign equality, and mutual respect. We remain ready to engage the British government in a mature, constructive relationship to resolve our mutual historic responsibilities. (Incidentally, it is only because, to an extent, we recognize British residual colonial responsibilities toward our country that we had up to now tolerate Mr. Hein's harmful utterances on our internal affairs). Mr Hein should realize that abusing us is not the answer. And worse still, it will not work. Morality and justice are on our side just as morality and justice were on our side when Mr. Hein joined us to fight the evil apartheid system.[85]

Analysis of the British Diplomatic Cargo Case

In the case of countries with cordial diplomatic relations, the contents of diplomatic cargo are only declared by the receiving embassy without the need for physical identification of the contents. Instead, the Zimbabwean government decided to physically verify the contents of the diplomatic cargo to ensure the contents complied with Zimbabwean law. There is no reason for the Zimbabwean government to complain about the incident because the British High Commission complied, although under protest. According to the British, the Zimbabwean government's action was in accordance with the Vienna Convention. However, it

---

85. *Minister of Foreign Affairs I.S.G. Mudenge, Zimbabwe-United Kingdom Relations, 15 March 2000.*

demonstrated the lack of trust and deteriorating Anglo-Zimbabwe diplomatic relations. The British also suspected the action was prompted by Zimbabwean accusation of British interference in Zimbabwe's internal affairs.

The British had no alternative except to recall their high commissioner for debriefing. There is no way the Zimbabwe customs department could have unilaterally decided to physically verify the contents of the diplomatic cargo without the concurrence of the ministry of foreign affairs. This action could be misconstrued for a punitive measure to demonstrate to the British that Zimbabwe was responsible for its destiny and to remind the British they were no longer accorded privileged status in Zimbabwe. Anglo-Zimbabwe relations had soured due to the land reform-related farm invasions by ex-combatants and their sympathizers as well as the breakdown in law and order. The British government could not obviously take a backseat while their kith and kin are being maimed and murdered in a country where the government is seen to be reluctant or is not capable of protecting them. Due to the cordial relations existing between the British High Commission and the Zimbabwe opposition MDC, the Zimbabwean government felt it was necessary—in the interest of state security—to verify the contents of the seven-ton British diplomatic cargo. Considering British credibility, there was no need for this diplomatic misunderstanding. In reality, the receiving state should be interested to know the contents of a seven-ton diplomatic cargo.

The international community declared the 2002 presidential elections not free and fair. As a result, the Republic of Zimbabwe was suspended from the Commonwealth for human rights abuse and the suppression of democracy. The suspension of Commonwealth membership resulted in Zimbabweans being required to obtain visas to enter or transit through the United Kingdom and other Commonwealth countries. The introduction of the visa regime against Zimbabweans was also due to large numbers of economic migrants escaping economic hardships at home, entering the United Kingdom on visitor visas, and disappearing or declaring political asylum status after evading political persecution in Zimbabwe. The Zimbabwean government reciprocated by imposing visa requirements on British subjects visiting Zimbabwe, maybe as a way to demonstrate the equality of sovereign states.[86]

---

86. Ibid.

16.0 New Land Acquisition Act and Impact of Land Invasions on Agriculture

The last act performed by the outgoing parliament on April 6, 2000, was enacting a historic amendment to the country's constitution. The amendment removed sections of the Lancaster House Agreement, which treated land as any other property. A main aspect of the constitutional amendment was transferring the responsibility of paying compensation for land set aside for resettlement from the Zimbabwean government to the former colonial power, the United Kingdom. The new amendment obliges the Zimbabwean government to pay for improvements only, that is, irrigation, dams, farmhouses, and so forth. Following the amendment, the Land Acquisition Act of 1992 was amended to comply with the new constitutional framework. That process was accomplished on May 23, 2000, when the Zimbabwean government, through a special gazette, published the new Land Acquisition Act. The impediments previously hindering the Zimbabwe government from quick acquisition of land for resettlement were removed. All of the program's critics were labeled as traitors who did "not have the interests of this country at heart" and "They are either people who reside outside Zimbabwe or are influenced from outside."[87]

The Zimbabwean government accelerated its land resettlement program and simultaneously issued a decree amending the country's Land Acquisition Act. White commercial farmers could now be forced off their land with immediate effect, and the takeover would be legitimized faster. President Mugabe decreed an amendment to Zimbabwe's Land Acquisition Act, totally changing the procedure for the occupants' takeover of white commercial farmers' land. Commercial farmers issued with acquisition orders by the government must immediately stop farming and will be confined to their houses, which they should also vacate within three months. The government immediately takes over ownership of the farm. As the land acquisition orders previously had to pass through the courts first, some 800 cases are awaiting a verdict. These farms must now be handed over immediately, and farming will have to cease or pass over to the occupants. The courts are now examining these cases retrospectively.

Patrick Chinamasa, Zimbabwean minister of justice, explained the move and the need to accelerate the land reform:

---

87. *New Land Acquisition Act," The Zimbabwe Herald, 6 April 2000.*

> We had power to confine the commercial farmers at their houses. We did not
> do this because we expected some co-operation from commercial farmers but
> it was not forthcoming. Now that we have removed ambiguity, the resettle-
> ment program will go ahead.[88]

Of course, reactions depend on those interviewed. The government newspaper, *The Herald*, published an interview with Hurungwe District war veterans'
chairman, Comrade John Dungiro, who welcomed the amendment. "The latest
move protects the new settlers, and they have to farm without interference," said
Mr. Dungiro. Referring to the landowner of the farm, he was occupying, he continued, "Commercial farmers of (Mr.) Roper's calibre have been on the forefront
creating tension and false information that new settlers were problematic." He
told *The Herald* he expected Mr. Roper to comply with the new law[89].

The country's white commercial farmers are more skeptical. According to the
BBC, Zimbabwe's white commercial farmers say farming is likely to stop immediately on nearly 800 farms, deepening the economic crisis of the country. An
estimated 1,700 commercial farms owned by white commercial farmers have
been occupied over the last year-and-a-half. These farms now are estimated to
house more than 200,000 Zimbabweans, mostly landless people. Under the
accelerated land resettlement program, more than 50,000 new, black, commercial farmers have emerged. Those are, however, mostly ruling party veterans.
With the new amendment, government is in an easier position to take over new
farms without the previous occupation by war vets. According to Patrick Chinamasa, the Zimbabwean government is set out to acquire a total of more than nine
million hectares for resettlement purposes. The government will increase the
number of judges at the Administrative Court from the current six to handle and
clear the land cases. The white commercial farmers have continued to "filibuster
the system contesting against the acquisition of their farms and slowing land
reforms," reported *The Herald*.[90]

Independent Comments on the Impact of Land Invasions on Agriculture

White commercial farmers in Zimbabwe's agricultural heartland resolved to
strike yesterday after another member of their community was killed. The 180
commercial farmers in the Karoi area, northwest of Harare, said they were stop-

---

88. *New Land Acquisition Act," The Zimbabwe Herald, 6 April 2000.*
89. *New Land Acquisition Act," The Zimbabwe Herald, 6 April 2000.*
90. *"New Land Acquisition Act," The Herald, 6 April 2000.*

ping work because police had failed to curb the latest outbreak of squatter violence. They were furious after a police chief responded to their complaints with threats of war. Black militants, who have stepped up their intimidation campaign amid impatience over government promises of land reform, have already closed forty-six farms in the Shamva area in protest at action. Landowners in Mazowe, Concession, Marondera, and Tengwe have also threatened to follow suit. Three hundred or more farms could soon be on strike in action, which could badly hit the national economy. Since squatters began their invasions in February, five white commercial farmers have been killed in the violence. On Sunday night, another man, Willem Botha, who was in his sixties, was beaten to death by suspected robbers. Although squatters were not accused of involvement, other commercial farmers blamed his death on the "breakdown of law and order" caused by the land invasions, which have been encouraged by President Mugabe.

In Karoi, commercial farmers and their black employees have been subjected to constant harassment this year. More than 1,000 cases of assault have been reported to the police, but not one arrest has been made. Trouble over the past few days has pushed the local commercial farmers' association into action. On the Vuka estate, Fin and Jane O'Donoghue awoke with their three children yesterday to find that squatters had barricaded them inside their home. "They said no one would be allowed in or out," said Mrs. O'Donoghue. "They started forming up in ranks. It looked like some military maneuver was beginning." The couple managed to flee with their eleven-year-old daughter and sons, aged five and ten. Alarmed by their inability to make radio contact with the O'Donoghues, fifteen neighbors demanded action from a local police chief, Superintendent Mabunda, and told him of their plans for a strike.

According to commercial farmers who met him, Superintendent Mabunda asked them, "Do you want war? If you want war, I will bring troops, and we can have war. I think we will have war today." They accused Superintendent Mabunda of collaborating with the squatters, although he managed to defuse the situation at Vuka two hours later. One farmer said, "Mabunda has been behind this all along. He went and told those guys to lay off for the day and come back tomorrow." On nearby Kutepa farm, Craig Stirling made three attempts to drive his tractor to his fields, but he was stopped by squatters each time. On Nassau farm, invaders ordered Dave Penny to stop all work. When he tried taking his tractors to the fields, they threatened to burn the vehicles. Karoi is Zimbabwe's most fertile corner. Its lush fields of wheat, maize, tobacco, and soya beans will be silent today. Irrigation systems will be switched off, and crops will neither be reaped nor sown. Mr Penny said, "It's going to have a great effect on the economy. We have to do it, and we have nothing to lose now." The resolve of land-owners was hardened by the news of Mr. Botha's murder near Beatrice, fifty miles south of Harare. His television was stolen. Few white commercial farmers believe the killing can be separated from the current crisis. A neighbor said, "Thanks to the land invasions, there is no law and order, and we are all considered fair game."[91]

After the enactment of the Land Acquisition Amendment Act, the commercial farmers realized nothing could stop the government from acquiring land within the law, hence the adoption of the strike action, which some viewed as counter-revolutionary action. On hearing news the commercial farmers were stopping work, the landless squatters and ex-combatants started invading and occupying the commercial farms. Like in the first Chimurenga, the violence on the commercial farms flared simultaneously like bush fire, from Karoi, northwest of Harare, to Shamva, where the commercial farmers, protesting to the farm invasions, closed forty-six farms. The farm invasions soon spread to Mazoe, Concession, Marondera, and into Beatrice near Harare. Unknown assailants were killing white commercial farmers. Yet, the police were unable to make even a single arrest. After the commercial farmers were barricaded in their house at Vuka estate, the local CFU approached the chief police superintendent and informed him they wanted to strike. In response, he asked them if they wanted to start a war. According to the law, the commercial farmers should have submitted a written application seeking authority to hold a public demonstration At that point and time, the commercial farmers realized there was a breakdown in law and order in the country, which they alleged to have been encouraged by President Mugabe.

The commercial farmers made a terrible mistake by resolving to strike with the idea that the action would force the government to stop the farm invasions to salvage the already ailing economy. Instead, they opened the door for the squatters and ex-combatants to come in and demand to work on the land. The fact of the matter was that the commercial farmers' strike was illegal. As such, the police could not support or protect those involved in an illegal action. If the government have taken steps to protect the commercial farmers, the squatters and ex-combatants could have seized the opportunity to unleash the violence against the government for collaborating with the commercial farmers. The commercial farmers failed to understand the perceived negative impact of their strike on the national economy was secondary to the political land acquisition pressure from

91.   *CFU, "Summary of impact on Agriculture-Land Invasions, 23 May 2000.*

the ex-combatants. The government was under threat of violence and even guerrilla warfare from the ex-combatants, legal suits, and economic paralysis from the commercial farmers. The government was apparently aware of the farm invasions, but it was not in control of the situation.[92]

92. *Ibid.*

17.0 MDC Threatens Strike as Government Announces the Fast-Track Approach

The accelerated Land Reform and Resettlement Implementation Plan Fast-Track approach commences today in all the eight provinces of the country. Following the amendment of the Constitution and the subsequent amendment of the Land Acquisition Act, which was followed by the gazetting of 804 commercial farms for acquisition by government, the Program has now gathered momentum. This legal framework has removed the impediments that had hindered government from quick acquisition of land for resettlement. Government has now adopted the fast-track approach. Under this approach, priority is given to land acquisition, demarcation, settler emplacement, and the provision of basic infrastructure such as water points and access roads. More comprehensive infrastructure and other support services will be provided later.

Identification of land for resettlement will be done according to established criteria as follows: derelict farms, underutilized farms, farms belonging to absentee landlords, farms adjacent to communal areas, farms under multiple ownership. Beneficiary selection is going to be done in accordance with the established Resettlement and Land Redistribution Policies and Procedures of government. Under these, local committees made up of traditional leaders, councilors, district administrators, provincial administrators, governors, representatives of war veterans, and other specially appointed individuals will carry out beneficiary selection. Further, government will shift the war veterans and peasants from farms that were not identified and those that are not suitable for resettlement

Contrary to our detractors' blatant lies that land redistribution is being implemented in a way designed to benefit politicians, government officials, and ZANU-PF supporters, the above committees provide checks and balances to ensure that beneficiaries are bona fide landless people. The whole process is designed to ensure fair and equitable redistribution of land to correct the racial imbalance in land apportionment created by former colonial regimes. Those who cry foul of this program do not have the interests of this country at heart. They are either people who reside outside Zimbabwe or are influenced from outside. The current resettlement program shall be based on the following order of priority: accelerated Fast-track resettlement to start immediately with the gazetted 804 farms based on the A1 Model volatized resettlement scheme and the 3-tier model for grazing in dry regions. This model is government's top priority. And, after covering mileage in the resettlement of people from congested communal areas, government will then embark on other models as follows: Model A2—self-contained units, as well as small- and medium-scale commercial farm units. And, finally, the large-scale commercial farm scheme, based on full cost recovery, for indigenous black people wishing to enter commercial agriculture.

Having realized that donors and some stakeholders, such as the CFU, were not genuinely interested in assisting government undertake a successful land reform and resettlement program, as demonstrated by their not honoring pledges made at the September 1998 International Donors' Conference, if need be, government is determined to go it alone using its own, limited resources to resettle people. However, government will accept the participation and contribution of other stakeholders and interested parties provided they do so under the established.[93]

Zimbabwean Government Land Redistribution Policies and Procedures

Zimbabwe is a sovereign state, and, as such, government will not accept suggestions coming from some foreign governments that they would want to make financial assistance available for resettlement outside government channels. Government will continue to hold dialogue with all stakeholders and any genuinely interested parties. Information has reached my office that the commercial farmers union has offered government over 400 farms for resettlement. The true position is that the commercial farmers union has provided me with a summary table comprising 180 farms measuring approximately 350,000 hectares with no farm names or an indication of their precise locations. Government still awaits detailed information on the names, location, and suitability of these farms for resettlement in the context of government's set targets. When government receives the appropriate list of farms, discussions on the mechanism of transferring the suitable farms to the resettlement program shall be held with the commercial farmers union and any other commercial farmers and individuals who have offered or are willing to offer land to government for resettlement.

Thank you. Vice President Joseph Msika.[94]

Zimbabwe's opposition leader warned President Mugabe yesterday that urban workers might join the strike of white commercial farmers, which began a week ago. As the protest spread to a second region—with other areas also considering action—Morgan Tsvangirai, president of the MDC, backed the landowners and threatened strike action in solidarity with their employees. His intervention came

---

93. *Vice President Joseph Msika, Statement announcing "fast-track" approach, 16 July 2000.*
94. *Resettlement and Land Redistribution Policies and Procedures.*

after squatters severely injured another white farmer, when a mob of forty set
upon him with sticks and clubs. With 237 commercial farmers now on strike,
Tim Henwood, the president of the commercial farmers union, said the protest
could spread nationwide because normal operations were becoming impossible.
He petitioned President Mugabe to halt the land invasions, which commenced in
February, and begin a fresh legal attempt to end his members' ordeal. Commercial farmers around Karoi, 150 miles northwest of Harare, began their strike at
6:00 AM yesterday. Irrigation systems were switched off, and the 27,000 workers
sat idle, although they will be paid for as long as possible. Fifty-seven commercial
farmers in neighboring Tengwe joined the protest. Alan Parsons, one of the striking landowners, said, "We want law and order back in our country. That's what
this is about. We can't continue in this state of anarchy any longer." He said a
nationwide strike was being planned. Some of Karoi's shops and garages closed in
solidarity with the landowners after Morgan Tsvangirai called the commercial
farmers' action justified. He said, "If this lawlessness continues, the protests may
spill into the urban areas, where workers will be forced to take action in solidarity
with farm workers who now live under constant fear of losing their lives or jobs."
Morgan Tsvangirai is a former secretary-general of the ZCTU, which has close
ties with the MDC. He led a series of national strikes in 1997 and 1998, and
senior figures in the MDC believe such action is necessary again. A member of
Morgan Tsvangirai's executive said, "What we need is a general protest, covering
every industry, until we return to the rule of law. I think it will happen soon."

Beleaguered commercial farmers, who have lost all confidence in the police,
were still shocked yesterday by the attack on Mr. Brand, one of the striking commercial farmers, outside his gates at Gremlin farm, Karoi. He said, "They came
and said they wanted to take my farm. I turned to go back to my security gate,
and that's when they started beating me. They hit me with sticks until I dropped
to the ground." Fellow commercial farmers rescued Mr. Brand and rushed him to
Chinhoyi hospital, where he was treated for a fractured arm, severe bruising, and
lacerations to his head and right ear. He told them the squatters had "got into a
frenzy and wanted to take vengeance on somebody." Commercial farmers are
reaching the end of their patience after an ordeal that has lasted for almost six
months. Mr. Henwood gave the CFU first warning of national action. He said,
"In the interests of the safety of our members and their workers, it may soon
become impossible for farming operations to continue nationwide. This drastic
action will have a serious impact on the economy of Zimbabwe, but it will be a
small price to pay to prevent further loss of life." Mr Henwood begged the presi-

dent "to intervene in bringing to an end the perils faced by all those involved in commercial farming."

The CFU asked the High Court to order the police to evict the squatters and act against violence. Judges have already granted this request twice, but their orders have been ignored. Few believe the third legal attempt to solve the crisis will meet with any more success. The government has scant sympathy for the commercial farmers. Joseph Made, the newly appointed agriculture minister, accused them of trying to sabotage land reform and warned against a strike. He told the official *Herald* newspaper, "I appeal to the commercial farmers not to go ahead with the demonstration. If the strike goes ahead, it will reaffirm the need for land redistribution in this country. We cannot have a few people threatening the majority."[95]

Mass Job Action Looms over Commercial Farm Violence

A fresh confrontation between the government and the ZCTU loomed after the labor movement's general council said it was considering tough measures, including mass job action, to end widening violence on commercial farms by pro-government followers. The violence, mostly beatings of commercial farmers and their workers, gathered momentum as mobs of self-styled independence war veterans and supporters of the ruling ZANU-PF party chased away commercial farmers from their properties. Other commercial farmers, fearful for their lives, halted all farming activities, sparking fears of severe food shortages in Zimbabwe, normally a food exporter.

"The general council is concerned, and the general membership is angry at this continued victimization of workers. A decision on what strong measures to take are going to be made at our meeting on Friday," ZCTU's acting spokesman, Isaac Mudzengere, told the *Financial Gazette*. Mudzengere refused to say what sort of measures the umbrella union would adopt, but he noted, "The government can easily stop this violence if it chooses to. But should it continue to watch workers being victimized and jobs being destroyed, then we as workers will be forced to resort to mass job action and demonstrations to show our anger."

Sources close to the labor movement said the ZCTU leadership was under pressure from its general members to take a tougher stance on the violence, which began in February 2000 when the veterans fanned across the country to seize hundreds of farms. The ZCTU is also unhappy at the widespread beatings of ordinary people in towns and cities by security forces, who the government says

---

95.   *David Blair, "Zimbabwe townsfolk may join farm strike," The Telegraph, 25 July 2000.*

have been deployed to keep law and order in the aftermath of the June 24–25, 2000 general elections. More than 12,000 jobs have already been lost in the agricultural sector, Zimbabwe's economic mainstay, as veterans continue disrupting farming operations.

The commercial farmers union, some of whose members stopped production in protest against the farm violence, say more jobs could be lost. Union sources said affiliates of the ZCTU were pushing the labor body to mobilize its international counterparts to press the government to end the violence. "Pressure is on the ZCTU leadership to act on this issue. In fact, the mood among ordinary workers is that the leadership has been too slow to react," one source said. Leaders of some affiliates of the ZCTU, while not unilaterally calling for mass job action, made it clear they were under mounting pressure from members to take a hard line. Mass job action by the ZCTU, which has successfully staged nationwide work stoppages in the past, could cripple Zimbabwe's already sickly economy.

David Shambare, Railway Artisans Union secretary-general, said members were deeply concerned by the violence in towns and on farms and would press the ZCTU council to act forcefully.

> It is workers or members of families who have borne the brunt of this violence. We are deeply concerned at this state of affairs and, as an affiliate of the ZCTU, we are going to put across our views at the Friday meeting.

There are 350,000 workers employed by the sector to loose their jobs unless law and order is urgently restored. ZCTU sources said their affiliates were pushing the labor body to mobilize its international counterparts to press the government to end the violence.

Shambare noted a drop in farming activities as commercial farmers flee the violence led to a drop in the tonnage transported by the National Railways of Zimbabwe and could eventually impact the viability of some jobs in the company.

The General Agriculture and Plantation Workers' Union (GAPWUZ) criticized the ZCTU leadership for being slow in its response to the anarchy on the farms. "The ZCTU should have taken a stronger stance as soon as it became clear that the present violence was targeting workers on farms and in towns," said Philip Munyanyi, GAPWUZ secretary-general . He said the rampaging mobs attacked white commercial farmers and workers and burned down their homes and properties in some instances. At least thirty-one people were killed in the violent run-up to Zimbabwe's general elections in June 2000. The veterans, who are now busy allocating themselves pieces of land on the farms they occupy, linked most of the deaths to the campaign to seize farms.[96]

Independent Comments on the National Strike in Support of Commercial Farmers

Morgan Tsvangirai, Zimbabwe's opposition leader, warned President Mugabe that urban workers might join the strike of commercial farmers, which was in progress at that time. As the commercial farmers protest spread to a second region, with other areas also considering action, Morgan Tsvangirai, president of the Movement for Democratic Change, backed the commercial farmers and threatened strike action in "solidarity" with their employees. Morgan Tsvangirai, who was by that time leader of the opposition MDC did not want to be seen to be threatening strike action in solidarity with the commercial farmers from a trade unionist point of view. In his capacity as president of the opposition MDC it could have been in order for him to come out openly in solidarity with the commercial farmers who also supported the opposition party. His intervention came after a white farmer was severely injured by squatters, when a mob of 40 set upon him with sticks and clubs The commercial farmers were not satisfied with the MDC president's announcement that the strike could become national in solidarity with the farm workers although a farmer had been injured. Tim Henwood, the president of the CFU, said the protest could spread nationwide because normal operations were becoming "impossible." Instead of the MDC taking the lead in making representations to the president, the president of the CFU petitioned President Mugabe to halt the land invasions, which commenced in February 2000, and began a fresh legal attempt to end his members' ordeal. The MDC and CFU wanted the commercial farmers strike to appear like a employers association industrial action affecting workers as well.

Mr. Henwood gave the CFU's first warning of national action. He said: "In the interests of the safety of our members and their workers it may soon become impossible for farming operations to continue nationwide. This drastic action will have a serious impact on the economy of Zimbabwe but will be a small price to pay to prevent further loss of life." Mr Henwood begged the president "to intervene in bringing to an end the perils faced by all those involved in commercial farming." The CFU asked the High Court to order the police to evict the squatters and act against violence. Judges have already granted this request twice,

---

96. *"Mass job action looms over farm violence,"* The Financial Gazette Staff Reporter, 26 July 2000.

but their orders have been ignored. The last resort was a Commercial farmers national strike action after they had failed to have the farm invasions dealt with legally. Joseph Made, the newly appointed Agriculture Minister, accused the commercial farmers of trying to sabotage land reform and warned against a strike. He told the official Herald newspaper: "I appeal to the commercial farmers not to go ahead with the demonstration. "If the strike goes ahead it will reaffirm the need for land redistribution in this country. We cannot have a few people threatening the majority. According to the Minister, the Commercial farmers should seat back while the farm invasions and occupation continue. The government did not promise legal action to have the farm invaders removed from the farms nor guarantee protection for the Commercial farmers.[97].

A fresh confrontation between the government and the Zimbabwe Congress of Trade Unions (ZCTU) loomed after the labor movement's general council announced that it was considering tough measures, including mass job action, to end widening violence on commercial farms by alleged pro-government followers. The violence, mostly beatings of commercial farmers and their workers, had gathered momentum in the past two weeks, with mobs of self-styled independence war veterans and supporters of the ruling ZANU-PF party chasing away commercial farmers from their properties. Other commercial farmers, fearful for their lives, have halted all farming activities, sparking fears of severe food shortages in Zimbabwe, normally a food exporter.

The CFU, some of whose members stopped production in protest against the farm violence, said more jobs could be lost. Union sources said affiliates of the ZCTU were pushing the labor body to mobilize its international counterparts to press the government to end the violence. "Pressure is on the ZCTU leadership to act on this issue. In fact, the mood among ordinary workers was that the leadership has been too slow to react," one source said. Leaders of some affiliates of the ZCTU, while not unilaterally calling for mass job action, made clear this week they were under mounting pressure from members to take a hard line. Mass job action by the ZCTU, which has successfully staged nationwide work stoppages in the past, could cripple Zimbabwe's already sickly economy.

The General Agriculture and Plantation Workers' Union (GAPWUZ) criticized the ZCTU leadership for being slow in its response to the anarchy on the farms. "The ZCTU should have taken a stronger stance as soon as it became clear that the present violence was targeting workers on farms and in towns," GAPWUZ secretary-general Philip Munyanyi said. He said the rampaging mobs had

---

97.   *Mugabe sued for farm invasions, Andrew Meldrum, The Guardian, 27 July 2000.*

attacked white commercial farmers and workers and burnt down their homes and properties in some instances. At least 31 people were killed in the violent run-up to Zimbabwe's general elections. The veterans, who are now busy allocating themselves pieces of land on the farms that they occupied, linked most of the deaths to the campaign to seize farms;

CFU Sue Mugabe for Role in Farm Invasions

The country's white commercial farmers lodged a lawsuit, accusing Zimbabwe's president of being directly responsible for the breakdown of law in the country. President Mugabe, the suit alleges, played "a material role in the persistence of the farm invasions," which has seen more than 1,400 farms occupied by supporters of the ruling ZANU-PF party. The action was filed by the commercial farmers Union, which represents 4,200 white-owned farms in the country. The suit said there has been "a major resurgence of farm invasions" since the June 2000 parliamentary elections, and more than fifty commercial farmers have been threatened with death. It alleges numerous commercial farmers have been ordered to leave their properties immediately, though the ZANU-PF supporters have "no legal authority" to issue such eviction notices. "Death threats are being issued with such vehemence and conviction that it would be foolhardy for anyone to ignore them," the CFU alleges. "The whole situation is greatly aggravated by totally inadequate police reaction." The lawsuit also names the country's police commissioner, Augustine Chihuri, and Chenjerai Hunzvi, the leader of the war veterans' group that has taken a leading role in the farm occupations.

The courts twice ruled the occupations were illegal, but President Mugabe ordered the police to take no action to end the squatting on the farms. The commercial farmers union says it will drop the legal proceedings against the president if he takes immediate action to end the occupations and restore law and order. The production of tobacco, maize, wheat, and other key crops has been disrupted. Tobacco is the country's key export commodity. In the northern Karoi area, 230 white-owned farms have closed, protesting the farm invasions. Most of the shops in Karoi have also shut to show solidarity with the white commercial farmers. A Karoi farmer, David Brand, was beaten unconscious by war veterans and was recovering. The opposition MDC went ahead with its legal challenge to twenty-eight parliamentary seats won by President Mugabe's ZANU-PF party in the June 24 and 25, 2000 elections. ZANU-PF won sixty-two of the one hundred twenty elected seats, and the MDC won fifty-seven. However, because President Mugabe can appoint thirty MPs, his party ended up holding ninety-two of the one hundred fifty parliamentary seats.

Large-scale electoral irregularities were alleged in the Mazowe east constituency, where officials were investigating the voting papers. Lawyers for the MDC claim that many people voted twice, and, in some cases, the dead cast ballots. The MDC is hoping to not only overturn several results, but also have some ZANU-PF candidates barred from office. The government raised the price of regular petrol by almost twenty-six percent. It also raised the price of kerosene—used by the poor for lighting and cooking—by 128 percent. With inflation already at seventy percent and unemployment at fifty percent, the increases are bound to raise hostility to the government.[98]

ZANU-PF Seeks to Rein in Squatters to Avert National Strike

In what was seen as a conciliatory gesture to Zimbabwe's striking white commercial farmers, a senior figure in President Mugabe's ZANU-PF party called for squatters to stop disrupting farming. After a new outbreak of militancy by the invaders, who claimed to be veterans of the war against white rule and now occupying about 1,100 properties, commercial farmers decided on drastic action. At least 237 went on strike. Hundreds more were to follow, and the commercial farmers union petitioned President Mugabe to defuse the situation while launching legal action against the police and the government.

The intervention by Nathan Shamuyarira, ZANU-PF's information secretary and a former cabinet minister, is the first sign this pressure is having an impact. He said, "We are appealing to both the war veterans and our members, who include war veterans and peasants, not to disrupt farming activities." Nathan Shamuyarira added that commercial farmers should continue production and he expected the squatters to take heed of the appeal. In another sign of growing unease in government circles over the farming crisis, *Herald*, the official newspaper, ran a leading article calling for a return to normality. The paper said, "The continued occupation of farms and the attendant violence and disruptions on some of the farms should not be allowed to continue. The war veterans have made their point." Chenjerai "Hitler" Hunzvi, the war veterans' leader and prime mover behind the land invasions, was pointedly excluded from President Mugabe's new cabinet, indicating the president is preparing to discard him. Yet, the government has made previous appeals for the squatters to allow normal work on white farms without taking any action to enforce it. President Mugabe made

---

98. *Andrew Meldrum, "Mugabe sued for role in farm invasions," The Guardian, 27 July 2000.*

this call in April, 2000 but he failed to curb a new outbreak of violence that claimed the lives of five commercial farmers.

Observers agree he is the only figure with sufficient authority to end the crisis. But President Mugabe has repeatedly pledged never to remove the squatters from the land they occupy and has even thanked them for their efforts. Unless he makes a public about-face, the crisis is likely to continue.[99].

Having said that ZANU-PF is the government policymaking political party, whose decision is normally transformed into government policy? The idea at this point and time was to portray an image supporting dialogue between the land invaders and the commercial farmers. The situation at that time was like a guerrilla warfare, whereby the government was not in a position to be seen to be with the ex-combatants and land invaders during the day, hence the intervention of the party through Shamuyarira. Using the power vested in him, the president could have called upon the police and, if necessary, the army to remove the said squatters and land invaders from the commercial farms. The government found itself in a difficult position because it was reluctant to come to the aide of the commercial farmers who had unilaterally decided to go on an illegal strike or the war veterans who had taken the law into their hands through launching illegal land invasions. The government had to take heed of the war veterans warnings of returning to guerrilla warfare if the government intervened in favor of the commercial farmers. The war veterans became an equal threat to the government and the commercial farmers.[100]

---

99. *David Blair, "ZANU-PF seeks to rein in squatters," The Telegraph, 27 July 2000.*
100. *Ibid.*

18.0 Zimbabwe National Strike in Solidarity with Commercial Farmers

The National Executive of the MDC held an emergency meeting at the party headquarters. The meeting was called to discuss the party's position on work stay-aways, in light of increasing calls by the public for a public demonstration demanding the restoration of law and order. A press conference was held immediately after the meeting to present the party's position. The party's statement, read by acting MDC President Gibson Sibanda, follows:

> We have been consulting stakeholders, who include NCA, ZCTU, women's groups, human rights organizations, and other civic groups. The message coming from all the stakeholders is that we should go for a stay-away. We are therefore adding our voice to the call for a stay-away, and we call upon all our members to participate in the stay-away. We have taken this position in the light of the intensification of lawlessness and anarchy in the country. To this end, government has to withdraw troops and its militias from the townships and rural areas. The government should also as a matter of urgency withdraw war veterans from the farms where they are busy raping, beating, and killing farm workers. We also point out that the call for a stay-away has nothing to do with land redistribution. It is a simple matter of the government restoring law and order. The general council of the ZCTU met yesterday and also discussed the issue of stay-aways.

Following that meeting, the ZCTU announced it would, in consultation with its members, push for a stay-away on Wednesday, Thursday, and Friday of the next week (August 2–4). Sibanda stated the MDC added its voice to this demand and called its members to stay away August 2–4. The party appeals to all the people to participate in the stay-away. In doing so, the party asks all people not to participate in any party meetings or demonstrations, but to stay at home peacefully during the days of the stay-away. The sole purpose of the stay-away is to force the government to perform its constitutional obligation of protecting every Zimbabwean against lawlessness and, consequently, restore law and order.[101]

ZCTU Back Strike in Support of Farm Workers

Zimbabwe's powerful trade union movement threw its weight behind embattled white commercial farmers by backing a general strike next week. The ZCTU's

---

101. *MDC calls for stay-away.-Patrick Bond*

decision to launch a mass protest over "the breakdown of law and order" substantially raises the stakes in President Mugabe's confrontation with the commercial farmers. At least 500,000 workers in thirty-five trade unions are expected to close down the national economy in the first general strike since 1998. After an all-day meeting in Harare, the congress's general council decided to launch the protest in sympathy with workers on white farms, who have been singled out for assault by the gangs of squatters now occupying approximately 1,100 properties. Police have failed to prevent violence that has seen more than 4,000 recorded cases of assault against black farm laborers. Nicholas Mudzengerere, acting secretary-general of the congress, said, "We are going on strike because of the beatings that are random in Zimbabwe, because the farm workers are being terrorized, and because of the state of lawlessness." The whole workforce will follow.

> Shops will be closed. Factories will fall silent. Public transport will come to a halt. Hospitals will provide emergency cover only, and teachers are expected to boycott schools. More than 300 white commercial farmers have already been mounting sporadic strikes during the past fortnight, and every landowner in Zimbabwe is expected to join the national protest, ensuring that all the pillars of the economy are closed down.

Mr Mudzengerere believes the government will be compelled to heed the workers' demands. He said:

> The stay-away has nothing to do with employment conditions or remuneration. It is about law and order. We are aware the government can stop this lawlessness. They must be forced to listen.

He described the congress's decision as a response to "overwhelming demands from our grassroots membership."

Beleaguered commercial farmers, who have endured nearly six months of harassment from squatters, are deeply moved by the resolve of black workers to rally behind their demand for the restoration of law and order. Chris Thorne, who helped organize a strike by commercial farmers in Glendale, said, "It's very encouraging to see us being joined by all sectors of Zimbabwean society, black and white, who want nothing more than the rule of law in our country." Thorne, whose Irenedale farm was invaded by 350 squatters yesterday, believes a general strike is the only way of forcing concessions from the government. He said, "We can't continue like this. We're at rock bottom now. Without law and order, there can be no recovery, and a national stoppage is the only way to make that point."

The congress has close ties with the MDC, the main opposition party. The memory of political violence that engulfed last month's parliamentary election and claimed thirty-seven lives is behind the decision of many unions to join the strike. Gift Chimanikire of the postal workers union said, "Mugabe is showing no willingness to bring the situation on the farms back to normal, and the only way we can put pressure on him is when all Zimbabweans demonstrate. We know this has nothing to do with land. The issue is violence. He must act to prevent it."[102]

A total of 3,000 of Zimbabwe's 5,000 white-owned farms will be seized soon, one of the country's cabinet ministers announced last night. Ignatius Chombo, the local government minister, was quoted on state television as saying the farms would be confiscated to ensure black settlers would be on the land before the start of the next rainy season in four months. The statement stunned farm union officials. "I cannot believe that such an outrageous statement would be official government policy," David Hasluck, director of the commercial farmers union, said. The immediate appropriation of more than sixty percent of white-owned farms would have a devastating effect on the country's already crippled economy. Hundreds of thousands of farm workers would be thrown out of work. Economists have said agricultural production would collapse, leading to severe food shortages.

The announcement is seen as a reflection of the chaos within President Mugabe's ruling ZANU-PF party, which must deal with a three-day countrywide shutdown this week called by the national labor movement to force the government to restore law and order on the country's commercial farms and remove soldiers from urban townships. If that was not enough, the regime is coping with the rise of a less dramatic, but still highly effective, form of opposition, which has captured the imagination of Zimbabwe's football-mad, militant urban populace. It is red, costs almost nothing, fits in your shirt pocket, and can be used to get rid of dictators responsible for foul deeds. At appropriate moments, such as the appearance of President Mugabe's twenty-four-vehicle motorcade, whip out the little plastic rectangle. Brandish it as the armor-plated, presidential Mercedes-Benz flashes past. It tells the seventy-six-year-old autocrat he has been red-carded and it is time to get off the field he has dominated for the past twenty years.

This cheeky piece of symbolism has caught on with those voting against President Mugabe's ZANU-PF party in last month's parliamentary elections. In Masvingo, about 180 miles south of Harare, I remarked to a petrol attendant,

---

102. *David Blair, "Zimbabwean unions back general strike," The Telegraph, 29 July 2000.*

William Mugari, that the town had voted against ZANU-PF. "We gave them the double red card," he said with a huge grin. When President Mugabe stepped out of the ceremonial 1936 Bentley ten days ago to open parliament, thousands of red cards flashed at him by MDC opposition supporters greeted him. When the anthem was played three weeks ago, before the start of the ill-fated football match between Zimbabwe and South Africa, the packed terraces of the 65,000-capacity national stadium twinkled with red cards. The first million, cut out of a thin sheet of shiny plastic and the same dimensions as the original wielded by football referees, are in such demand that the MDC is having three million more produced. The device grew out of the referendum in February on a draft of a new national constitution, which was manipulated by ZANU-PF. Rejected outright, township wags said they had "given Mugabe the yellow card." MDC campaign workers gave it its logical extension in their call to show him the red card in the parliamentary elections and send him off. Since the cards first appeared at the final campaign rally on June 18 of the MDC leader, Morgan Tsvangirai, they have got up the noses of ZANU-PF leaders

Topper Whitehead, the MDC coordinator, says that, along with three million red cards, a million whistles will soon be delivered to signify the end of the game for ZANU-PF. Five weeks after the elections, it is still unwise to be found with a red card in rural areas where pro-Mugabe thugs maintain a rule of fear. Equally risky is the MDC's open-hand salute that says the greeter comes in friendship and without weapons, in contrast to the clenched fist of ZANU-PF that threatens violence. On Friday, the commercial farmers union reported a farm guard was badly injured by so-called guerrilla war veterans for making MDC gestures.[103]

MDC Endorses National Strike in Support of Commercial Farmers and Workers

The General Council of the ZCTU met on June 28, 2003, and discussed the issue of stay-aways. Following that meeting, the ZCTU announced it would, in consultation with its members, push for a stay-away on Wednesday, Thursday and Friday (August 2–4). The acting president of the MDC Mr. Gibson Sibanda stated that the MDC had added its voice to this demand, and is calling on its members to stay away August 2–4. The MDC appealed to all the people to take part in the stay-away. In doing so, the party asked all people not to participate in any party meetings or demonstrations, but to stay at home peacefully during the days of the stay-away. According to the MDC the sole purpose of the stay-away

103. *Jan Raath, "3,000 white farms 'will be seized'," The Times, 31 July 2000.*

was to force the government to perform its constitutional obligation of protecting every Zimbabwean against lawlessness, and consequently to restore law and order in the country. The MDC asked the government to withdraw troops and its militias from the townships and rural areas. The MDC demanded that government should, also as a matter of urgency withdraw war veterans from the farms where they were alleged to be busy raping, beating and killing commercial farmers and farm workers. The opposition party also made it clear that the call for a stay-away had nothing to do with land redistribution. The government was given a month notice of the impending strike and as such had sufficient time to prepare for any consequences resulting from the national strike.

The commercial farmers protesting against the land invasions started the strike and the national strike was an escalation of the commercial farmers strike although ZCTU member unions maintained that the strike was intended to force the government to restore law and order in the country. In the eyes of the government, the endorsement of the nationwide strike was tantamount to a declaration of war. This is one of the reasons why the Zimbabwe service chiefs declared that they were not prepared to serve under a government of civilians who did not participate in the armed struggle. Through the propaganda machinery, the MDC was perceived as a group of political malcontents and puppets of the former colonial masters who only wanted to enrich themselves at the expense of the toiling masses[104].

MDC Alleges National Stay-Away Was for the Restoration of Law and Order

The ZCTU, representing the majority of trade unions, including GAPWUZ, have called for a National Stay-Away on Wednesday, Thursday, and Friday of this week (August 2–4, 2000) in a mass call for the restoration of law and order in our country. This particularly refers to the beatings and intimidation in the high-density townships and the invasions of farms by war veterans. The CFU, therefore, supports the call for a National Stay-Away and calls on all commercial farmers to observe the shutdown. Clearly, the situation under which commercial farmers find themselves, including six months of ongoing invasions, stoppages, threats, theft, poaching, and attendant ills, is intolerable and cannot be sustained any longer.

Our appeal to the leadership to save this country at the eleventh hour must, therefore, be a universal, unequivocal clarion call for justice and fairness and the

---

104. *Ibid.*

rights of protection under the law. We are not isolated in this dilemma, and the Zimbabwean people are, by their actions, calling for nothing less. I know there are many and varied circumstances on each farm and no one operator is the same as the next, but we can follow certain principles in impacting the shutdown without irretrievably destroying the basis for production. I believe, for the period, there should be nothing off the farms in the way of produce and nothing onto the farms in the way of inputs. There should be no business conducted with the banks or other sections of industry, service providers or suppliers. There should be no other activities related to the business of farming, except notable exceptions. I also believe there should be no threat to the welfare of livestock, which must obviously be fed and watered, milked, treated, bedded, or whatever else is required while plants (nurseries, seedbeds, greenhouses, and so forth) must be maintained as normal.

Importantly, all labor is paid for the period of the shutdown. And, as commercial farmers, we show solidarity with our workers who have suffered the brunt of the brutality since the invasions began. I know, too, this is costly for commercial farmers, who can ill-afford to risk their businesses any further, but, without a return to the rule of law, there can be no future for any of us in Zimbabwe. And our country, as we know and love it, is at the crossroads. Now is the time to stand united and resolute for what we believe in.[105]

The ZCTU said yesterday the three-day stay-away planned for tomorrow will go ahead because of continuing lawlessness in Zimbabwe. Isaac Matongo, the acting secretary-general of the ZCTU, said the government had refused to restore law and order, so cancellation of the mass action was not warranted. "We have not gone back on the stay-away," said Matongo. "Nothing has changed. People are still being beaten up and harassed." He said the ZCTU held a meeting yesterday to spread word about the mass action. Matongo said most of the ZCTU affiliate unions had been informed about the stay-away. The union has said the stay-away is in protest against lawlessness, particularly on the farms. War veterans, occupying more than 1,600 farms, have stepped up the terror campaign against commercial farmers and workers since the June 24–25 election. The ZCTU said it was also concerned soldiers and the police were beating up people in the high-density suburbs. Matongo said, despite dissent by veterans and other organizations, the stay-away would go ahead.

The message about the action is going all over," said Matongo. "Those who do not believe the stay-away is on will see for themselves on Wednesday. Commer-

---

105. *CFU, National Stay-away, 1 August 2000.*

cial farmers and workers were expected to join tomorrow's action after calling off
a mass shutdown of farms organized for yesterday by the CFU.

The proposed action has gained support from several quarters. The Agricultural Labor Bureau (ALB) said yesterday they supported the proposed mass stay-
away. "The ALB has decided to support the three-day stay-away because commercial farmers, farm workers, and their families have been the main victims of
the failure on the part of the state to uphold the rule of law and an economy that
is not supported by the law of the country and its agencies on the road to collapse," ALB said in a statement. The Zimbabwe National Students Union
(ZINASU) yesterday called on its members to join the stay away;

Hopewell Gumbo, president of ZINASU, said, "ZINASU call on all its member student organizations to join the stay-away planned to start on Wednesday to
press the ZANU-PF government to immediately restore the rule of law in the
country." The executive committee of the Employers Confederation of Zimbabwe (EMCOZ) met yesterday to discuss the proposed action. Justin Nyoka, president of EMCOZ, said, "EMCOZ believes that timely action by the authorities
can still avert the stay-away. We are concerned that, if it goes ahead, it will do
untold damage to the economy." Presidential spokesman George Charamba said
yesterday the government would not interfere with the mass action if it was
peaceful.[106]

Mugabe Confirms Plan to Seize More Land in Retaliation

President Mugabe, in the most desperate move yet in his self-declared war against
Zimbabwe's white commercial farmers, has announced his government will take
more than 60 percent of their land. Vice President Joseph Msika, in charge of
President Mugabe's land seizure committee, said, in addition to the 804 farms
listed for compulsory acquisition in June, another 2,237 properties have been
identified for nationalization. The legal process of gazetting and formally taking
possession of them was at an advanced stage. The twelve million acres President
Mugabe has set as his target will leave commercial farmers with only 7 million of
the 19 million they now own.

The CFU and economists say, even though the bankrupt government does
not have any hope of settling even a tiny proportion of the target of 500,000 families, the announcement has delivered what probably will be a fatal blow to the
confidence of the commercial farmers whose production drives the country's
economy. They predict economic collapse in the coming months. "It is a recipe

---

106. *"Strike on tomorrow," Zimbabwe Daily News, 1 August 2000.*

for absolute economic disaster," Jerry Grant, deputy director of the CFU, said. Meanwhile, Simba Makoni, the finance minister, announced the national currency is to be devalued from Z$38 to the American dollar to Z$50, with immediate effect.[107]

With two-thirds majority in parliament, the government was in a position to amend any act through parliament. In order to end farm acquisition delays due to notice and other delay tactics enshrined in the constitution, the government amended the Land Acquisition Act. The amendment drastically reduced the chances of any farmer taking the government to court over land acquisition, reduced the eviction notice from ninety days to seven days, and increased the fine for resisting eviction from Z$20,000 equivalent USD 400 to Z$100,000 equivalent USD 2,000.

In reality, the commercial farmers wasted their time fighting the government in court. They should have combined their efforts with the government in making representations to the British government. For unknown reasons, they never believed the landless majority really needed land and were convinced their experience in tilling the land was more important to the government than land redistribution. The commercial farmers failed to understand the executive, and the judiciary understood the land issue in the same way and appreciated the efforts the executive made to peacefully solve the problem. At the same time, the learned judges were aware the land also legally belonged to the commercial farmers in accordance with the existing constitution of Zimbabwe.

The proposed transfer of land to the landless was constitutional, subject to the government paying reasonable compensation for developments made on the land. Politically, the intent of the government action was to disrupt farming activities and weaken the MDC main financial power base before the presidential elections. It would appear the commercial farmers were being punished for their financial and material support of the opposition, resulting in the constitutional referendum defeat of the government and the challenge posed by the opposition's gains during the 2000 parliamentary elections. The government could no longer sit back and wait to see the results of the proposed nationwide strike. Instead, it supported the attack position by harassing the commercial farmers and their workers and, wherever possible, instill fear in the opposition to neutralize the impact of the industrial action.[108]

---

107. *Jan Raath, "Mugabe to seize more land" The Times (UK), 2 August 2000.*
108. *Ibid.*

Zimbabwean Government Alleges Army and Police Mobilized to Keep Peace

Zimbabwe prepared itself yesterday for a crippling, potentially violent national strike today to protest the failure of President Mugabe's government to stop months of violence. The one-day action is a protest against attacks on opposition supporters and the illegal occupation of white-owned farms by war veterans. The stay-away promises to be successful. By last night, more than fifty civic society groups had endorsed it. Several businesses had served notice they would be shut for the day. Government sources said the entire Zimbabwe National Army and Air Force of Zimbabwe had been put on standby to disperse any strike gatherings. The organizers scaled back the planned action, from three days to one, yesterday. "We want to give the government time to respond. If it does not, we will go on a much longer strike," said Nicholas Mudzengerere, acting secretary-general of the ZCTU, the strike's main sponsor. The war veterans intensified their threats against commercial farmers and farm workers yesterday. Dave Hasluck, the director of the CFU, said some farm workers had been threatened with death if they joined the strike action. He said new occupations had also been reported in the province of Mashonaland. "It is ironic that the war veterans have been disrupting and stopping farming activities. Now that the commercial farmers want to stop farming, they are then ordered by the same war veterans to go to work."

Tim Henwood, the CFU's president, said the organization had been left with no alternative except joining the call for the restoration of law and order through the strike. On Monday, the government officially confirmed reports it had identified more than 3,000 white-owned farms for redistribution to black Zimbabweans. Nkosana Moyo, the minister of industry and international trade, said the strike would hurt Zimbabwe's limping economy. He said the ZCTU should have opted for dialogue with the government. A ZCTU spokesman, meanwhile, expressed his anger at the decision by South Africa's president, Thabo Mbeki, to visit Zimbabwe on the day of the strike, saying he should have postponed his visit. Mr Mbeki has been criticized for his open support for President Mugabe during the farm occupation crisis.[109]

---

109. *Basildon Peta, "Army mobilized to keep peace in Zimbabwe," The UK Independent, 2 August 2000.*

MDC Alleges Government Mobilizes Army for Huge Farm Invasion

Zimbabwe is mobilizing its army to rapidly resettle several million black peasants on white-owned farms after the government said it would now seize about two-thirds of all white land. In a move that dashed hopes of a compromise, the vice president, Joseph Msika, confirmed the government would dramatically increase the number of farms targeted for confiscation without compensation from the 804 earmarked in May to more than 3,000. President Mugabe's administration says it plans to resettle 500,000 black families on the land before the beginning of the rainy season just a few weeks away. The local government minister, Ignatius Chombo, said Zimbabwe's 40,000-strong army will provide transport and other logistics for the operation.

"It has the vehicles needed to move people from one point to the other. It will also establish a communications center to ensure decisions are made fast and are implemented," he told the state-run *Herald* newspaper. Mr Chombo said the legal procedures to seize the first 211 farms would begin by Friday. That land will be used to resettle 37,000 families. The move further antagonized the government's opponents ahead of a nationwide general strike today backed by trade unions, the main opposition party, and white commercial farmers to protest the handling of land redistribution and the police's failure to respond to growing political violence.

The strike is expected to shut down all of Zimbabwe's major cities, where there is growing anger at the president's heavy-handed response to the surge in opposition support in June's parliamentary election and disillusionment at the economic consequences of the government's policies. Long petrol queues have reemerged since the election. Agriculture and tourism are facing collapse, and power cuts loom. The government plans to take twelve million acres without compensation, nearly two-thirds of all agricultural land owned by whites. It is seizing farms under new legislation that demands the United Kingdom pay the impacted commercial farmers on the grounds they are of British descent. There are strong doubts about the planned role for the army, particularly with so many of its resources tied up in the DRC. However, it would only take a few dozen owners to be forced off their farms at gunpoint for many white landowners to give up any last hope of clinging to their land.

Earlier this week, the CFU, which represents most of Zimbabwe's more than 4,000 white commercial farmers, noted soldiers had been spotted visiting farms, particularly in Mashonaland, where a high proportion of land has been earmarked for confiscation. "At this stage, this seems to be little more than an intelligence-gathering operation," the union said. The CFU is throwing its weight behind the strike led by the ZCTU today to protest the land confiscations and soldiers routinely beating up opposition supporters in townships. But the union appeared to lose its nerve yesterday and scaled back a planned three-day action to just twenty-four hours, despite the powerful backing of the opposition group, MDC, which nearly beat the ruling party in June's elections. The union said it did not want to do further damage to the economy.

"We want to give the government time to respond. If the government does not respond, we will go on a much longer strike," said Nicholas Mudzengerere, acting secretary-general. "We have taken this decision because we want to use the strike as a warning shot, and we think one day would be adequate." Morgan Tsvangirai, the MDC leader, urged all Zimbabweans to support the strike and accused President Mugabe of pursuing a political vendetta against opposition supporters. "There is no need to pursue political vendettas in a manner that destroys the social and economic fabric. There is no need for suicidal policies just because things did not go well for him during the elections," he said. In London, the foreign office said the latest reports, if confirmed and acted upon, were very disturbing. Foreign office ministers are anxious to not become embroiled in another propaganda war with President Mugabe. However, officials warned last night:

> Mass acquisitions would not help the people of Zimbabwe. We have always said we are willing to cooperate in a program of genuine land reform, including by offering cash. However, mass acquisitions would not be fair to the commercial farmers of Zimbabwe and not the fresh start that Zimbabwe so badly needs after the elections.

The CFU hoped to meet President Mugabe on Monday to reach a compromise on land distribution, but the president canceled the appointment.[110]

In anticipation of a total breakdown in law and order due to the planned nationwide strike action, the government mobilized the army and the air force. From lessons learned from other countries, national strikes of that nature ended up becoming demonstrations, deteriorating into looting sprees and government takeover, as was in the case of Romania and Yugoslavia. To render the strike ineffective, the war veterans ordered the same commercial farmers they wanted out of the land to go back and work. They even threatened the farm workers with death

---

110. *Chris McGreal and Patrick Wintour, "Mugabe mobilizes army for huge farm invasion," The Guardian, 2 August 2000.*

for joining the nationwide strike. According to the government, the army was being mobilized to assist in the resettlement of 500,000 landless peasants on approximately twelve million acres of land to be acquired without compensation, nearly two-thirds of all agricultural land owned by whites at that time. This operation was supposed to be conducted with the assistance of the armed forces transporting the landless into the white commercial farms.

This move was also intended to instill fear in the minds of the commercial farmers, trade unionists, and the opposition. The government even threatened to set up farm occupation command posts in the districts. The government was not convinced the strike was a stay-away from work, as the ZCTU advertised. Due to lack of intelligence on the activities of the ZCTU, the government thought there was a secret agenda to turn the stay-away into a mass demonstration and popular uprising, hence the reason to prepare mechanisms to crush such a revolt. The reasons given for the military deployment were quite genuine from a national perspective, but, according to the international community, the army was being deployed to suppress the proposed national strike. Supporting this theory was the fact that tear gas was used to disperse the crowds, and the army was seen patrolling the townships. In Bulawayo, one of the MDC strongholds, the government deployed the border gezi militias to threaten the population. The militias are not trained in the rule of law and human rights. They are only there to support the ideals and policies of the government in power. During the Zimbabwe-Rhodesia government, the same militia concept suppressed and intimidated the local population against supporting the same revolutionary movement, which is now employing the same political tactics against the people. The army should not have been called from the barracks until such time when the police were unable to contain the security situation in the country.

According to the international community, in a democratic state, the police are a sufficient force to control a stay-away from work whose organizers had issued specific instructions for the workers not attend party meetings during the stay-away. The army was brought into the African townships during the time of the illegal Smith regime to suppress nationwide stay-aways, which the trade unions and the nationalists supported. The Zimbabwe service chiefs declared they were not prepared to serve under a leader who was not involved in the armed struggle based on party propaganda against the agenda of the MDC. The same type of mentality resulted in General Peter Walls and other military commanders of the Zimbabwe-Rhodesia army to plot a coup d'état in the event of ZANU-PF winning the 1980 elections. Likewise, they were not confident of their personal security under what they saw as a terrorist communist-led government. The planned coup was averted by elevating Lieutenant General Peter Walls to general. Despite this declaration, any democratic army would not stand by, watching the economy slide into the doldrums just because of loyalty to a particular group of the national leadership. The service chiefs are receiving salaries sufficient to sustain their families and are unsure if a new government would cater for their personal needs in the same way the ZANU-PF government is doing. The point here is fear of the unknown, hence their support for perpetual leadership of the government and party.

The government also needed the army and war veteran support to continue in power. This is why the Zimbabwean government agreed to the payment of pensions and allowances to ex-combatants, even though there was no economic justification for such payments. War veterans capitalized on this government weakness to press for new demands, including land. The ex-combatants were made happy at the expense of the economic development of the country, transparency, accountability, and international image. The Zimbabwean government is now being blamed for suppressing democracy, economic mismanagement, breakdown in law and order, and breach of human rights in its capacity of custodian of the law.[111]

The Zimbabwe National Strike Halts Commerce and Industry

Factories, farms, and businesses across Zimbabwe shut down on Wednesday as the vast majority of Zimbabwe's 1.4 million workers observed the one-day strike the ZCTU called. Union officials claimed eighty to ninety percent support for the stoppage, but government offices and institutions were open, as were many small businesses. Large companies and the country's main manufacturing industries were closed, along with the banks along with leading supermarkets and retailers. The stay-away was peaceful with few reports of violence or intimidation. The ZCTU called the strike, with the support of the CFU, to protest the breakdown of law and order in Zimbabwe in urban areas as well as on commercial farms.

Well-supported though it was, the stoppage is unlikely to influence government policy. The best hope white commercial farmers now have of reversing the government's plans to take over 3,100 white-owned commercial farms covering five million hectares seems to be pressure from South Africa commercial farmers and business leaders, who are waiting anxiously to see if President Mugabe will soften his stance on land expropriation without compensation, following

---

111. Ibid.

Wednesday's discussions in Harare with President Thabo Mbeki of South Africa and senior South African cabinet ministers. Western governments and foreign investors in southern Africa hope President Mbeki is pressing President Mugabe in private to restore the rule of law in Zimbabwe. However, President Mbeki has refused to criticize President Mugabe in public, and the Pretoria government has even held out the possibility of loans to prop up the economy. On Wednesday, President Mugabe said the war veterans illegally occupying white-owned farms would be removed by the end of the month. However, observers said it was doubtful how he would honor this pledge. In the past, he has said he would not use the army to remove the veterans from occupied land. The best news the country's beleaguered, 4,500, white commercial farmers have had for some time was Tuesday's decision to devalue the Zimbabwe dollar by almost twenty-five percent to Z$50 to USD 1 unit from Z$38 to USD 1 previously.

Businessmen and the tobacco industry welcomed the devaluation, even though some economists believed the government should have gone further to eliminate the free-market premium altogether. Foreign exchange dealers said they expected the free-market rate, which had been as high as Z$68 to the American dollar, to narrow, perhaps to about Z$60 equivalent USD 1.5. This would leave a twenty percent premium at the new official rate, according to some stockbrokers. The MDC welcomed the devaluation, but it warned the overdue adjustment did not go far enough to give the country a competitive real exchange rate. Economists said, while devaluation lowered the trade-weighted real effective exchange rate, making Zimbabwe's exports more competitive, the real rate was still twenty percent higher than it was at the end of last year and nearly double its levels of January 1999. Bankers say a further downward adjustment is inevitable and could come within two months. Much will depend on supplementary measures to be announced soon by Simba Makoni, finance minister. The main beneficiaries will be the tobacco and gold sectors. Other exporters, including the tourist sector, had been selling currency earnings at the free-market rate and could be temporarily worse off if, as dealers predict, the free-market premium declines over the next few weeks. Economists are unanimous in predicting a sharp increase in the inflation rate. Zimbabwe imports all its petroleum and forty percent of its electricity. These increased costs will have to be passed on to the consumer. One bank economist expects devaluation to add some eight percent to consumer prices over the next two to three months, which, with second-round effects and the worsening shortages partly caused by the land crisis, would push inflation above seventy percent by September.[112]

Zimbabwe's town centers fell silent yesterday as a general strike called to protest the breakdown of law and order, joined by white commercial farmers for the first time, and paralyzed the economy. Factories closed, shops were shut, and streets emptied of traffic. The usually bustling bus stations were silent, and Harare's main shopping areas were empty. The ZCTU claimed that ninety percent of the workforce had joined the strike, although government departments were largely unaffected and most schools and hospitals continued as normal. The CFU confirmed that virtually all of the 4,000 white commercial farmers in every province had joined the protest, even as squatters, who sparked the closure by illegally occupying 1,600 properties and mounting a terror campaign against President Mugabe's opponents, singled out striking landowners for a new wave of intimidation. Riot police armed with batons and tear gas were deployed in strategic positions around Harare. A military helicopter flew overhead, even though no violence was reported.

Nicholas Mudzengerere, acting secretary-general of the congress, said, "I am very pleased by the response to the stay-away. We are waiting for the government to reply to our demands and guarantee a return to law and order." Mr Mudzengerere said the congress's general council would meet on Saturday, adding, "If the government does not respond, I cannot rule out another stay-away." In Harare's black townships, Mbare and Highfield, streets were filled with striking workers enjoying an extra day off. Moses Sibanda, a bank clerk, was clear about the purpose of the protest. He said, "We have got to stop those guys on the farms from beating people. All the time, they are beating people, and the government does nothing. We support the white commercial farmers because our entire economy comes from them." Fields in Zimbabwe's agricultural heartland were deserted as many commercial farmers defied intimidation to join the strike. Squatters in the Karoi area, 150 miles northwest of Harare, issued dozens of threats. A farmer said, "They are telling us, 'You've closed now, so you're closed for ever. We will take your farm.' They've told our workers never to come to work again if they down tools today."

Paul Stidolph was trapped by a mob of forty armed with clubs and axes at the gates of his Grand Parade farm. He said, "I told them I was joining the stay-away, and they shouted, 'You are an enemy of the government. We've been ordered to take your farm.'" Only a rescue mission by neighboring commercial farmers, who have formed a rapid reaction unit and use a light aircraft to track the squatters,

---

112. *Tony Hawkins and Victor Mallet, "Zimbabwe strike hits businesses," The Financial
Times, 3 August 2000.*

drove away the gang and saved Paul Stidolph. He said, "It's exactly this sort of intimidation and harassment that we want to stop. I'm all for this stoppage because it's the only way to make that point." Other commercial farmers paid a heavy price for their determination to join the strike. Irvine Reid, whose Calgary farm has been occupied by fourteen men he believes to be police and army officers, was ordered to leave his property. He said, "The first question they asked was 'Is the farm working today?' Then they told me to go or else." Irvine Reid and his family fled for the safety of Harare. Jack Callow fled from his Naryvale farm after being threatened by a mob of twelve who screamed, "We want the whites out of Zimbabwe. You whites must go." After a meeting yesterday with President Mbeki of South Africa, President Mugabe injected more uncertainty into the farm crisis. He repeated promises by ministers that squatters would be removed from farms that have not been listed for resettlement, despite failing to enforce previous pledges of a return to normality on Zimbabwe's white-owned farms. President Mugabe said, "We will be removing the war veterans from the farms we are not resettling." Asked when this would happen, he replied, "Within the next month." Past performance means few landowners will take comfort from his latest comment.[113]

Analysis of the Reasons behind the Failure of the National Stay-Away

The introduction of the army into the national strike made the ZCTU reduce the strike from the proposed three days to two days, hoping the government would bend down to the mass stay-away and choose the negotiation path as an alternative to all-out confrontation with the workers. At the same time, the ZCTU also diluted the effects of the strike by asking its members to stay at home and not attend any meetings. If they were serious, they should have encouraged their members to go into the streets and demonstrate to show their anger. This passive resistance resulted in the government taking advantage by injecting the available military resources into the streets to reinforce the police. Looters, who masqueraded as demonstrators, broke into shops and even went to the extent of looting butchery shops, spoiling the stay-away. Many people were arrested for looting. At the end of the strike, the police and army recovered a lot of property, including furniture and carcasses of beef.

The strike was a success, but it failed to achieve the desired effect. The government accused the trade union of economic sabotage due to the negative economic effects of farming, industrial, and commercial activities throughout the country.

---

113. *David Blair, "Protest strike halts Zimbabwe," The Telegraph, 3 August 2000.*

The ZCTU argued the objective of the stay-away was to send a message to the government on the state of the economy and rule of law. The stay-away was supposed to force the government into abandoning the land reform program and compromise to the idea of a government of national unity and maybe take over the government through mass action. The government realized the opposition was a formidable force to be reckoned with. The alliance among the commercial farmers, the workers, and the intellectuals became clearly defined. Indeed, the government managed averting a planned mass uprising, which could have resulted in demonstrations and popular uprising. The government also learned the nationwide strike lacked a political agenda to remove the government and was just a national disobedience action, despite the intelligence information on the government table of a planned mass uprising. The government implemented mechanisms to avert the perceived uprising, but, according to the international community, the government was suppressing democracy and freedom of expression. In addition to international concern, Africa and the subregion were also concerned about the Zimbabwean situation to the extent the South African president visited Zimbabwe during the time of the strike. The Zimbabwean president promised to remove squatters and war veterans from lands not marked for resettlement.

The MDC lost a golden opportunity to force the government to the negotiation table leading to free and fair elections. The opposition failed to take the risk of being arrested and attract international attention to the problems facing Zimbabwe. A revolution is not like an industrial action against an employer. It needs more commitment, even being prepared to make the maximum sacrifice price. The Zimbabwean people are waiting for the MDC leadership to take the lead in effecting change through democratic means. The government alleged the MDC leadership was planning to assassinate the president with the objective of distracting the opposition from planning any government change by popular uprising. The government realized the opposition leadership was not prepared to face personal persecution through imprisonment for encouraging public disobedience. The MDC must remember ZANU-PF leaders suffered imprisonment and detention without trial for the achievement of the independence of Zimbabwe.[114]

---

114. Ibid.

19.0 The Zimbabwe Land Reform Crisis on the Regional Agenda

President Mugabe denied he had given any pledge to force an end to illegal farm invasions and even held out the prospect of further extending his land grab program. After appearing to be ready for compromise, President Mugabe's return to a hard-line dashed hopes of an economic and political turnaround in the southern African country. President Mugabe announced after talks with South African President Mbeki that liberation war veterans who began seizing white farms would be moved off them by the end of the month. Zimbabwe's mainly white commercial farmers and its hard-pressed financial markets had welcomed the statement, but President Mugabe said in a speech to black, commercial farmers in Bindura that he had never undertaken to end the invasions. "I didn't say war veterans should be removed," he said. Mugabe reaffirmed his intention to take more than 3,000 farms from white owners without compensation for the value of the land and added, "Whatever we do after the 3,000 farms will be purely complementary, but we are not stopping there.' The farm invasions, which have hobbled the country's crucial agriculture industry and Zimbabwe's participation in a civil war in the DRC have driven the economy to the brink of collapse.

With foreign reserves down to approximately one day's imports, unemployment at fifty percent, inflation at sixty percent, and interest rates around seventy percent, the country is in a deep recession. Political violence unleashed by supporters of the ruling ZANU-PF ahead of parliamentary elections in June and President Mugabe's antiwhite rhetoric has compounded investor concerns.[115]

There was little cheer for southern African leaders who met in Windhoek, the Namibian capital, for their annual summit. The financial and political crisis in Zimbabwe, one of the region's biggest economies, and civil war in the DRC has blighted economic prospects for the fourteen-nation SADC. The spread of AIDS has also undermined hopes for rapid development. Among the few signs of progress is the planned adoption of a free-trade protocol by eleven SADC members. The participants intend to eliminate tariffs for eighty-five percent of intra-SADC trade by 2008 and have a full free-trade area by 2012. Only Angola and the DRC, both embroiled in war, and the Seychelles, have yet to sign. "Our businesspeople and their counterparts in other parts of the globe are looking to this trade arrangement as the critical pillar of this region's economic growth," said Hidipo Hamutenya, Namibian trade minister. However, international and

---

115. *Cris Chinaka, "Zimbabwe's Mugabe Dashes Hopes for Reform," Reuters, 3 August 2000.*

regional investors are more concerned about the damage caused by President
Mugabe's policies in Zimbabwe than a trade accord that will impact only about
$7 billion of annual trade between SADC members and be fully effective only
after more than a decade. President Mbeki of South Africa, the dominant economy in SADC, has tried persuading President Mugabe to restore the rule of law
in Zimbabwe, but he has been repeatedly rebuffed. President Mugabe, ignoring
court orders and warnings from members of his own ZANU-PF party about the
disastrous economic consequences of destroying Zimbabwe's agricultural sector,
has vowed to seize more than 3,000 white-owned commercial farms to resettle
black Zimbabweans. The latest land proposals have not been properly planned,
and they appear to be President Mugabe's angry response to the strong opposition showing in the SADC. Long dismissed by business executives as an ineffective bureaucracy, it seems powerless to take the lead in promoting the region's
interests. Yet again, SADC officials have postponed restructuring plans. One
reform, backed by South Africa, would have brought the semiautonomous
"organ for politics, defense and security"—chaired by President Mugabe and
used by him as a power base—under the control of SADC governments.

War in the DRC is another source of conflict within SADC. South Africa is
pushing for an United Nations-led peacekeeping operation, while Zimbabwe,
Angola, and Namibia are reluctant to withdraw the troops they have sent to support President Kabila in his fight against rebels backed by Rwanda and Uganda.
SADC comprises Angola, Botswana, the DRC, Lesotho, Malawi, Mauritius,
Mozambique, Namibia, the Seychelles, South Africa, Swaziland, Tanzania, Zambia, and Zimbabwe.[116]

---

116. *Victor Mallet, SADC looks for the positive, Financial Times, 7 August 2000.*

20.0 Zimbabwe Launches Donor-Recommended National Economic Revival Program

Following up on the Harare donor conference recommendations, the government launched the much-awaited National Economic Revival Program, which seeks to promote economic growth through homegrown solutions to various challenges facing the country, the *Herald* newspaper said. Speaking at the unveiling ceremony in Harare, Dr. Herbert Murerwa, the minister of finance and economic development, said the new measures were a sign of government's comprehensive response to its obligations under the Tripartite Negotiating Forum. "This is a full and broad-based program that was produced in full consultation with business and labor, and we hope that it will slow down the negative growth in our economy," he said. The new measures are expected to boost production and slow down the negative economic growth by at least two percent from the projected 10.3 percent for this year. According to the policy document, the country was facing severe socioeconomic challenges.

> These have been compounded by a hostile external and domestic environment, arising from our detractors' opposition to our Land and Agrarian Reform Program. Sanctions imposed on Zimbabwe have seen important sources of foreign exchange—donor funding for development projects, banks' lines of credit, foreign direct and portfolio investment—dry up. This, coupled with worsening export performance, has heightened failure to adequately provide for fuel, electricity, food, drugs as well as spares, capital and equipment, among others. If not urgently addressed, foreign exchange unavailability will lead to national instability and pose a threat to national security.

The ten-point plan President Mugabe enunciated sets the tone for the sectoral-driven economic revival growth strategy.

> This, however, needs to be complemented by measures that enhance the country's capacity to generate foreign exchange. These measures are also central to the success of agrarian reforms—the cornerstone of government's economic and social transformation.

The plan comes against the background of a deteriorating economy that has declined a cumulative 19.3 percent over the past three years. The rapid expansion in money supply to around 150 percent by December 2002, a result of increased bank lending to the public sector, was also a major cause of concern. The plan notes the unsustainable high inflation, which accelerated to 208.1 percent in January 2003, remained Zimbabwe's prime macroeconomic challenge. According to the policy document, the government will introduce several programs to boost production in the agriculture, manufacturing, mining, tourism, transport, energy, science, and technology sectors. The government, through the Reserve Bank, will avail Z $50 billion to exporters and producers on a revolving basis under the productive and export facilities while the financial and banking communities were expected to mobilize an additional Z$50 billion. As an additional measure to prop up production, the government, in conjunction with its social partners has launched the National Productivity Centre at the Scientific Industrial Research and Development Centre (SIRDC). Furthermore, the government was resuscitating the Business Linkages Program in partnership with interested business organizations to address deindustrialization in the country. The new policy, which hinged on the success of the agrarian reform, will see the government through the minister of lands, agriculture, and rural resettlement announcing viable pre- and postplanting producer prices of key commodities while postharvest prices were going to be announced where necessary.

In addition, a dairy and livestock development program would be introduced to revive and enhance growth in the two industries through the establishment of financial facilities with the banking sector. Other measures include the introduction of seasonal contract farming for agro-processors and seed houses in conjunction with commercial farmers. In tourism, the government will promote the development of the sector through the introduction of urban center duty-free shopping malls as well as agro, ecotourism, and tourism development zones, which enjoy similar incentives as export processing zones enterprises. The new policy framework was also geared at supporting the small- to medium-scale enterprise sector through the introduction of new legislation and the reduction of import duties to encourage the growth of cross-border traders. Other measures outlined in the policy document include the scrapping of duty on buses and spare parts. In the entertainment industry, the government will facilitate duty-free imports of music, film, video equipment, and studios for music and film recording. Scrap metal exports have been banned as all aluminium and copper waste scrap are now being reserved for local foundries. The government will also narrow the current high spreads between deposit and lending rates in line with international practices, review upwards deposit interest rates for the benefit of savers, review upwards rates on consumption and speculative activities, and review the proliferation of service charges levied on depositors. Individuals will be allowed to import a maximum of 200 liters of fuel per vehicle at entry, provided they comply with safety regulations. As a temporary measure to alleviate the plight of commuters, rural bus operators and noncommercial transport owners will be allowed to carry passengers to and from work between Monday and Friday during peak hours. To support its initiatives to fight hunger, the government will review upwards import thresholds so that individuals can import foodstuffs such as maize meal, flour, rice, cooking oil, and so forth without having to pay for import permits. The government has already adopted a two-tier exchange rate policy, which would see exporters getting Z$800 for every US$1 they remit to the Reserve Bank.[117]

---

117. *Government Launches National Economic Revival Program, Zimbabwe Herald.*

21.0 UN Secretary General Special Envoy Visit to Zimbabwe.

Formal opening remarks, I wish to welcome you all to this dinner, which I have hosted in honor of Mr. Mark Malloch Brown, the UNDP Administrator. May I take this opportunity to welcome Mr. Mark Brown not only to this dinner, but also to Zimbabwe? I am aware that he has gone through a very busy and tight program of consultations with a number of my colleagues. Tomorrow, Mr. Brown will deliver an important message to His Excellency The President as well as meet other personalities in the fields of politics, agriculture, and finance. Mr. Administrator, you are here on an important mission on behalf of the international community and Zimbabwe, a mission to reestablish cooperation between Zimbabwe and the donor community on the land issue. On behalf of the Government of Zimbabwe, I wish to assure you that we will do what we can to ensure that your mission succeeds. So, please feel free in all your interaction with us. I know you have been well-briefed by your team that recently visited our country and as a result of your discussions today with my colleagues. Therefore, I do not propose to restate the reasons for land reform in Zimbabwe and the processes thereto. I will only make a few comments of a general nature. The first comment is to underline that the approach we have now adopted to resolve the colonial injustice associated with our land question is not the one we would have freely chosen had the colonial power lived up to its commitments it undertook at Lancaster House in 1979. Between 1980 and 1999, we followed a different path to the one we have now been forced to adopt as a result of the former colonial power reneging on its commitments. If the United Kingdom had honored its obligations then, Mr. Administrator, your mission to Zimbabwe would be a very different one.

In choosing the approach we took, we were guided by principles of justice, fair play, and equity. We wanted to bring justice and equity to all our people. We sort the fairest way of doing just that. We articulated just and equitable criteria to guide us in carrying out this difficult but necessary task. I know you are aware of these criteria, which guide our program. It is because we have tried our utmost to be fair and open in our approach that we feel secure in our conviction that what we are doing is right. Mr. Administrator, we have a powerful ally in our land reform program, namely, a clear conscience. Yes, we know that our cause is just. Morality bids us to correct the present, skewed land system. The poverty of our people congested in the communal lands enjoins us to act. The sad social and economic condition of our people brooks no delay. Over a century of humiliation and deprivation have to come to an end now…nay…yesterday. We are on a fast track to eradicate that condition, even if we do not have all the requisite financial resources to do a perfect job.

Even the promises made at the 1998 Land Conference did not give any new life to the resettlement program. Between October 1998 and June 2000, no land was acquired for resettlement due to resource constraints and an unfavorable international perception about the effects the resettlement program would have upon the huge investments, which the remaining 4,500 white commercial farmers had made on their farms. Admittedly, a speedier process of land acquisition and the resettlement of the indigenous landless people does cut the matrices of networks between the commercial farmers, the producers of agricultural inputs and implements, the market, the banks, and insurance houses—all of which are dominated by the same people, and a minority for that matter.

The network spreads further afield into the international capital arena. It is our just concern that the interests of this sophisticated network are allowed to overshadow the morally legitimate cry of the impoverished and landless majority in postcolonial Zimbabwe. On the ground, this results in the continuation of debilitating land hunger and poverty among the 500,000 rural households clamoring for land and economic relevance. Ladies and Gentlemen, in response to the withdrawal of the international donor community from the land reform and resettlement program, especially after the 1998 Donors Conference, and in order to respond to the explosive political restlessness and massive farm occupation, the Government of Zimbabwe embarked on the Fast-Track Resettlement Program. The current phase of the Resettlement Program is characterized by fast approaches and processes to: The identification and acquisition of the remaining five million hectares needed to resettle the 500,000 households on the waiting list; Plan, demarcate the land so acquired; Emplace the settlers on planned and demarcated land; Deal with all legal questions related to the entire land acquisition process. The fast-track program demonstrates the government's commitment to resolve land injustice once and for all and in the shortest period possible. Our time frame for the completion of this phase is June 2000 to December 2001.

We are pursuing this phase in the fullest knowledge and awareness of our financial, logistical, and manpower limitations. We have decided to go ahead, with speed and within our limited resource constraints. Our people appreciate the depth of our resolve and have demonstrated a firm commitment to work with us. This Zimbabwean train is on the move. To borrow the words of a famous American actor: "Let the dogs bark, the caravan moves on." The land resettlement program we have embarked on is irreversible and unstoppable. All who want to assist us will be assisting a train in motion to go forward.

We shall not hide the fact that the fast-track program has room for improvement. For example, the settlers require access roads, water supplies, schools, clinics, dip tanks, drought power, initial seeds and fertilizers, extension services, training, and many more, which the government is unable to provide at present. If we get help, some of these facilities can be provided to the settlers. It is against the background of the reality of the donors' reluctance to assist the pace and efficacy of the program, that the government has made the choice to go ahead with the fast-track program, albeit against obvious shortfalls in resources and program efficiency. The people need justice. They need it now. The people need land. They need it now. The country needs order and stability. It needs these now. The peoples' patience cannot stretch a year, a month, nor even a week longer, without land, whatever the reasons of delay.

We are fully aware, as well, of the need to integrate economic sense into the entire resettlement program. We are mindful, for example, not to disrupt the agricultural sector irreparably. Those of the 4,500 commercial farmers who wish to remain on the land will be afforded the opportunity to continue. Mr. Administrator, the Zimbabwean government is not unmindful of the concerns of the commercial farmers on the question of fair and adequate compensation. It is for that reason that we have accepted to compensate them for improvements they effected on our soil. But, when it comes to paying for the soil itself, we have said to the commercial farmers we will try our best to get the former colonial power that robbed the land from us to live up to the obligations it assumed at Lancaster House to provide adequate resources to enable us to pay for the land originally robbed from us. If the former colonial power does not provide the resources, then we will only honor our commitment as regards improvements. However, it is the hope of many in this country that your mission may provide an opportunity for a breakthrough to this vexed question.

In conclusion, may I note with profound appreciation the ongoing efforts of the UN secretary-general, Mr. Kofi Annan, aimed at finding a common ground of understanding between the Government of Zimbabwe, the international donor community, and other national players in the current efforts by the government to fast-track the land reform and resettlement program. I want to thank you for the efforts you have yourself exerted to try to find a solution to this problem. I am aware that, on one occasion, you found yourself in quite a tricky position. But as we say here in Africa, "diamonds are found in the mud."[118]

United Nations Intervention in the Land Redistribution Crisis

In September 2000, President Mugabe met the United Nations secretary-general, Kofi Annan, in New York City and discussed the land issue in Zimbabwe and a possible role for the United Nations. A technical mission to Zimbabwe under the aegis of the United Nations Development Program (UNDP) was dispatched in October that year. The mission was mandated to carry out a technical review into measures necessary for a "sound technical process to take the land reform forward." The UNDP Technical Mission conceded that, while a framework for the legal and administrative process for compulsory acquisition of land through the Land Acquisition Act of 1992 was in place, the government had failed to acquire that land principally on account of technical and administrative considerations arising from legal challenges launched by white commercial farmers.

As a follow up to the UNDP Technical Mission and the subsequent visit of its administrator, Mr. Mark Brown, in December 2000, written communication was exchanged with the government. Through this medium, the government was given the assurance the United Nation's secretary-general's consultations with President Mbeki of South Africa, Olusegun Obasanjo of Nigeria, other regional leaders, as well as key western donors, including the World Bank, gave him confidence the UNDP could generate the requisite support for the land reform program. However, as was previously the case, conditions were placed on the government once more. The secretary-general could only persuade the donor community to come on board once "outstanding law and order issues are being brought under control." The government was therefore requested to make a choice between continuing with its fast-track land reform program and adopting "a more systematic, investment-backed approach," which the United Nations supported. In the letter, Mr. Brown conceded the second approach entailed a slow start and the delay of resettlement until confidence-building measures were implemented to secure a resumption of donor funding. The government through the foreign minister, Dr. I. S. G. Mudenge, responded in March 2001 to Mr. Brown, agreeing with most of his proposals. It, however, rejected the second approach, which would have entailed the abandonment of the fast-track program. It was also put to Mr. Brown that, if the donor community had responded in a timely manner with the required resources to implement the agreement reached at the 1998 Land Donor Conference and had the commercial farmers not resorted to legal actions aimed at frustrating the land resettlement program,

---

118. *Minister Mudenge Honors the Special Envoy of the UN secretary-general, 30 November 2000.*

significant progress could have been achieved by that time. The government indicated a unique opportunity had been missed. It is worth noting that, while expressing disquiet over unrelated political questions and conditions from some donors, the government accepted the following proposals submitted by Mr. Brown:

> Enhancement of capacity in government and other stakeholders in the land reform program to speed up consultations, land delivery, settler emplacement, and support
> Encouragement of continuing dialogue between government and other national stakeholders
> Establishment of prominent Zimbabwean citizens and institution to put up a revolving fund to acquire land for resettlement
> Establishment of a land reforms technical team within the UNDP office in Harare to assist the government in capacity building and planning and land reform. It was emphasized that the team should not seek to restart the ongoing fast-track program, but only to enhance its capacity to deliver land to the poor within the objectives, targets and timeframe of the government program
> Establishment of a land reform trust fund, subject to further consultations

At the same time, the government appealed to the United Nations secretary-general "for urgent assistance by the various UN Agencies, as well as willing donors and NGOs to assist the resettled commercial farmers who find themselves in dire need to infrastructure and social facilities."

Following yet another round of consultations with the United Nations, the UNDP resident representative in Harare, Mr. J. Victor Angelo, responded in July 2001 to the government's response to the March 2001 communication by proposing the formation of yet another assessment team to visit Zimbabwe. Principally, the assessment team would "produce a comprehensive report with all necessary technical information and will make recommendations on the possible establishment of an information mechanism for the land reform program." The proposed assessment was seen as part of a "possible partnership building process between the Government of Zimbabwe, the donor community, and local stakeholders." It was further seen that such an assessment would be useful in establishing the facts as far as the fast-track program was concerned.

The government rejected the proposal, which appeared to be a further attempt to delay addressing a very urgent and highly volatile land issue.[119] The United Nations believed the Zimbabwean government was genuinely in need of a sus-

---

119. *Government of Zimbabwe—UNDP communications on land redistribution.*

tainable, economically justified solution to the land redistribution program. The Zimbabwean government, at that point, was content with a political justification of the land issue, but it needed an endorsement from the United Nations.

22.0 Future Uncertainty Grips Commercial Farm Workers

Under Zimbabwe's Land Acquisition Act, the government has gazetted 804 farms for immediate occupation. The land is being haphazardly demarcated and parceled out to landless peasants and among themselves. Meanwhile, the country's estimated one million commercial farmers and their families are sitting tight, wondering what lies ahead. Zimbabwe's estimated one million farm workers and their families are waiting to see if they will still have jobs and what their quality of life will be like after the government implements its accelerated land resettlement program it formed last year. Following the rejection of a government-sponsored referendum on a draft constitution in February last year, war veterans, along with landless supporters of the ruling party ZANU-PF, have occupied more than 1,600 white-owned farms, vowing to stay put until they are properly resettled. They are demanding back what they claim is their ancestral land. After the referendum, the government came up with the Land Acquisition Act, which allows the government to acquire land without compensation. At present, the government has gazetted 804 farms for immediate occupation. In the confusion that has prevailed in the farms, the former fighters have haphazardly demarcated vast tracts of farmland and parceled them out to landless peasants and among themselves. "If this is the way land is going to come, then let the war veterans have it to themselves," says thirty-year-old Tapera Kufa. "Our future hangs in the balance because we don't know what is going to happen to us after all the farm has been taken over."

However, many farm workers doubt if those being allocated land will be able to utilize it productively. The government has not provided infrastructure such as roads, schools, and clinics. People are being resettled on land without water sources. And peasant commercial farmers do not have title to the land so that they cannot use it as collateral to borrow money from the bank. Analysts foresee a reduction in productivity of most farms being resettled. The government has also not come up with clear policies on how to tackle the plight of farm workers, the bulk of who consist of migrant workers. The GAPWUZ wants the Land Acquisition Act to be amended to include a clause compensating farm workers who lose their jobs after the farms have been acquired for resettlement. GAPWUZ, which says its members were not consulted when the Act was formulated, estimates that 50,000 jobs are threatened if the government resettles people on all the 804 farms it has gazetted.

"We support fair and orderly land redistribution," says Philip Munyanyi, GAPWUZ president. "There is nothing in place for the workers, some of whom have lived on these farms for the rest of their lives. If nothing is done, otherwise, we will only be repeating what happened in 1890 when settlers displaced villagers in order to establish their own settlements." Despite official assurance the workers would not be excluded from the resettlement exercise, the future of this disadvantaged group remains unclear. The workers' fear of war veterans pervades the farming community. This reporter conducted an interview with the farm workers' representative at a farm out in the bush, forty kilometers from Bulawayo, Zimbabwe's second-largest city.

"But, if the white man goes, will the government give us loans to run the farms?" asked the representative. "After all, there is going to be nepotism in the land redistribution program. If you closely follow the events, its only ZANU-PF supporters, youth, and war veterans who are benefiting." He, however, noted his sympathy with the white commercial farmers, saying some were third-generation Zimbabweans being punished for the sins of their fathers. He said some bought the properties on the market as opposed to having inherited it from their forefathers.

Fear, intimidation, and uncertainty grip thousands of farm workers as they recall the brutality they endured in the hands of war veterans over the past year, violence that was actually condoned by President Mugabe. His government has snubbed three court orders to stop further invasions. In the run-up to last June's parliamentary elections, thousands of farm workers were assaulted for their alleged loyalty to the opposition MDC. The workers were also forced to attend war veteran's all-night "reeducation" rallies held by war veterans, while other workers had their homesteads gutted to the ground for their suspected allegiance to MDC.

The ruling ZANU-PF, which managed to scrape together sixty-two seats against the opposition's fifty-eight, believes farm workers are opposition party supporters because ZANU-PF tends to associate white commercial farmers with MDC. "To be quite frank, we are treated as second-class citizens in this country," says Job Kundiona, an elderly farm worker. "Nobody cares for our welfare, as we are referred to as mere farm laborers. But still ZANU-PF expects our votes." President Mugabe's appointed governor for Matebeleland North, Obert Mpofu, recently told ZANU-PF supporters that no one from the opposition would be tolerated in the scheme But 4,000 white commercial farmers own seventy percent of the country's fertile land while seventy percent of the black population is

crammed on overused and useless land. These are the disparities that President
Mugabe says he is addressing.

"We want our jobs, but we are a forgotten lot," says migrant worker Renes
Mwale. "You know, if two elephants fight, it is always the grass which suffers.
"Mwale has been living on Yorkshire Farm, east of Harare, for forty years. He
says this has become his home, yet his future is doomed because the farm has
been invaded. He cannot go back to Malawi because he has long forgotten the
way back. Unlike Mwale, Timothy Khupe, also a migrant worker, feels that white
commercial farmers had it coming. Says Khupe, "These Boers are rough. They
treat their dogs better than us, so we are also happy there is some form of revenge
against them." He is however equally skeptical when it comes to whether farm
workers will be resettled because "most are a powerless and ignorant lot." GAP-
WUZ's Munyanyi feels, if the plight of the farm workers is not solved, they may
soon start talking of having been displaced. "They have the right to the land as
much as anyone else."[120]

Some of the farm workers are a second generation of workers—born, educated, and employed on the farms. Most of them are of foreign origin, whose parents came to Zimbabwe to work on the farms during the time of the Federation
of Rhodesia and Nyasaland. These people have nowhere to resettle after being
evicted from the farms together with their employers. The Analytic Report by the
United Nations secretary-general (February 1992) describes internally displaced
persons as persons who have been forced to flee their homes, suddenly or unex-
pectedly, in large numbers as a result of armed conflict, internal strife, and systematic violations of human rights or natural or man-made disasters, and who are
within the territory of their own country. The ex-farm workers will also need to
be resettled like any other landless persons. The problem is that most of the farm
workers have become specialized workers in agriculture and are not capable of
general management of a farm. The government should guarantee the farm
workers employment with the new farm owners and attempt to improve their
conditions of service. The welfare and protection of internally displaced persons
is the responsibility of the government assisted by humanitarian agencies.[121]

---

120. *Zimbabwe Land rights, Rodrick Mukumbira AFRICANEWS—from Africa 58 (January
2001).*
121. *Ibid.*

Commercial Farmers Start Receiving Positive Judgments from the Judiciary

Commercial farmers are receiving positive judgments from the Zimbabwean judiciary, even though an insidious campaign of intimidation against the legal profession unfolds. These attacks, reported in the press in the last few weeks, are not isolated incidents. They are part of a pattern of intimidation meant to enforce judicial and legal support for the government's policies or failing this to declare it irrelevant. With these developments, yet another barrier has been placed in the road to a return to the rule of law.

President Mugabe continues usurping any and all speaking opportunities to pretend that no single-owned farms are being acquired and his government is abiding by its criteria. As this release is written, Andy and Sharon Kockott, who won their legal battle to retain their farm, stand by and watch as their coffee plantation is uprooted to make way for illegal settlers' huts. The Carter families on unlisted Wye Farm were last allowed in their Raffingora home in January 2002. They grew Virginia tobacco, paprika, and maize. Smith Mereki, a war veteran evicted them, scoffing at their High Court order granting them the right to continue farming. These are a few of the 1,024 single-owned farms listed for acquisition and, in most cases, illegally evicted by war veterans. Many will win their cases and be permitted to return to their farms, but the battle to win their right to a livelihood continues.

Justice for Agriculture (JAG) calls on our president to explain why there is such a chasm between his words and the deeds of the settlers on the ground. We call on him to accept he has compromised agricultural trade for shameful aid and reduced proud Zimbabweans to piteous beggars in just two years. More and more, land that was once productive lies fallow. This as the dams are seventy-five percent full. As to the land reform program, we demand an explanation why he is not accountable to his constitution and to the legal instruments ignored in implementing the land reform program. The program communicated in the People First policy document is also being ignored, despite the fact it was recognized by the Supreme Court as a sound program. Land is being handed out willy-nilly to the politically correct with scant regard to sustainable development or even to legalizing the position of settlers on the land so that they can speedily grow crops to feed Zimbabwe.

JAG has test cases challenging the amendments to the Land Acquisition Act before the courts. These amendments, which came in through the back door of parliament by ignoring standing orders, are odds with the Zimbabwean constitution. JAG will continue to advocate for agricultural stakeholders to continue testing the judiciary in the hopes this will unlock the way forward for a return to the rule of law and true peace and productivity in Zimbabwe. Meanwhile, Ministers Made (lands and agriculture), Chombo (local government and national housing affairs) and Chinamasa (justice, legal, and parliamentary affairs) continue insisting settlers from both the A1 (villagized) and A2 (commercial) take up land allocated to them by the lands and agriculture ministry. In so doing, they are forcing the shutting down and eviction of farm operators and their staff. The ministers are also silent on the provision of any legal rights on the land allocated.

Under current legislation, no government minister can give out legal rights in state property, including any land acquired by the state, except in terms of a power given to him by a statute. The statute in question, the Agricultural Land Settlement Act Ch 20:01 requires the Agricultural Land Settlement Board considers every application for a lease and makes its recommendations and report before the minister makes a decision to allocate land. This board has to take into account various matters specified in the Act and keep a record of its proceedings. No members of parliament can be involved, and any board member who has any interests himself or through family or business interests has to declare this interest. He can then take no further part in the process.

Despite this, when the chairman and secretary of the board were subpoenaed to attend a court in Harare last week, the ministry of lands advised it had not been working and had not considered any applications and the identities of the chairman and secretary were not even known there, finally confirming mounting suspicions the law on allocations was being totally disregarded. All the allocations are instead being made by land task force committees chaired by the provincial governors, who fall under the ministry of local government and housing, whose minister is Ignatius Chombo, himself an illegal invader of a farm in Mashonaland West.

Apparently, all new settlers are being asked to begin cropping on land they have no legal rights on. The legal opinion is the allocation letters, signed by Minister Made and made available to beneficiaries, have been prepared and are issued without any consideration or recommendation from the board. This adds another legal problem for settlers, particularly those trying to raise funds from financial institutions. Already, if the minister fails to prove a case against the owner in the Administrative Court (where cases concerning about 2,500 pieces of land are pending), the Land Acquisition Act obliges the court to order its return to the owner. The Act makes no provision for any payment to be made for standing crops by either the owner or government, and it is thought to be very unlikely the law could help them at all in terms of restitution of losses. The government has also been urging settlers to quit their jobs before they move onto the land. The Act requires new settlers use the land themselves, precluding them from handing over possession to another. As government ministers, we presume the above ministers are well aware of the Act. It is referenced in the official land reform program and in various forms being handed out. Their motives for ignoring it in practice and creating a situation in which settlers are using land only "by grace and favor" are unknown.

The decisions on what land to take and who will get it are incorrectly being made by the unauthorized people, instead of the court first deciding what should be taken and the board considering who will be able to use it. No effort is being made to calculate the cost or stay within the budget for acquisitions. The result is that, contrary to the official program aimed at underutilized land, the best developed land is usually being targeted, existing farm businesses are being shut down, and commercial farmers are seen being chased from their homes—while the country is believed to be racking up debts for compensation that will burden it for years to come. JAG is also in the process of putting together a group action to sue for losses in terms of stolen assets and loss in earnings for both owners and employees. Estimates available indicate the amount in question could far exceed Z$20 billion equivalent USD 400,000.[122]

Amendments to Land Acquisition Act Approved

President Mugabe signed into law the second amendment of the Land Acquisition Act. The amendments are meant to close the loopholes identified in the implementation of the country's land reform program. The government decided to amend the Act after some white commercial farmers challenged certain sections of the law pertaining to the serving of eviction notices. At the request of these commercial farmers, the High Court nullified eviction notices that were improperly served on seventy commercial farmers. The government was supposed to issue both the commercial farmers and bondholders with the Section 5 preliminary notices of acquiring land. In some cases, the government overlooked this procedure and only served preliminary notices to commercial farmers only. As a result of the amendment, Section 5 of the Land Acquisition Act now provides that failure or an oversight on the part of the acquiring authority to serve preliminary notices on bondholders shall not render final notices issued under

---

122. *Justice for Agriculture (JAG), Land Acquisition by Grace and Favor news release, 4 September 2002.*

Section 8 invalid. Bondholders who have not yet received Section 5 notices can now be served with them and would have to lodge their claims with the acquiring authority within thirty days.

However, what is particularly important is the period of notice to vacate land following a reissue of an order is now seven days from the date of issue. Before the amendment, it was ninety days. Under the amendment, it is not necessary for the government to prove rural land is suitable for agricultural resettlement if it is to be acquired for that purpose. Besides validating many preliminary acquisition orders issued under Section 5, where bondholders were advised late, the amendment also increased fines for those who resist eviction from $20,000 to $100,000.[123]

---

123. "Amendments to Land Acquisition Act approved," 11 August 2002.

23.0 Land Reform and Imperialist Hypocrisy

Zimbabwe today is a country on the brink of famine and total economic collapse. Since last year, inflation has skyrocketed at a rate of 228 percent, and unemployment stands at more than sixty percent. Tobacco production, which generates thirty-one percent of the country's foreign currency, is projected to plummet by a third. Moreover, without any seed for corn, Zimbabwe's primary food source, at least sixty percent of the population faces food shortages. This in a country that was once one of Africa's largest exporters of foodstuffs. When the government, pressed for funds, raised gas prices by at least 200 percent, the ZCTU launched a three-day general strike in late April. To which, the government responded in its usual repressive fashion, using troops to force closed shops to open. Dozens of ZCTU officials have been rounded up, including nearly the entire union leadership in the city of Bulawayo. The previous month, the British-supported MDC staged a two-day strike. A government crackdown followed, in which hundreds of MDC supporters were arrested.

The current crisis in Zimbabwe is largely a product of the imperialists cut off of economic aid for the country after President Mugabe initiated his program of seizing land owned by white commercial farmers, remnants of the former colonial occupation. The bourgeois press in the United Kingdom, Zimbabwe's former colonial master, has accused the African leader of unleashing "mob savagery" against the white population. In the United States, Republican Congressman Ed Royce, chairman of the House Committee on Africa, denounced President Mugabe as "a power-crazed, aged dictator literally burning his country down." Yet, for nearly two decades, President Mugabe was regarded and occasionally praised by London and Washington as a moderate African leader because he perpetuated the economic dominance in both agriculture and industry of the former white colonialists. Western bourgeois politicians and the media scarcely noticed, much less protested, when, in the mid-1980s, the Mugabe regime waged a war of extermination against the forces of a rival nationalist movement based on the minority Ndebele people. At the time, the Zimbabwean army massacred an estimated 10,000 to 20,000 villagers in Matebeleland, homeland of the Ndebele. As long as Mugabe's regime did not touch, indeed enhanced, the wealth of the white propertied classes, the men who run the City of London and Wall Street could not care less what he did to Zimbabwe's workers and peasants.

The backdrop to the current crisis was the economic austerity program carried out by the Mugabe regime in the early- to mid-1990s at the dictate of the IMF and World Bank. This provoked a series of mass strikes spearheaded by government employees like teachers and nurses. So, in the name of fast-track land reform, President Mugabe sought to divert popular hostility away from his own regime and toward the white commercial farmers, the core of the former colonial ruling class in what was then called Southern Rhodesia, who still owned seventy percent of the country's most fertile land. Almost all of the older white commercial farmers had been officers or non-coms in the Rhodesian army, which fought the black liberation forces led by Mugabe and others. These white colonialists killed some 40,000 black Africans, many of them unarmed, defenseless, rural villagers. A Dutch journalist of evident left-wing sympathies, Bram Posthumus, neatly cut through the cant and hypocrisy on both sides, "Most Rhodies are unreformed racists, and I would not want to be in the company of any of them." On the other hand, the ZANU-PF top brass was cashing in on white largesse when it suited them. They did not question the economic models they now claim the IMF and World Bank foisted upon them. Why should they? Capitalism has suited them fine ever since they came into power. "The point here is, very basically, that neither of these two groups, white commercial farmers and ZANU-PF chiefs, deserves a shred of sympathy, let alone support."[124]

The land seizures in Zimbabwe have resonated strongly in South Africa, where white commercial farmers still own eighty percent of the land, even though Nelson Mandela's bourgeois-nationalist African National Congress (ANC) replaced the white supremacist government in 1994. Indeed, in the countryside, the black toilers' conditions have changed little from the days of apartheid. In some ways, they are even worse. Seeking to forestall land seizures, white commercial farmers have evicted increasing numbers of blacks from land they have worked for generations. At the same time, South African President Mbeki has acted as the "soft cop" for British and American imperialism, vis-à-vis President Mugabe. While President Mbeki and Nigerian President Olusegun Obasanjo are unwilling to publicly denounce President Mugabe, as this would reveal them as pawns of the imperialists in Africa, they are currently embarked on a visit to the Zimbabwean capital of Harare to press President Mugabe to resign. An article by our comrades of Spartacist South Africa, titled "Hue and Cry over Land Seizures in Zimbabwe"[125]:

---

124. *Zimbabwe: Land Reform and Imperialist Hypocrisy, Workers Vanguard 803 (9 May 2003).*

125. *Spartacist South Africa, titled "Hue and Cry over Land Seizures in Zimbabwe" WV No. 741, 8 September 2000,*

In countries such as Zimbabwe and South Africa, the burning democratic tasks such as agrarian revolution, equality for women and tribal/ethnic minorities, and breaking the yoke of imperialist domination can only be realized through the Trotskyist program of permanent revolution: the seizure of state power by the proletariat standing at the head of the peasantry and all the oppressed...

Especially in a small country like Zimbabwe, a socialist revolution would inevitably and almost immediately pose the task of international extension—in the first instance to neighboring South Africa, which supplies most of Zimbabwe's petrol and electrical power, and beyond that to the imperialist centers.

South Africa holds the key to the future of all of sub-Saharan Africa. The rule of the capitalist ANC means continued brutal exploitation and oppression of South Africa's black, colored (historically derived from the offspring of Boer settlers and the indigenous Khoi people and later Malay slaves), and Indian working masses by the white, racist bourgeoisie and the enforcing of the imperialists' plundering of the region. Under a workers' government, South Africa's industrial and mineral wealth, as part of an international planned economy, would be used to develop the vast resources of the region for the benefit of the former colonial slaves in a socialist federation of southern Africa.[126]

The counterpart to the current hostility of Western, especially British, imperialism to the Mugabe regime is the imperialists' support for the MDC. The MDC is an unholy alliance between black trade-union bureaucrats, represented by former ZCTU head Morgan Tsvangirai, white capitalists, and commercial farmers. The regime is currently staging a sham trial of Tsvangirai, who, during last year's presidential elections, was riding a wave of popular support as an MDC candidate. Tsvangirai and two others are accused of plotting to kill President Mugabe. The regime's star witness in this frame-up is a former secret service agent who admits to being on President Mugabe's payroll. For its part, the MDC's main economic spokesman is Eddie Cross, former vice president of the Confederation of Zimbabwe Industries, who is an ardent champion of free-market neoliberalism and a strong advocate of IMF/World Bank guardianship over the Zimbabwean economy. The MDC receives financing from the likes of the London-based Westminster Foundation for Democracy, which, in turn, the British government partly funds.

A group occupying the left fringe of the MDC until recently is the Zimbabwean International Socialist Organization (ISO), part of the British-centered

---

126. *Zimbabwe: Land Reform and Imperialist Hypocrisy, Workers Vanguard 803 (9 May 2003).*

international tendency founded and led for many decades by the late Tony Cliff. While claiming, at times, to uphold the Leninist and Trotskyist tradition, the Cliffites are, in fact, left social democrats, that is, a pro-capitalist, pro-imperialist tendency falsely claiming to represent the interests of the working class. The social-democratic character of the Cliffite tendency was clearly exposed in Zimbabwe, where they were in a political bloc with the colonial-derived and imperialist-backed white, propertied classes against the Mugabe regime. In 2000, Munyaradzi Gwisai, then a senior leader of the Zimbabwean ISO, ran for and was elected to parliament as a representative of the MDC for the Highfield district of Harare. At the time, Gwisai and company portrayed the MDC as some kind of workers party, which could be pressured into carrying out radical socialist policies. An ISO action program for the first MDC congress proclaimed, "MDC is primarily a working people's party, that is, workers, the unemployed, peasants, and students. And it is they who must fund and lead the party."[127] Although the mass of white commercial farmers supported (and some joined the MDC), the Cliffites ludicrously demanded its parliamentary representatives "must vote in support of the taking of farms without paying compensation for the land."[128] By the time of last year's presidential elections, it was no longer credible to deny the MDC was a right-wing, pro-imperialist bourgeois party. Alex Callinicos, a central leader of the Cliffite tendency internationally, now lamented Tsvangirai had fallen under the influence of evil advisers, "Despite his origins as a union leader, MDC leader Morgan Tsvangirai has, with the encouragement of both Western governments and local bosses, adopted a neoliberal program that amounts to handing the economy over to the IMF[129] Nonetheless, the Zimbabwean ISO still supported the MDC leader in the election against President Mugabe. Gwisai stated, "We will vote for Tsvangirai because it will mean more space for us to operate…We want to strengthen the anticapitalist elements in the MDC."[130] Interestingly, Callinicos came from the white colonial stratum in Rhodesia/Zimbabwe before immigrating to England. There is, of course, nothing reprehensible in that. Many left-wing leaders, including Engels, Lenin, the anarchist Peter Kropotkin, and militants came from socially privileged backgrounds. But they then sought to lead the struggles of the exploited and oppressed against the propertied classes into which they were born. However, Callinicos and his Zimbabwean colleagues were in a bloc with white landowners against a black bourgeois-national-

127. *Socialist Worker [Zimbabwe], December 1999*
128. *Socialist Worker [Zimbabwe], August 2000*
129. *(Socialist Worker [Britain], 19 January 2002)*
130. *(Socialist Worker [Britain], 9 March 2002)*

ist regime, which, for its own ignoble reasons, is expropriating them. The April 2002 issue of *International Socialism*, the main Cliffite theoretical journal, has a major article, "Crisis in Zimbabwe," by Leo Zeilig. Predictably, he directs almost all his fire at President Mugabe with only the mildest criticism of the MDC, specifically it "holds none of the answers to the poverty and misery crippling Zimbabwe."[131] This is scarcely surprising for a party, which represents the main body of (white) agrarian and industrial capitalists in Zimbabwe and their British imperialist godfathers.

Zeilig points to and implicitly criticizes the propaganda campaign in British ruling circles against President Mugabe. But he then concludes in this regard, "There is not much to choose between the violence and repression of a dying regime, and the hypocrisy and colonial morality of [Britain's] New Labor."[132] This self-styled revolutionary socialist here equates British imperialism with a bourgeois-nationalist government in an African neocolonial country. That is, he equates an imperialist state with a semicolonial country. But, in fact, Zeilig, Callinicos, and Gwisai do choose between British imperialism and the Zimbabwean government. They choose the former. Indeed, in his article, Zeilig boasts of Gwisai's parliamentary victory in 2000 as a representative of the MDC, a party openly financed by the British ruling class, writing, "The International Socialist Organization (ISO) won an important seat in a working class area of Harare in the 2000 parliamentary elections as part of the MDC and, despite continued opposition from the party leadership, remains in the organization."[133] As is often the case, what the *International Socialism* article omits is just as telling politically as its content. Zeilig does not mention that all Western governments have cut off economic aid to Zimbabwe, mainly to strengthen the hand of the MDC against President Mugabe. Nor does he mention the Blair government in the United Kingdom is campaigning for international economic sanctions against Zimbabwe. These omissions amount to tacit support or at least nonopposition to imperialist economic warfare against the impoverished southern African country.[134]

Having preserved and protected the white commercial farmers for almost two decades, why did President Mugabe then turn on them, thereby provoking the

---

131. *Zimbabwe: Land Reform and Imperialist Hypocrisy, Workers Vanguard 803 (9 May 2003*

132. *Socialist Worker [Britain], 9 March 2002)*

133. *Zimbabwe: Land Reform and Imperialist Hypocrisy, Workers Vanguard 803 (9 May 2003).*

134. *Zimbabwe: Land Reform and Imperialist Hypocrisy, Workers Vanguard 803 (9 May 2003).*

wrath of British and American imperialism? To answer that question, it is necessary to review the history of Southern Rhodesia/Zimbabwe from the last period
of colonial rule through the present. In the mid 1960s, the United Kingdom,
with America's backing, moved toward a standard neocolonial solution in Southern Rhodesia, that is, the smooth transfer of governmental office to a pliant black
regime. However, under the leadership of Ian Smith—who professed his support
for the MDC in 1999 the white colonialist stratum, though only four percent of
the population, rebelled against this policy and declared "unilateral independence" from the United Kingdom. White supremacist South Africa, the most
powerful state in the region, economically supported "independent" Rhodesia.

Seeking to overthrow white colonialist rule, the Black Nationalist forces
launched a rural-based guerrilla insurgency, which convulsed the country during
the 1970s. However, the Ian Smith regime, with South Africa's backing, held the
black insurgency at bay while resisting pressure from London and Washington to
come to terms with the insurgency's leaders. A murderously hostile tribalism division between President Mugabe's ZANU, based on the majority Shona people,
and Joshua Nkomo's ZAPU, based on the Ndebele, weakened the black liberation struggle. Finally, in 1979, Thatcher's United Kingdom brokered a compromise, the Lancaster House Agreement. President Mugabe's ZANU took over the
government while the whites retained control of the economy. The Lancaster
House Agreement stipulated that, for ten years, the government could not take
over white farmland without the consent of the owners. Then, compensation had
to be in "hard" (that is, Western) currency. The property rights of the white colonialists were also written into Zimbabwe's new constitution.

A recent book on the Zimbabwean economy by two British academics
described the structure of ownership at the time of independence:

> Although they made up only 3.8 percent of the population, at independence,
> the modern sector of the economy was almost entirely owned and managed by
> whites. For example, over ninety percent of marketed output came from
> white- or foreign-owned farms, which provided thirty-five percent of formal-
> sector employment and over one-third of exports. The manufacturing and
> financial sectors were also almost exclusively a white preserve.[135]

---

135. *"Zimbabwe: Land Reform and Imperialist Hypocrisy, Workers Vanguard 803 (9 May
    2003).*

Land Seizures and Economic Collapse

In the decade after independence, little had changed in this respect. Academic studies in the United Kingdom indicated the white propertied classes were economically better off after ten years of President Mugabe's rule than they had been in the last years of the Ian Smith regime. While maintaining the wealth of the white propertied classes, the Mugabe regime also built up privileged black elite via the state treasury. A large government bureaucracy was formed under ZANU-PF's patronage. Outright corruption was systemic and massive while the government set up and financed numerous black-owned businesses. The Mugabe regime therefore consistently ran large government budget deficits, even in fairly prosperous years. Borrowing heavily from City of London and Wall Street banks at commercial rates of interest initially financed these deficits. Consequently, the burden of foreign debt doubled from one-third of Zimbabwe's GDP in 1986 to two-thirds of its GDP by 1994.

The counterrevolutionary destruction of the Soviet Union in 1991 and 1992 led to the intensification of imperialist bloodsucking in Africa, thereby increasing starvation and bloodshed. Specifically, the IMF and World Bank demanded payment on the money they had previously given to these African countries as a counterweight to Soviet influence during the Cold War. In order to roll over Zimbabwe's foreign loans, the IMF and World Bank demanded the standard combination of fiscal austerity and free-market liberalization: slashing expenditure for social programs; eliminating or cutting back the wide array of government subsidies; and dismantling tariff protection for the country's manufacturing industries like textiles, clothing, and footwear.

The effects were predictably devastating for almost all sectors of the urban-based labor force. Employment in the textile industry fell by half, from 25,300 in 1990 to 12,400 in 1995. Also hit hard were the more privileged (middle class) sections of the black populace, which had, until then, been the core support for the Mugabe regime—government functionaries, university students expecting upon graduation to get government or government-subsidized jobs. Some 25,000 civil service jobs were eliminated by 1995. The stage was thus set for mass labor struggles for the first time since the black bourgeois-nationalist regime replaced white colonial rule fifteen years before. A successful strike of public sector employees in 1996 was followed by a general strike, with broad popular support, against increased taxation at the end of 1997. Immediately thereafter, food riots led by working-class women erupted in Harare. The ZCTU emerged as a potent oppositional force enjoying substantial and increasing popular authority, especially in the cities.

President Mugabe responded by seeking to refurbish the regime's nationalist credentials by declaring economic warfare on the white commercial farmers. The ZANU-PF tops demagogically revived the rhetoric of the 1970s independence struggle, denouncing white racism, Western imperialism, and the heritage of colonialism. The ZCTU bureaucracy under Morgan Tsvangirai played into the regime's hands, especially among the peasant masses, by forming a political bloc with the white commercial farmers and other capitalists through the MDC.[136]

The land seizures began in early 2000 with the invasion of white commercial farms by veterans of the independence struggle and unemployed urban youth. In several instances, this caused violent clashes with farm workers who were fearful of losing their jobs. Today, almost all the white farmland has been taken over. Many of the former owners have left the country. An apologist for the Mugabe regime, Gregory Elich, recently declared:

> Temporary economic dislocation is an unavoidable by-product of land reform, but genuine and lasting progress in Zimbabwe can only be achieved through land redistribution. In the West, the gross imbalance imposed by colonial theft is accepted as the natural order in Zimbabwe, with the indigenous population lacking any claim to the land. The government's fast-track land reform is intended to rectify historical injustices and to ensure a more equitable division of the land.[137]

To begin, the red vision of the land has been far from equitable. Of the first 600 white farms taken over three years ago, 200 of the largest were given free of charge to officials of the ZANU-PF as well as President Mugabe's cronies and relatives, including his wife. Inspecting her new 2,500-acre estate, Grace Mugabe announced to the assembled agricultural laborers, "I am taking over this farm."[138] Only such members of the postcolonial black ruling elite have the money to operate the commercial farms at a profit. The mass of black peasants who now occupy much of this land in most cases do not even have seeds to plant next year's crop to feed their families.

---

136. *Zimbabwe: Land Reform and Imperialist Hypocrisy, Workers Vanguard 803 (9 May 2003)*.

137. Zimbabwe Under Siege by Gregory Elich, considered Mugabe apologist August 26, 2002.

138. Guardian Weekly [London], 21–27 November 2002

Let us consider the arguments of President Mugabe apologists, like Gregory Elich, at face value and assume the Zimbabwean government is genuinely committed to bettering the conditions of the black peasantry through an equitable division of land. Where would it get the financial resources to supply seeds, fertilizer, and farm machinery to hundreds of impoverished black smallholders? The country is already massively in debt to British and American banks. And one can hardly expect the British ruling class to subsidize the expropriation of Zimbabwe's white commercial farmers with whom, in some cases, they have family as well as financial ties.

In an interview in December with the state-controlled newspaper *The Herald*, President Mugabe admitted, "We took it for granted that the supplies would be adequate." He continued, "It then proved that we were mistaken. Seed is short, fertilizer is short, and tillage is inadequate." According to United Nations sources, more than half the government's tractor fleet, which was supposed to plow fields for poor commercial farmers, is out of service because of shortages of spare parts and fuel.

During the 1990s, Zimbabwe produced an average annual grain (corn and wheat) crop of almost two million metric tons. Last year, the grain crop was less than half a million tons. (A contributing factor was lack of rainfall, resulting in crop failures throughout southern Africa.) One does not need to be an apologist for the white commercial farmers or Western imperialists to recognize that millions of people in Zimbabwe now face conditions of famine. Indeed, it is a measure of the bankruptcy of President Mugabe's neocolonial regime that the transparently direct benefactors of British imperialism, the MDC, could have any level of popular support.[139]

Land is no longer the most valuable resource in agricultural production. In his Zimbabwe *Herald* interview, President Mugabe triumphantly proclaimed, "For us, the most valuable resource and source of our wealth is our land." But land as such is no longer the most valuable non-labor resource in agricultural production. Chemical fertilizer can enhance the natural fertility of the soil. Irrigation can supplement inadequate rainfall. In general, a modern commercial farm, producing for the world market, employs a level of technology comparable to that of an industrial enterprise producing for the world market. To effectively manage such a "factory in the field" requires years of specialized education and training. The development of modern agriculture was projected a century ago by Karl

---

139. Zimbabwe: Land Reform and Imperialist Hypocrisy, Workers Vanguard 803 (9 May 2003).

Kautsky, then considered the leading Marxist theorist, in a major work, *The Agrarian Question* (1900). Lenin regarded *The Agrarian Question* as a very important contribution to a Marxist understanding of the changing world capitalist economy. (Kautsky's later rightist revisionism and hostility to the Bolshevik Revolution does not negate the value of his earlier works.) Kautsky recognized that, just as developments in science and technology had transformed small-scale handicraft manufacturing into large-scale mechanized industry, similar developments—albeit later and more slowly—were occurring in agriculture:

> Within a few years agriculture, traditionally the most conservative of occupations, nearly devoid of progress for almost an entire millennium and utterly devoid for several centuries, suddenly became one of the most revolutionary branches of modern industry, if not the most revolutionary. This transformation meant that agriculture progressed from being a *handicraft*, whose routines were passed down through the generations, to being a *science*, or rather a complex of sciences, undergoing a rapid expansion in both its empirical and theoretical knowledge. Any farmer not fully at home with such sciences, the mere "practician," will be helpless and baffled in the face of current innovations, yet cannot continue in the old ways. [140]

Kautsky noted the economic size of a modern capitalist farm is to be measured not in acreage per se. Instead, it should be measured in capital per acre, which is directly related to crop yield per acre:

> The law according to which the more intensive the cultivation of the farm, the smaller its area must be for a given volume of capital also works in the same direction. An intensively farmed small estate represents a larger enterprise than a large, extensively cultivated one[141].

While Kautsky foresaw the direction of agricultural development, he misjudged its pace. Small-scale, traditional peasant farming remained economically viable even in Western and Central Europe, not to speak of more backward regions of the world, for several decades. His description of a scientifically managed, mechanized farm was not so much an empirical picture of European agriculture at the time as an anticipation of the future. Following World War II, the

140. Zimbabwe: Land Reform and Imperialist Hypocrisy, Workers Vanguard 803 (9 May 2003).
141. Zimbabwe: Land Reform and Imperialist Hypocrisy, Workers Vanguard 803 (9 May 2003).

revolution in agricultural technology, the beginnings of which Kautsky had ana-lyzed, radically altered both the structure of agricultural production and pattern of trade throughout the capitalist world. The United States began dominating the world market for basic foodstuffs, including rice and soybeans, the traditional staples of East Asian civilization. At the same time, many major third world countries—Mexico, South Korea, and Indonesia—now export industrial prod-ucts and cash crops and import foodstuffs, mainly from North America.[142]

The desperate plight of Zimbabwean peasants who now occupy the former white-owned commercial farms was described in Kautsky's classic work on the agrarian question:

> The independent peasant farm has become untenable: it can only continue by being associated with a large establishment. If a nearby large industrial enter-prise employs peasants as wage-laborers, or specialized workers, they will become its slaves. Where no such establishment exists, the peasant needs a large agricultural enterprise to avoid sinking into extreme poverty[143].

In all likelihood, most peasants on the former white farms will revert to the kind of subsistence agriculture, which they practiced on the so-called communal lands. Because agricultural produce, especially tobacco, has accounted for half of Zimbabwe's export earnings, a large-scale reversion to subsistence farming will lead to further massive contraction of the modern urban-based sectors, from fac-tories to universities. What then is to be done? The answer does not lie purely within the boundaries of this poor southern African country. However, across Zimbabwe's southern border is South Africa, the one relatively industrialized country in sub-Saharan Africa. For example, South Africa generates more than half the electric power in the entire continent. The key force for social progress throughout the region is South Africa's large, powerful, and combative proletar-iat, predominantly black but with important colored and Indian components. What is key is to mobilize that power in a struggle for socialist revolution.

To realize that program, black workers must be broken from their current political allegiance to the ANC regime, the black front men for the white capital-ists who still own the country's factories, mines, and farms. Spartacist South Africa, section of the International Communist League, seeks to build a Bolshe-

---

142. Zimbabwe: Land Reform and Imperialist Hypocrisy, Workers Vanguard 803 (9 May 2003).
143. Zimbabwe: Land Reform and Imperialist Hypocrisy, Workers Vanguard 803 (9 May 2003).

vik workers party that will lead the struggle against all forms of national and social oppression, including the mass homelessness in the black townships, the hideous conditions of millions still trapped in the former tribal reserves (Bantustans), the degradation of women through reactionary tribal traditions such as *lobola* (the bride price), as well as government persecution of and vigilante attacks on immigrants from other African countries. The land question is an important motor force for socialist revolution in South Africa. Some 55,000 white commercial farmers own 250 million acres of the most fertile land. Approximately a million black agricultural laborers and their families work upon these land. At the same time, 1.2 million black households, numbering some seven million people, are crowded into forty million acres in the former tribal reserves. Here are concentrated the poorest of South Africa's poor. Mainly women, children, and the aged, remittances from husbands, brothers, sons, and other relatives working in the country's factories and mines mainly support them. Insofar as the inhabitants of the former reserves earn their own money, it is mainly from seasonal, migrant labor on nearby white-owned farms. The large majority of South Africa's rural toilers are thus agricultural proletarians, rather than smallholding peasants. A workers' revolution in South Africa would expropriate the highly mechanized, capital-intensive, white-owned farms and transform them into modern, large-scale collective and state farms, thereby providing a decent living for South Africa's rural toilers.

The agrarian question in Zimbabwe and elsewhere in southern Africa is significantly different. While 350,000 agricultural laborers and their families worked on the white-owned commercial farms, their number was dwarfed by the six to seven million peasants engaged mainly in subsistence farming in the communal lands. As we have seen, the Mugabe regime exploited and manipulated the land hunger of these dispossessed peasants against the MDC opposition (and also against the agricultural laborers). A workers' and peasants' government in Zimbabwe, in the context of a socialist federation of southern Africa, would establish soviets (councils) of rural toilers, both poor peasants and agricultural laborers, which would democratically determine which land was organized as collective or state farms and which was kept by (or distributed to) individual peasant families. However, a workers state in such a backward country will be immediately faced with the problem of how to acquire items like tractors and other farm machinery, essential to the collectivization of agriculture. The solution to this fundamentally lies outside the borders of Zimbabwe or, indeed, southern Africa as a whole. Only an expanding collectivized economy, based on the necessary extension of proletarian revolution to the advanced industrial countries and an internationally planned economy, could provide the necessary resources and technology to free rural workers from backbreaking labor while absorbing in industry or construction those former peasants and agricultural workers no longer needed to work the land.

Not only the land question unites the Zimbabwean and South African masses. The Ndebele people, for example, reside on both sides of the border, arbitrarily drawn according to the interests of British colonialism. Furthermore, Zimbabweans make up a sizable proportion of migrant workers who slave in the mines and on the commercial farms of South Africa. These face constant persecution and deportations by the state and murderous attacks by anti-immigrant vigilantes. The ANC uses them as scapegoats for the massive unemployment. At the same time, the migrant workers are a living link between the South African proletariat and the toiling masses throughout the region. Spartacist South Africa fights for the labor movement to take up the defense of migrant workers and all immigrants, demanding full citizenship rights for all immigrants.[144]

This is part of our larger struggle for a socialist federation of southern Africa, in which there will be a place for all the myriad peoples of the region, including those whites accepting the rule of a government centrally based on the black proletariat and rural toilers. Only workers rule can break the yoke of imperialist domination. This program is necessarily linked to the perspective of proletarian revolution in the advanced capitalist countries of North America, Western Europe, and Japan. A workers' revolution in Zimbabwe would spark revolutionary upheavals throughout the area, particularly in South Africa.[145]

The Rise and Fall of Socialism

A discussion of the history of socialism for the past 200 years should be as dreary as reading *Communist Manifesto or Das Capital*. Incredibly, this book is not. Before reading any book, it is advisable to have an idea from where the author is coming. This author was born and raised in an American socialist family. He was the national chairman of the Young People's Socialist League from 1968 until 1973. He is presently a resident scholar at the American Enterprise Institute. Quite a shift!

---

144. Zimbabwe: Land Reform and Imperialist Hypocrisy, Workers Vanguard 803 (9 May 2003).
145. Carolyn Jenkins and John Knight, The Economic Decline of Zimbabwe: Neither Growth Nor Equity (2002).

Yet, he gives a true believer's lively account of socialism by telling us about the lives and ideas of the thinkers and leaders who had the greatest impact in developing the theories of socialism. He also details the virtually always disastrous results of the application of those theories. Knowledge of the results is necessary to discuss these theories.

The book's title comes from Moses Hess, the man who fired up Marx and Engels about socialism. Hess wrote:

> The Christian...imagines the better future of the human species...in the image of heavenly joy...We (socialists) on the other hand, will have this heaven on earth[146].

Therein lies socialism's great appeal. The people the author chooses to highlight in this evolutionary history of socialism are Gracchus Babeuf, Robert Owen, Friedrich Engels, Karl Marx, Benito Mussolini, Clement Attlee, Julius Nyerere, Samuel Gompers, George Meany, Mikhail Gorbachev, Deng Xiaoping, and Tony Blair, the current prime minister of the United Kingdom. Through chapters about each, he explains and documents 200 years of socialism.

The French revolutionary Babeuf developed the idea of outlawing private property so that all could be equal. "Liberty, equality, fraternity," said the French revolutionaries. It was very different from the American "Life, liberty, and the pursuit of happiness." Whereas the American founders wanted equality of opportunity, the French socialists promised equality of outcomes, that is, heaven on earth. Huge difference!

Robert Owen, who coined the term *socialist*, is one of the very few socialists who ever actually created wealth for himself and others. He made his fortune in textiles during the industrial revolution in the early 1800s in England. Whereas Babeuf thought one must take by force through the power of the state to implement socialism, Owen recognized, if someone just gave land and capital, a socialist community could be set up. Because he had the money, he set one up in the American Midwest. Owen believed no human "is responsible for his will or his own actions."[147] He thought he could shape people into working collectively for the higher good by educating (indoctrinating) them from the age of one. He never seemed to have noticed his socialist experiment failed miserably and it seemed to attract the less industrious—even after it cost him his fortune! Engels developed the idea that all private property is theft and competition and capital

---

146. The Life and Ideas of Robert Owen, pp. 73-76, 81, 123-124, 134-135, 164-165.]
147. *The Life and Ideas of Robert Owen, pp. 73-76, 81, 123-124, 134-135, 164-165.]*

led to a concentration of wealth, despite all the evidence to the contrary. It is fitting that Karl Marx is the most famous socialist of all. Muravchik details how much of a deadbeat he was and how he spent his entire life mooching off others, like many socialists. Further, he had virtually no contact with—nor did he want anything to do with—the poor, working man he claimed to want to help. Lenin was another pampered brat who lived off others. Like many so-called intellectuals, he thought socialism should be "created for the workers, not by them!" He realized he would have to terrorize the working man into collectivism. He did so at the cost of tens of millions of lives. Stalin, his heir, started out as Lenin's fundraiser. He robbed banks. Unsurprisingly, he followed in Lenin's brutal footsteps.

Mussolini, a draft dodger, modified socialism. He realized Lenin's violent methods worked best, but he noticed Italy was not yet industrialized. So, to get elected, he decided to modify socialism into something called fascism. Under fascism, he would wait until entrepreneurs had created something of value worth taking, then nationalize it or create so many rules and regulations that he could force the private entrepreneur to do whatever he (the government) decided. Mussolini said he hated communism, yet mimicked it as often as he could. Hitler and his National Socialists differed from other socialists in that they were nationalistic in their looting of wealth. When Hitler took power, he immediately set up four-year plans, so that no one would think he was copying the Soviet Union's five-year plans.

After World War II, Clement Attlee, another pampered socialist, was elected prime minister of the United Kingdom. He decided to socialize and nationalize the United Kingdom, bit by bit, evoking the class struggle and envy of the rich approach that works so well today in the United States for the Democratic party. Muravchik thinks socialism is dead because it has failed just about everywhere. And Margaret Thatcher's Tory government reversed many of Atlee's socialist nationalizations. Lastly, the socialist Labor Party of the United Kingdom got Tony Blair elected by campaigning on a platform that was antisocialist. However, socialism has yet to disappear in the United Kingdom. The author details Nyerere's socialization of Tanzania, one of the first African colonies to gain independence. Nyerere subsidized commercial farmers, took over the education system to teach people to work for the common good, and so forth. Despite massive aid from the developed world and China, the economy shrunk for the twenty-three years he was in power. Muravchik says socialism never got a foothold in America and then explains how Samuel Gompers, the most significant organizer of labor unions, and George Meany, president of the AFL-CIO, the country's largest union, kept the socialists/communists from taking total control of the unions in this country. Gompers and Meany were from working-class backgrounds and were acutely aware that socialists would subordinate the workers' goals to someone else's goals. They knew the workers would starve without the capitalist owners and government intervention was socialist. They had no use for middle-class theorists who appointed themselves to lead labor. They were anticommunist and rightly referred to Stalin as a brutal, fascist dictator.

China's Communist dictators Mao and Deng both came from privileged backgrounds. After almost forty years of Mao's socialist experiments and millions of deaths, Deng noticed that giving people personal responsibility and rewards for their efforts worked better than collectivization. He turned Communist China into a Fascist dictatorship and began allowing private ownership and a market economy. For Deng, the dictatorship of the party was the essence of socialism. All else was negotiable.

Gorbachev's siblings and grandparents died, along with millions of others in the 1932–1933 collectivizing of the Ukraine. Once he traveled to the West, he knew he had to do something different. His conclusion: If he could just clean up the corruption and inefficient bureaucracy, socialism would work. He thought he could do this by allowing a little democracy. It had never occurred to him that it was maybe the system causing the corruption, inefficiency, and horrible living conditions in most socialist societies. Yet, even today, he remains a committed socialist.

Why then has socialism continued to have such popularity? My wife, who grew up in a socialist family, says its eternal appeal is that it makes people feel good about themselves. It is particularly popular with people who would never directly help their fellow man, but they claim the higher moral ground by declaring to want to help their fellow man by taking someone else's hard-earned money and redistributing it to someone else who has not earned it. Muravchik says socialism was popular because "Not only did it vow to deliver the goods in this world rather than the next, but it asked little in return."[148] He thinks socialism is dead. A look at our own government suggests he is wrong. Our government promises medical care and social security, expropriates private property without due process, subsidizes or pays special interests not to produce, fixes prices, and controls production of certain commodities. It increasingly intrudes in our private lives, uses welfare to strip people of their dignity as unique persons by asking

---

148. Mr. Davis is president of AIA. He is married to the niece of the head of Chile's Communist Party and spent time in jail in Communist/Socialist countries, never having been charged with a crime.

nothing in return, and so forth. These are all socialist/fascist programs and should be called as such.

These examples demonstrate how socialism goes against human nature and how it has virtually always hurt the poor the most. It has caused 100 million deaths in the twentieth century and billions of people to live in horrible conditions. But it still sounds nice to idealistic people who have not experienced it first-hand or studied its horrible results. That is why socialist ideas are still so popular in universities throughout the world. These ideas are also popular with politicians because taking other people's money and taking credit for giving it to someone else is how they get elected. Government employees also usually like politicians who give them more money. Having experienced firsthand the lack of liberty and brutality of living under a socialist government, I was disappointed the author glossed over how horrible it is to live under socialism.[149]

The Lancaster House Independence Constitution Democratic Road Map

Like in any guerrilla war, the strategy is to boldly defy the ruling class laws, rob the rich, and distribute the wealth to those who did not work for it in exchange for popular support and power. The ZANU-PF socialist independence election manifesto promised the electorate heaven on earth, guaranteeing free health and education. The Zimbabwean government dropped the socialist ideology in pursuance of the Lancaster House Constitution and the collapse of the Soviet Union. Members of ZANU-PF continue addressing one another as comrades, even though they severed all ideological links with communism and socialism.

The Zimbabwe International Socialist Organization, under the MDC umbrella, supported the Zimbabwean government's land acquisition by force without compensation and its redistribution to the landless. Munyaradzi Gwisai, the revolutionary socialist MP who was elected to Zimbabwe's parliament in 2000 with the backing of the opposition MDC, was stripped of his seat. Emmerson Mnangagwa, the speaker of parliament, declared the constituency vacant on December 3 after the MDC informed him that Gwisai had been expelled from the party. Gwisai was elected to represent the Harare electorate of Highfield as a high-profile member of the International Socialist Organization of Zimbabwe (ISOZ). The ISOZ, along with Zimbabwe's trade unions and other militants,

---

149. Mr. Davis is president of AIA. He is married to the niece of the head of Chile's Communist Party and spent time in jail in Communist/Socialist countries, never having been charged with a crime.

played an important role in the creation of the MDC. However, as the MDC leadership became dominated by members of Zimbabwe's capitalist class and increasingly embraced neoliberalism, Gwisai and the ISOZ often clashed with the MDC tops. Gwisai has survived several attempts by the MDC leadership to have him expelled in the past. The MDC leadership finally expelled Gwisai on November 22, 2002. The MDC national executive found him guilty of contravening the party's constitution. However, Gwisai's real crime was to support radical land distribution and oppose the MDC's moves to form a "government of national unity" with the hated authoritarian regime of President Mugabe. Gwisai and the ISOZ also sharply criticized the MDC's unwillingness to support mass action by workers, peasants, and urban dweller to challenge President Mugabe's rule.

On December 5, 2002 Gwisai accused the MDC's leaders of dividing the opposition movement "at a time when unity of purpose and focus in the struggle was required from all democratic forces." "Millions of our people face starvation, are unemployed, and the prices of basic goods are skyrocketing," Gwisai noted.[150] He added the MDC leadership had taken the party from its working-class founders and handed it to the employers. Gwisai said he would not appeal his ejection from parliament.

> Parliament is only one—and increasingly irrelevant—arena of the great struggle to smash the Mugabe dictatorship. Capitalist poverty will not be fought in that august house, but in the factories, offices, classrooms, streets and mines, as they were fought in Madagascar, Serbia, and Indonesia.[151]

However, Gwisai refused to disclose if he was going to contest the by-election for Highfield as a candidate for the ISOZ, saying only that "we will cross the bridge when we get there."

The opposition MDC expelled its member of Parliament from Highfield, Munyaradzi Gwisai, for his continued criticism of the party's policy on both the

---

150. *From Green Left Weekly, December 11, 2002. ZIMBABWE: Socialist MP expelled from parliament BY NORM DIXON Munyaradzi Gwisai, the revolutionary socialist MP of the opposition Movement for Democratic Change, was stripped of his seat. Emmerson Mnangagwa, the speaker of parliament, declared the constituency vacant on December 3, 2002*

151. *From Green Left Weekly, December 11, 2002. ZIMBABWE: Socialist MP Munyaradzi Gwisai expelled from parliament BY NORM DIXON December 3 the MDC informed parliament that Gwisai had been expelled from the party.—Gwisai exit speech*

social and economic fronts. Paul Themba-Nyati, the MDC spokesman, told a press conference in Harare recently that his party had raised six key allegations against Gwisai. The allegations included his critical remarks on the opposition party's land policy and threats to resign over the MDC's continued participation in elections. The Highfield legislator is also a staunch supporter of the ongoing land reform program and, in the past, made it very clear there was no need to compensate the affected white commercial farmers because they forcibly grabbed the land from blacks. On the other hand, the MDC, siding with its British masters, has been criticizing the land reform program. This is unsurprising because the white commercial farmers and the British sponsor the opposition party. "What the national executive did was to relieve Mr. Gwisai of the burden of putting up with a party whose ideology he is strongly opposed to," Mr. Nyati said. Constitutionally, once a constituency MP elected on a party ticket ceases to belong to that party, the seat is declared vacant, and by-election would be held. Some political analysts have questioned whether expelling from a party for holding different views is the most democratic thing to do. They said, if the MDC failed to talk and unite with Gwisai, there is no way it can talk to or engage ZANU-PF.[152] The withdrawal of the socialists marked the end of the marriage between the socialists, workers, and capitalists.

The Rise and Fall of Socialism by James F. Davies clearly demonstrates the socialist objective is similar to religion in which the faithful ones go to the extent of sacrificing themselves with the hope of being rewarded in the next world, except socialism promises to reward the converted through the creation of capital forcibly acquired from the minority rich and powerful classes and redistribute it to the poor. The fact the great USSR dismally collapsed under economic pressure makes us doubt the thought of envisaging a southern Africa socialist federation. The socialist ideology strives on the foundations of an economically viable capitalist and corrupt base, creating conducive conditions for a mass uprising. Through socialist encouragement, those without wealth are more than prepared to join the socialists with the objective of sharing the wealth they did not work for. The socialist ideology will result in a violent revolution in which all economic activities will be nationalized, looted, destroyed, and services disrupted with no development bringing suffering to the people. At the end of the day, the same people will turn against the socialists as in the case of the fall of Nazi Germany, Mussolini Italy, disintegration of the former Soviet Union, and the Romania

---

152. Norm Dixon, "Gwisai expelled from MDC," *Green Left Weekly*, 11 December 2002.

uprising. The best example we have in southern Africa was the postindependence socialist revolution in Mozambique in which the government nationalized all land and property, resulting in social and economic hardships. It only recovered after the government became more liberal after the fall of the Soviet Union. The FRELIMO government adopted political conditions conducive for investment, resulting in the Mozambique economy being one of the most buoyant in southern Africa after South Africa. Talking about socialism at this day and time in the new world order is like wishing a dream to come true.[153]

---

153. *Ibid.*

24.0 President Thabo Mbeki Justifies Seizure of White Farmland as Perhaps Inevitable

President Mbeki shocked foreign diplomats and some local observers by justifying Zimbabwean President Mugabe's forcible seizure of white farmland as perhaps inevitable. They have also reacted with dismay to what they called President Mbeki's deeply offensive remarks written in his weekly electronic letter in his party's Web site journal, *ANC Today*. These include the charge that the United Kingdom opposed Zimbabwe's readmission to the Commonwealth this week merely to protect its "white, settler, colonial kith and kin." And those Western powers are using the demand for President Mugabe to respect human rights merely as a tool for regime change in Zimbabwe. President Mbeki used his weekly letter to mount a major broadside assault on those, especially the United Kingdom, who opposed Zimbabwe's readmission. Zimbabwe has since quit the Commonwealth over its extended suspension. The Democratic Alliance called President Mbeki's letter "a disgusting defense of a disgraceful tyrant." On Saturday, Nigeria dismissed South African criticism the Commonwealth summit in Nigeria this week had steamrollered a decision to keep Zimbabwe suspended from the organization. President Mbeki complained in his newsletter that the land issue, which was central to the Zimbabwe crisis, had not been discussed at the Abuja summit. He concluded President Mugabe's forcible seizure of white farmland in 2000 had become perhaps inevitable because the United Kingdom and other Western countries had broken promises, dating from 1979, to fund peaceful land redistribution. In the past, the United Kingdom firmly rejected such charges, insisting it did donate money for land redistribution until it became apparent the land was going to President Mugabe's cronies and not needy peasants. President Mugabe charged the United Kingdom and other Western powers had reneged on their promises to fund land redistribution. The United Kingdom and the United States promised this at the Lancaster House negotiations on Zimbabwe's independence in 1979. "The large sums of money promised by both the British and American governments to enable the new government to buy land for African settlement never materialized," President Mbeki said.[154] South Africa and others had called an international land conference in Zimbabwe in 1998, at which the United Kingdom, the United Nations, the European Union, and others agreed to help finance the program of land redistribution. "Nothing came of these commitments," President Mbeki said.[155] Later, South Africa again:

---

154. Mbeki's Zim comments, Sunday Independent (SA), 14 December 2003.

intervened to help solve the Zimbabwe land question. We managed to get pledges from various countries, other than the UK, to provide this £9 million (R100 million). Having handed this matter over to the UN, it collapsed in the intricacies of the UN bureaucracy. Though there were willing sellers and willing buyers and the necessary funds, the 118 farms were not bought. With everything having failed to restore the land to its original owners in a peaceful manner, a forcible process of land redistribution perhaps became inevitable[156].

British government sources said President Mbeki's newsletter was being digested in London, which would decide whether and how to respond. However, in the past, the United Kingdom has denied criticism it broke its promises to fund land redistribution. On the United Kingdom's foreign office Web site it says, "Between 1980 and 1985, the UK provided £47 million equivalent USD 94 million for land reform."[157] The British foreign office Web site said the United Kingdom took part in a 1998 land conference and agreed to give more funds, provided the Zimbabwean government observed the principles it agreed to there. "Those principles included the need for transparency, respect for the rule of law, poverty reduction, affordability, and consistency with Zimbabwe's wider economic interests." the United Kingdom said its preparations to fund the program were "interrupted by the illegal farm occupations and the subsequent violence in the run-up to the 2000 parliamentary elections."

In his letter, President Mbeki insists the United Kingdom's real motive in Zimbabwe is still to protect its own people and suggests that ZANU-PF are the real democrats. "Those who fought for a democratic Zimbabwe, with thousands paying the supreme price during the struggle, and forgave their oppressors and torturers in a spirit of national reconciliation, have been turned into repugnant enemies of democracy."[158] President Mbeki adds that those campaigning for human rights in Zimbabwe are really just using human rights "as a tool for overthrowing the government of Zimbabwe and rebuilding Zimbabwe as they wish." [159]Graham McIntosh, the Democratic Alliance's spokesperson on Africa, said President Mbeki's letter "offers a fascinating but frightening insight into the pres-

155. Mbeki's Zim comments, Sunday Independent (SA), 14 December 2003.
156. Mbeki's Zim comments, Sunday Independent (SA), 14 December 2003.
157. UK and Commonwealth Office Foreign Policy on Zimbabwe
158. Shock at Mbeki's Zim comments, Sunday Independent (SA), 14 December 2003.
159. Shock at Mbeki's Zim comments, Sunday Independent (SA), 14 December 2003.

ident's disturbed logic and devotion to lost causes." [160]He said, as with the AIDS issue, President Mbeki revealed a dissident view on Zimbabwe.

McIntosh said:

> Any informed individual who has visited Zimbabwe and seen the reality of the Mugabe regime's disastrous policies and programs will agree that the sentiment expressed by President Mbeki is utter nonsense. The president's letter is a disgusting defense of a disgraceful tyrant. He should be ashamed of the way he has used race and smear tactics against the other members of the Commonwealth and its secretary-general and the astonishing trashing of the world's commitment to human rights as 'a tool of US foreign policy.'[161]

The Land Ownership Issue Is a Regional Problem

President Mbeki of South Africa believes the British and the international community, under the pretext of human rights violation and oppression of democratic change, are demonizing Zimbabwe. The truth of the matter is that the land reform is being impeded due to the British moral wish to protect their kith and kin in Zimbabwe through creating conditions for the overthrow of the ZANU-PF government and effect a regime change. This is what the independent commentators see in the formation of the opposition MDC, which openly took sides with the commercial farmers during the nationwide strike. The South African president is only trying to make the conflicting parties understand logic and develop a solution that will prevent military confrontation in southern Africa. President Mbeki is also aware that supporting the isolation of Zimbabwe will be tantamount to abandoning a brother and comrade at arms at the eleventh hour. With the passage of time, South Africa is very likely to find itself in the midst of land-related racial confrontation if the Zimbabwe land issue ends without a negotiated settlement. The lessons learned from the Zimbabwe land redistribution process would form the basis of dealing with a potential similar situation should need arise in future South Africa. In 1913, the South Africa British Dominion passed the Land Act, which took away the best farming lands from the indigenous population. In response to this injustice, the South Africa Native Congress, forerunner to the ANC, was formed. The ANC originally petitioned the British and engaged in peaceful protests against seizure of African land, but its methods

---

160. British sources said Mbeki's newsletter was being 'digested' in London" "Shock at Mbeki's 'offensive' Zim comments, Sunday Independent (SA), 14 December 2003.
161. "British sources said Mbeki's newsletter was being 'digested' in London" "Shock at Mbeki's 'offensive' Zim comments, Sunday Independent (SA), 14 December 2003.

were ineffective. In 1948, the Afrikaaner-dominated Nationalist Party swept the elections and formalized apartheid. In 1952, the Bantu Authorities Act created African Homelands. The apartheid regime appropriated eighty-seven percent of the country's richest farmlands while Africans became citizens of impoverished Bantustans. History has a tendency of repeating itself. It will be recalled, when the United Nations imposed sanctions against the illegal Rhodesian government, the like-minded apartheid regime of South Africa assisted the Rhodesia government in sanctions bursting. President Mbeki is now being accused of protecting a leader who allegedly degenerated into a tyrant and dictator. There must be compromise between the British and Zimbabwe governments in dealing with the land dispute to prevent the land invasions from spilling into neighboring countries, especially South Africa and Namibia. Two main stakeholders are directly involved in the Zimbabwe land issue, the British government on behalf of the commercial farmers and the Zimbabwean government on behalf of the landless people of Zimbabwe. To achieve a sustainable solution, the commercial farmers and the landless majority should have been represented by the Zimbabwean government under a united front to negotiate with the British government. There are chances of the Zimbabwe land redistribution through invasions and occupation being repeated in South Africa and Namibia if positive measures are not put in place.[162]

---

162. Ibid.

25.0 Land Reform Seen as Vote-Buying Gimmick

Most Zimbabweans still view President Mugabe's land reform program as a vote-buying exercise, which has failed to gain credibility among members of the public, a survey has revealed. The survey, conducted recently by the Mass Public Opinion Institute (MPOI) and titled *Zimbabwe's Land Reform: An Audit of the Public Perception*, was compiled between August and last month with input from more than 1,400 people across the country. Funded by the Konrad Adenauer Foundation, the survey shows, although awareness of the land reform was very high, this was not matched by access to land itself. Respondents acknowledged the debilitating effects of the reform process on the country's socioeconomic fabric.

More than ninety-six percent of those interviewed said they were aware of the land reform program, but only fourteen percent had access to land, which was monopolized by ZANU-PF followers. "Awareness of the program is nationwide (96.2 percent) but is not matched by access to land (14 percent)," the report says. The report attributed the low percentage of access to land by the general populace, especially in congested communal areas, to politicization of the program. "Considering that one of the objectives of land reform was to decongest the rural areas, it is important to note that the people who benefited from the land allocations are the elite or people with political connections to the ruling party," said the report. The majority of Zimbabweans have understood the intention of government to use the land reform program as a vote-buying gimmick, the survey established. The land reform program, as conducted by government, is viewed by significant percentages as a vote-buying exercise that is likely to fail. People feel the exercise was hurried and unplanned. The survey also established there were fears of worsening food shortages due to the instability and uncertainty brought about by the land program. It emerged through the survey that less than sixty-five percent of households allocated land had occupied it, with even fewer engaged in any meaningful production. "One of the strongest criticism of the land reform process is its negative effect on production. Respondents point to the lack of equipment and inputs as stumbling blocks," the report said. Those interviewed also lambasted government for subverting the rule of law in the implementation of the land reform for political gain.

The controversy about the number of people resettled also came out strongly during the survey. "There is considerable controversy on the number of people who have been allocated land. The government claims that over 300,000 people were allocated land, yet reports from governors submitted to the portfolio com-

mittee dealing with land recorded about 129,000 people and the Utete Committee recorded a figure of 127,000. The discrepancies over the actual figures of
people allocated farms point to the irregularities surrounding the allocation of
farms."

The majority of the beneficiaries are aged over thirty-one years and more
between forty-one and fifty years. The youth appear to have been sidelined, even
though they are the future of this country, the report noted. President Mugabe
unleashed his supporters onto white-owned farms in February 2000 after the
rejection of the government-backed draft constitution. An orgy of violence
ensued, and President Mugabe converted the chaotic occupations into a process
aimed at redressing historical land imbalances, characterized by subversion of the
rule of law. Coupled with drought conditions in the region, the chaotic land
reform has resulted in massive food shortages.[163]

Land Issue: The Legal History Since 1980
Why Mugabe Has Waited Until Now

The Communal Land Act of 1991 changed the tribal trust lands into communal
areas and shifted land authority from traditional rulers to local authorities.

The 1995:Land Acquisition Act, though drawn in the spirit of the 1979 Lancaster House "willing-seller, willing-buyer" clause (which could not be changed
for ten years), gave the government the first right to purchase excess land for
redistribution to the landless. The Act, however, had a limited impact largely
because the government did not have the money to pay compensation to landowners. In addition, white commercial farmers mounted a vigorous opposition to
the Act. Some were plainly unwilling to sell any excess land. Others overpriced
their land twice or thrice over. Because of the "willing-seller, willing-buyer"
clause, the government was powerless in the face of the commercial farmers' resistance. As a result, between 1980 and 1990, only 71,000 families out of a target of
162,000 were resettled.

1992: The Land Acquisition Act was enacted to speed up the land reform process by removing the "willing-seller, willing-buyer" clause. The Act empowered
the government to buy land compulsorily for redistribution, and a fair compensation was to be paid for land acquired. Landowners were given the right to go to
court if they did not agree to the price set by the acquiring authority. Opposition
by landowners increased throughout the period of 1992 to 1997. The United

---

163. Land Reform Seen As Vote-Buying Gimmick, Itai Dzamara Zimbabwe Independent, 19 December 2003.

Kingdom withdrew aid to the land reform program, accusing President Mugabe of giving the land to his cronies. (London now claims to have contributed £44m, but Timothy Stamp, Zimbabwe's finance minister, who is white, says £17million equivalent USD 34 million.

1997 (November): As part of the implementation of the 1992 Land Acquisition Act, the government published a list of 1,471 farmlands it intended to buy compulsorily for redistribution. The list came out of a nationwide land identification exercise undertaken throughout the year. Landowners were given thirty days (as the 1992 Act demanded) to submit written objections.

1998 (June): The government published its policy framework on the Land Reform and Resettlement Program Phase II (LRRP II), which envisaged the compulsory purchase over five years of five million hectares from the 11.2 million hectares owned by commercial farmers (both black and white), parastatal corporations, churches, NGOs, and multinational companies. Broken down, the five million hectares meant that, every year (between 1998 and 2003), the government intended to purchase one million hectares for redistribution

1998 (September): The government called a donors conference in Harare on land reform (LRRP II). Forty-eight countries and international organizations attended. The objective was to inform and involve the donor community in the program. The donors unanimously endorsed the land program, saying it was essential for poverty reduction, political stability, and economic growth. They particularly appreciated the political imperative and urgency of the land reform and agreed the "inception phase" covering twenty-four months should start immediately.

1999: The CFU freely offered for sale to the government 1.5 million hectares for redistribution. But the program had to move on. Landowners once again dragged their feet. As frustration set in on both sides, the government drafted a new constitution with a clause to compulsorily acquire land for redistribution without paying compensation. The drafting stage of the constitution was largely boycotted by the opposition (supported by the landowners), claiming President Mugabe only wanted a new constitution to entrench himself politically.

February 2000: The government organized a referendum on the new constitution. If it had been approved, the new constitution would have empowered the government to acquire land compulsorily without compensation. Naturally, the country's powerful, landed gentry (mostly white, who also control the economy) threw its weight and money behind the disparate opposition and human rights groups who formed a united front to fight against the new constitution. Calling themselves the Movement for Democratic Change (MDC), the united front won fifty-five percent of the votes as against the ruling ZANU-PF's forty-five percent. There was wild jubilation by the MDC's local and foreign supporters, prompting "End of Mugabe" headlines in the British media. Two weeks later, the pro-Mugabe War Veterans Association organized like-minded people of (not necessarily war veterans as many of them were too young to have fought in the liberation war) to march on white-owned farmlands, initially with drums, song, and dance. They claimed to have "seized" the farmlands.

February 2000: The United Kingdom throws its weight behind the white commercial farmers (20,000 of whom have British ancestry and the right to live in the United Kingdom). At first, London and its media resorted to bluff and bullying. They tried using diversionary tactics by focusing on human rights, elections, and the current economic difficulties in Zimbabwe. It was all an attempt to sidetrack the main issue of land reform.

March 2000: The diversionary tactics having misfired badly, London now upped the ante by trying to organize its European Union and other Western allies to put pressure on President Mugabe. The Conservative party called for Zimbabwe to be suspended from the Commonwealth, as the British media loudly condemned President Mugabe and called him all sorts of names. Meanwhile the farm "invasions" continued. The CFU went to court and won an injunction, calling on the police to evict the squatters. However, the police chief refused to move, claiming he did not have the manpower to implement the court's order. He appealed against the ruling and lost. Still the police would not move.

April 2000: The farm invasions turned nasty. First, a black policeman was killed. The British media nearly ignored it (mentioning it in a sentence here and there). Then, one white farmer was killed, and all hell broke lose in the British media. President Mugabe returned from a conference in Cuba and refused to order the squatters off white farmlands. The British and South African media increased their attacks on him in the most blatantly one-sided, fact-twisting coverage the world has seen in many a year. Their bias only stiffened President Mugabe's resolve.[164]

---

164. Land issue: the legal history since 1980 (New African IC Publications Limited 2001, 2000).

26.0 The Role of Food Shortages in the 2005 Parliamentary Elections

Negotiating the 2005 election maze, food shortages in the former "breadbasket of southern Africa" have become the burning issue of Zimbabwe elections, writes Andrew Meldrum. President Mugabe's claims of the triumph of his seizures of white-owned farms ring hollow at campaign rallies where people are hungry. For the first time while campaigning, confronted by unenthusiastic crowds, President Mugabe admitted the country is confronted by widespread food shortages. Meanwhile, police have threatened to jail a civic leader who has charged the government is withholding food from areas supporting the opposition. But the food shortages are undeniable. Maize meal supplies have been erratic in both rural and urban areas over the past month, as supermarkets in the cities do not have stocks for days. Zimbabwean residents say large areas of planted crops stand dry and damaged, and international agencies estimate that more than four million Zimbabweans are in need of food aid.

Speaking in Zimbabwe's rural heartland, President Mugabe was forced to acknowledge the people were suffering from a lack of maize, the country's staple grain. At a rally for his ZANU-PF party on March 17, 2005 in Gutu in south-eastern Zimbabwe, President Mugabe blamed the shortages on the failure of the seasonal rains. "The main problem we are facing is one of drought and the shortage of food. We are going to work out a hunger alleviation program…I promise you that no one will starve," President Mugabe told a listless crowd of 7,000, according to Reuters.[165] The villagers sat through President Mugabe's forty-minute speech, many with blank faces. International aid agencies say at least four million people, a third of the population, will need food aid this year after a bad harvest due to poor utilization of the lands seized from white farmers, scant rainfall, and inadequate supplies of seed and fertilizer to small rural farmers. Leading civic rights group, the National Constitutional Assembly (NCA), charged on March 17, 2005 that President Mugabe's ruling party was using food as a political tool, as people in areas short of food had to produce party cards to get supplies.

Campaigning candidates from ZANU-PF threaten hungry villages that they will not get state food supplies if they do not vote for the ruling party, according to a report issued on March 21, 2005 by Human Rights Watch. President Mugabe denies his land seizure policy has sparked the country's worst economic

---

165. President Mugabe address in Gutu—Harold Newspaper 18 March 2005

crisis, instead blaming the sanctions imposed on his government by some Western governments. "We had tried in the farming sector, but the drought has let us down. I have made a promise to your traditional leaders that we are not going to let you down," President Mugabe said in Gutu. The regional famine early warning system has cautioned since last year that Zimbabwe would be facing food shortages. Last month, the agency reported the most serious shortages were in the drought-prone provinces of Matabeleland, Manicaland, and Masvingo, where analysts say, if President Mugabe's party loses any support, it could swing the vote in favor of the main opposition party, the MDC. For more than a year, President Mugabe has adamantly maintained the land seizures have been an unqualified success and the country has enjoyed a bumper harvest. Last year, President Mugabe stopped international donors from distributing food to rural areas. "We are not hungry. Why foist this food on us? We don't want to be choked on your aid," an indignant President Mugabe said on state television.

Critics say his main reason for blocking the aid was to give his government total control over all food supplies during the election period. The state Grain Marketing Board (GMB) has a legislated monopoly over all sales and transportation of maize. Political analysts say ZANU-PF, which draws most of its support from rural people who comprise more than sixty percent of the population, must show it can handle the food crisis competently or risk losing this support. "The hunger is very real, and the shortages are obvious," said a Harare-based commentator. "Even the state media can no longer mask it. He's compelled to say something." The MDC said the country urgently needed 1.5 million tons of the staple maize to avert hunger. Renson Gasela, shadow minister for agriculture, said Zimbabwe required urgent food aid and President Mugabe's government could not handle an unfolding crisis. Mr. Gasela said the government did not have any foreign currency and could not mobilize donor support because it lacked legitimacy. Also, international aid agencies would be reluctant to help Zimbabwe after President Mugabe stopped donors from distributing food last year. Mr. Gasela charged that ZANU-PF was politicizing food, especially in the drought-prone Matabeleland and Midlands regions, known as areas of MDC support, and most people attending opposition rallies complained of hunger.

The NCA repeated the charges that President Mugabe's party used food as an elections weapon. "The use of food as a tool for campaigning is noted as a cause for concern because clearly it is a violation and it would appear to constitute vote-buying," said Spokeswoman Jessie Majome, presenting the NCA report to Harare-based diplomats.[166] Police later threatened to arrest Lovemore Madhuku, NCA leader, for the allegations in the report.

"I stand by every detail in our report," Mr. Madhuku told *Guardian Unlimited*. "I am prepared to defend the accusations in court. "Everyone knows there is not enough food and that people are going hungry. Everyone knows that you must be ZANU-PF to buy maize meal from the Grain Marketing Board."

The NCA said it obtained its information from community monitors in eight of the country's ten provinces and they backed the allegations of food supply manipulation. The NCA is a loose coalition of churches, student and labor unions, as well as business and rights groups that has lobbied for a new constitution to replace one it says entrenches President Mugabe's power. The group denies charges it is antigovernment. International rights group, Amnesty International, has also accused President Mugabe's government of manipulating the GMB. It said GMB officials limit access to maize meal purchases to ZANU-PF members and control shipments of maize meal to create artificial shortages in opposition-dominated areas. The government has denied the charges.[167]

It's an often repeated refrain in President Mugabe's campaign: The opposition is a tool of white imperialists who want to recolonize Zimbabwe. While they were a visible force in the last two elections, Zimbabwe's increasingly wary white residents have rarely been seen in the run-up to March 31, 2005, Thursday's parliamentary vote. Analysts say this was a strategic decision by the main opposition, MDC, which has been hurt by the ruling party's accusations. But the change also reflects growing unease by the tiny, white population that remains in the country after an often-violent campaign to redistribute white-owned farms to black Zimbabweans. "I think they felt that there'd been a backlash because of their participation last time and that it's more opportune to keep their heads down," said Brian Raftopoulos, a development studies professor at the University of Zimbabwe. In the early days of the MDC, founded in 1999, the party received financial and logistical backing from white farmers, who were threatened by the government's land reform program.

"If, as a black person, you vote for the MDC, know that you are a sellout," President Mugabe said at a rally in March 2005. But analysts say the ruling party has exaggerated the role of whites to discredit the opposition, whose most significant power base is among young, black, urban voters. "Whites played an insignificant role," said Arnold Tsunga, executive director of Zimbabwe Lawyers for Human Rights. "The MDC comes largely from the labor movement." Three of

---

166. Zimbabwe Movement for Democratic on line news Thu March 17, 2005
167. Andrew Meldrum, "Food shortages in the former 'breadbasket of Southern Africa' have become the burning issue of Zimbabwe elections," 29 March 2005.

the party's fifty-one current lawmakers are white, including one who is serving a year in prison for brawling with two cabinet ministers. The party has fielded five white candidates in this election, all of them running in predominantly black constituencies. "They're outdated," said Justice Svosve, twenty-six, of the ruling ZANU-PF party's antiwhite slogans. "War, war, war. That's all they talk about. What we want is food, water, jobs."[168]

At a Sunday in March 2005 rally, a young white man in an MDC T-shirt dashed in front of the stage, shouting the party's slogan, "Change! Change!" The almost exclusively black crowd responded with a roaring cheer.[169]

"We've had this unrelenting diet of racist propaganda spewed out by ZANU in the last five years. But, as demonstrated by our rallies, where the audiences are ninety-nine percent black, it hasn't worked," said David Coltart, a white opposition lawmaker who represents a ninety percent black district in the city of Bulawayo. Whites have fled the country in droves in recent years. There are no official statistics on the racial composition of the country's population of nearly twelve million, but observers estimate 25,000 whites are probably left, down from about 70,000 five years ago and 200,000 at the end of white rule in 1980. Those remaining retain a disproportionate amount of Zimbabwe's wealth. The charge whites fund the MDC has resonated with the leaders of some neighboring African countries, which also have influential white minorities. Most have remained largely supportive of President Mugabe, despite his authoritarianism.[170] Paul Themba Nyathi, MDC spokesman, said President Mugabe's rhetoric about whites was an attempt to distract voters. "The issues in Zimbabwe have noting to do with white and black. They have to do with twenty-five years of misrule," said Nyathi.[171]

American Government Challenges African Governments over 2005 Zimbabwe Elections

The American government has challenged southern African governments to back their claims that Zimbabwe's March 31, 2005, parliamentary poll was free and

---

168. Andrew Meldrum, "Food shortages in the former 'breadbasket of Southern Africa' 29 March 2005.

169. Andrew Meldrum, "Food shortages in the former 'breadbasket of Southern Africa'29 March 2005.

170. Andrew Meldrum, "Food shortages in the former 'breadbasket of Southern Africa'29 March 2005.

171. Zimbabwe Experiences Exodus of Whites By MICHAEL HARTNACK, Associated Press Writer

fair. In a statement today, the American state department spokesman, Richard Boucher, said the American government—together with the United Kingdom, the European Union, independent local observers, and the defeated opposition—disputed the election outcome. "I would have to ask them what they think their basis is for saying that. We've put out what we think is the basis for viewing this election as seriously tainted and not free and fair," he said.

President Mugabe's ruling ZANU-PF party won a comfortable majority of the 120 parliamentary seats contested in the poll, according to the country's electoral commission, which was set up a few months before the election, to meet the SADC protocol on holding free and fair polls, which Zimbabwe signed in Mauritius last August. As a result of the ZANU-PF win, President Mugabe, who turned eighty-one last month, is now able to appoint thirty additional lawmakers to the 150-seat legislature. That will give him the two-thirds majority he needs to amend the constitution to further bolster his rule, according to observers watching the election.

The opposition MDC rejected the official results, which gave it forty-one seats to ZANU-PF's seventy-eight. It called for new elections, claiming intimidation and ballot-rigging. Protests, which police were quick to thwart, have so far been held in Harare against President Mugabe, whose twenty-five-year tenure and controversial land redistribution policies have left the former British colony's economy in tatters. MDC leader Morgan Tsvangirai said his party would challenge the results in court. African governments gave a thumbs-up to the election, stating it was an indication of the will of the Zimbabweans. They ignored criticism from Western capitals, human rights groups, and many Zimbabweans themselves, who argued the whole had been flawed because it favored the ruling party from the onset. President Mugabe, who has been engaged in a verbal war for years with critical Western governments, refused to allow Western monitors to observe the poll.

African Union observers declared the elections transparent, while those from regional governments comprising the fourteen-member SADC also said the vote reflected the will of the people. "The poll was peaceful, transparent, credible, and well-managed," said a statement issued by the SADC observer team, led by Phumzile Mlambo Ngcuka, a South African cabinet minister, now facing criticism from home after making unacceptable comments after the poll. She said all disputes related to the election had to be dealt with by Zimbabweans themselves because SADC observers did not have time for that because they were now homesick and wanted to leave for their respective countries to rest.

South Africa, the region's economic powerhouse that provides power to impoverished Zimbabwe, also sent a separate team of parliamentary observers. That team's leader, Labor Minister Membathisi Mdladlana, a lawmaker from the ruling ANC, issued a statement saying, "mission unanimously agreed that the elections were credible, legitimate, free and fair." However, representatives of other political parties distanced themselves from the verdict. One of those parties, the Democratic Alliance, accused the ANC government of deciding in advance to endorse the elections.

Criticism also came from Zimbabwean civil society groups. A local observer mission, the Zimbabwe Election Support Network, said there had been huge discrepancies between the number of people who voted and the final vote tallies. In some places, as many as a quarter of voters were turned away because they either did not appear on the voters' roll or failed to present proper identification, said the mission's chairman, Reginald Matchaba-Hove. "The polls took place in a climate of fear," he added.

While it was generally accepted the campaign had been less violent than previous ones in 2000 and 2002, other aspects of the campaign and the election itself however drew criticism from the American secretary of state, Condoleezza Rice. She said the "electoral playing field was heavily tilted in the government's favor." As many as ten percent of voters were turned away from polling stations due to irregularities with voter registration rolls, she said.[172]

---

172. The Daily News (online newspaper), 7 April 2005.

27.0 Present Zimbabwe Land Reform Crisis Comments and Conclusions

The Rudd Concession, signed in 1888 between King Lobengula and Cecil John Rhodes, provided the BSAC with the momentum to obtain a royal charter in 1889, granting the company authority to administer and govern the region encompassing present-day Zimbabwe. The charter was granted, notwithstanding King Lobengula's protestations he had been deceived. King Lobengula repudiated the Rudd Concession, stating he would "not recognize the paper, as it contains neither my words nor the words of those who got it." The response by Queen Victoria Advisor to King Lobengula's protestation to this development was that it "would be unwise to exclude white men." Based on the royal charter, the BSAC assembled an occupation force in 1890, composed of men from all walks of life, including soldiers; occupied Zimbabwe; displaced the natives from the fertile lands to barren, sandy areas; seized their cattle; and introduced development tax and forced labor. In 1893, the BSAC declared war against King Lobengula, occupied Matebeleland, and nullified the pledges made in the Rudd Concession. The occupation was justified in the interest of spreading Christianity and civilization. The BSAC occupation signaled the beginning of the British-Zimbabwean century-old land ownership conflict in Zimbabwe. In 1896, the natives rebelled against foreign occupation of their land and domination, but they were defeated and subdued, only to rise up again in the 1960s during the second Chimurenga war.

With the coming into power of the Rhodesian Front Party in 1962, any pretense at accommodating blacks was abandoned. Segregation would henceforth be pursued with increasing vigor. This process culminated in the 1969 Land Tenure Act, which, while repealing the Land Appointment Act, reenacted and strengthened its provisions by dividing the land in half with 44.9 million acres allocated to each race. The policy was entrenched in a new constitution. These measures led to further overstocking, very high population densities, serious environmental degradation, reduced agricultural productivity, and poverty in the communal areas. Overcrowding led many people to settle on riverbanks, steep slopes, grazing areas, and fragile land, thereby posing great environmental risks. It is therefore against this background that land ranked highest among the grievances motivating the indigenous black majority to launch the Second Chimurenga/Imfazwe to free the country from colonial oppression. Notably, in the period preceding the liberation war, "mwana wevhu/umntwana womhlabati (child of the soil) became the nationalists' rallying call. Herbert Chitepo, chairman of ZANU party, it succinctly when he said the following:

> I could go into the whole theories of discrimination, in legislation, in resi-
> dency, in economic opportunities, in education. I could go into that, but I
> will restrict myself to the question of land because I think this is very basic. To
> us the essence of exploitation, the essence of white domination, is domination
> over land.[173]

The Eastern Bloc portion of the Cold War supported the armed struggle against British colonialism as well as provided military training and arms of war. Alternatively, the West directly and indirectly supplied military logistics to the Rhodesian government under the pretext of fighting communism. That is the real issue.[174] Herbert Chitepo must have turned in his grave when the Patriotic Front signed the Lancaster House Agreement with the clause on freedom from deprivation of property.

The intensification of the armed struggle resulted in negotiations leading to the signing of the Lancaster House Agreement in 1979. The Lancaster House Agreement clause on freedom from deprivation of property was the most critical to independent Zimbabwe. President Mugabe and Joshua Nkomo were allegedly deceived into signing the Lancaster House Agreement based on land acquisition pledges the British and American governments made. Lord Carrington, chairman of the Lancaster House conference, acknowledged the centrality of the land issue and the enormity of the resources needed to redress the colonial legacy in a statement issued on October 11, 1979:

> We recognize that the future of Zimbabwe, whatever its political complexion,
> will wish to extend land ownership. The costs would be very substantial
> indeed, well beyond the capacity, in our judgement, of any individual donor
> country. And the British government cannot commit itself at this stage to a
> specific share in them. We should however be ready to support the efforts of
> the Government of Independent Zimbabwe to obtain international assistance
> for these purposes.[175]

The final agreement did not address the land problem adequately. The Patriotic Front accepted it on the understanding the United Kingdom, the United

---

173. Herbert Chitepo speech on a trip to Australia in 1973.
174. Herbert Chitepo speech on a trip to Australia in 1973.
175. Partial record of the 1979 Lancaster House Zimbabwe Independence negotiations.

States, and other donor nations would pay for land needed for resettlement. Julius Nyerere, then-president of Tanzania, during a press conference on October 16, 1979, believed the land issue would be impossible for an independent government in Zimbabwe.

> To tax Zimbabweans in order to compensate people who took it away from them through the gun. Really the British cannot have it both ways. They made this an issue, and they are now making vague remarks mixing rural development aid with the question of land compensation…The two are separate…The British paid money to Kenya. That the future government of Zimbabwe must pay compensation is a British demand, and the British must promise in London to make the money available.[176]

Clearly, the history of colonialism in Zimbabwe had been largely a story in which Europeans used their control over land to secure a position of economic and political dominance for themselves. No black government could be expected to uphold this racially skewed land structure. Addressing the Catholic IMBISA Plenary Assembly in Harare on July 30, 2001, President Mugabe described the situation obtaining in the country, which, however, was no different to that at pre-independence:

> As in the past, the basis of conflict in contemporary Zimbabwe is the unresolved national question of land. It is also the basis of peace and all other rights that we wish for in a democracy. Its solutions would enable us to end the two-nation, two-race model we inherited from colonialism. It would create opportunities for everyone and give a stake to the majority of our people. Indeed, it is the way to the recovery of our economy. This is why land reform is at the heart of the current struggle. We cannot relent on this one, and we hope the Church will stand with and by us in resolving it.[177]

Given the land reform legal history since 1980, apparently, since independence, the Zimbabwean government was making concerted efforts to have the land issue resolved amicably through the legal and diplomatic framework. The Communal Land Act of 1991 changed the tribal trust lands into communal areas and shifted land authority from traditional rulers to local authorities. The Land Acquisition Act of 1995, though drawn in the spirit of the 1979 Lancaster House "willing-seller, willing-buyer" clause (which could not be changed for ten years),

---

176. President Julius Nyerere of Tanzania, press conference on October 16, 1997.
177. President Mugabe, address ti the Catholic IMBISA Plenary Assembly, 30 July 2001.

gave the government the first right to purchase excess land for redistribution to the landless. The Act, however, had a limited impact, largely because the government did not have the money to pay compensation to landowners. In addition, white commercial farmers mounted a vigorous opposition to the Act. Some were plainly unwilling to sell any excess land. Others overpriced their land twice or thrice over. Because of the "willing-seller, willing-buyer" clause, the government was powerless in the face of the commercial farmers' resistance. As a result, between 1980 and 1990, only 71,000 families out of a target of 162,000 were resettled.

The Land Acquisition Act of 1996 was enacted to speed up the land reform process by removing the "willing-seller, willing-buyer" clause. The Act empowered the government to buy land compulsorily for redistribution, and a fair compensation was to be paid for land acquired. Landowners were given the right to go to court if they did not agree to the price set by the acquiring authority. Opposition by landowners increased throughout the period from 1992 to 1997. The United Kingdom withdrew aid to the land reform program, accusing President Mugabe of giving the land to his cronies. (London now claims to have contributed £44m, but Timothy Stamp, Zimbabwe's former minister, who is white, said £17million equivalent USD 34 million. The British Conservative government under John Major agreed to assist with further funding for land reform in 1996. However, due to Tony Blair's Labor government coming to power in 1997, matters came to a head. The Labor government refused to advance the process of land reform, in effect revoking the United Kingdom's obligations as per the Lancaster House understanding. In a letter to the Zimbabwean minister of agriculture, Mr. Kumbirai Kangai, then-secretary of state for international development, Claire Short stated:

> I should make it clear that we do not accept that Britain has a special responsibility to meet the costs of land purchase in Zimbabwe. We are a new government from diverse backgrounds without links to former colonial interests. My own origins are Irish, and, as you know, we were colonized, not colonizers.

This unprecedented stance by the British government marked the beginning of worsening relations between the two governments. No further funds were made available to Zimbabwe's land reform program.[178]

---

178. Claire Short, British secretaryof state for international development—letter to Zimbabwe Minister of Agriculture.

This change of international relations policy should have been made from the British prime minister to the Zimbabwe head of state, not from a secretary of state for economic development to a Zimbabwe minister of agriculture. The fact that Claire Short was of Irish origin and her country was also colonized had nothing to do with the Lancaster House Agreement pledges the United Kingdom made. Sir Shridath's response in the already cited BBC program gives context to this turn of events. Asked whether Zimbabweans were let down by the British, he said, "Britain let them down. Britain did not fulfill its promises, and they found all sorts of ways to wriggle out. And that was very unfortunate, and that it is what had led to some of the bitterness..." In November 1997, as part of the implementation of the 1992 Land Acquisition Act, the government published a list of 1,471 farmlands it intended to buy compulsorily for redistribution. The list came out of a nationwide land identification exercise undertaken throughout the year. Landowners were given thirty days (as the 1992 Act demanded) to submit written objections.

In June 1998, the government published its policy framework on the Land Reform and Resettlement Program Phase II (LRRP II), which envisaged the compulsory purchase over five years of five million hectares from the 11.2 million hectares owned by commercial farmers (both black and white), parastatal corporations, churches, NGOs, and multinational companies. Broken down, the five million hectares meant, every year between 1998 and 2003, the government intended to purchase one million hectares for redistribution In September 1998, the government called a donors conference in Harare on land reform (LRRP II). Forty-eight countries and international organizations attended. The objective was to inform and involve the donor community in the program. The donors unanimously endorsed the land program, saying it was essential for poverty reduction, political stability, and economic growth. They particularly appreciated the political imperative and urgency of the land reform and agreed the inception phase covering twenty-four months should start immediately. In 1998, the CFU freely offered for sale to the government 1.5 million hectares for redistribution. But the program had to move on. Landowners once again dragged their feet.

As frustration set in on both sides, the government drafted a new constitution with a clause to compulsorily acquire land for redistribution without paying compensation. The drafting stage of the constitution was largely boycotted by the opposition (supported by the commercial farmers), claiming President Mugabe only wanted a new constitution to entrench himself politically. The new constitution would have empowered the government to acquire land compulsorily without compensation. Naturally, the country's powerful, landed gentry (mostly

white, who also control the economy) threw its weight and money behind the
desperate opposition and human rights groups who formed a united front to
fight against the new constitution. Calling themselves the Movement for Democratic Change (MDC), the united front won fifty-five percent of the votes as
against the ruling ZANU-PF's forty-five percent. There was wild jubilation by
the MDC's local and foreign supporters, prompting "End of Mugabe" headlines
in the British media. Professor Jonathan Moyo, an ardent critic of President
Mugabe, joined the government and became minister of information. Two weeks
later, the pro-Mugabe War Veterans Association organized like-minded people
(not necessarily war veterans because many of them were too young to have
fought in the liberation war) to march on white-owned farmlands, initially with
drums, song, and dance. They claimed to have "seized" the farmlands.

the United Kingdom threw its weight behind the white commercial farmers in
February 2000. (20,000 of whom have British ancestry and the right to live in the
United Kingdom.) At first, London and its media resorted to bluff and bullying.
They tried using diversionary tactics by focusing on human rights, elections, and
the current economic difficulties in Zimbabwe. It was all an attempt to sidetrack
the main issue of land reform. The diversionary tactics, having misfired badly in
March 2000, London now upped the ante by trying to organize its European
Union and other Western allies to put pressure on President Mugabe. The Conservative party called for Zimbabwe to be suspended from the Commonwealth as
the British media loudly condemned President Mugabe and called him all sorts of
names. Meanwhile, the farm invasions continued. The CFU went to court and
won an injunction, calling on the police to evict the squatters. However, the
police chief refused to move, claiming he did not have the manpower to implement the court's order. He appealed against the ruling and lost. Still the police
would not move.

The farm invasions turned nasty in April 2000. First, a black policeman was
killed. The British media almost ignored it as it mentioned it in a sentence here
and there. Then, one white farmer was killed, and all hell broke lose in the British
media. President Mugabe returned from a conference in Cuba and refused to
order the squatters off white farmlands. The British and South African media
increased their attacks on him in the most blatantly one-sided, fact-twisting coverage the world has seen in many a year. Their bias only stiffened President
Mugabe's resolve.[179]

179. Land issue: the legal history since 1980 (New African IC Publications Limited 2001,
     2000).

In September 2000, President Mugabe met the United Nations secretary-general, Kofi Annan, in New York City and discussed the land issue in Zimbabwe and a possible role for the United Nations. A technical mission to Zimbabwe under the aegis of the United Nations Development Program (UNDP) was dispatched in October that year. The mission was mandated to carry out a technical review into measures necessary for a "sound technical process to take the land reform forward." The UNDP Technical Mission conceded, while a framework for the legal and administrative process for compulsory acquisition of land through the Land Acquisition Act of 1992 was in place, government had failed to acquire that land principally on account of technical and administrative considerations arising from legal challenges launched by white commercial farmers.

As a follow-up to the UNDP Technical Mission and the subsequent visit of its administrator, Mr. Mark Brown, in December 2000, written communication was exchanged with the government. Through this medium, the government was given the assurance the United Nations secretary-general's consultations with President Mbeki of South Africa, Olusegun Obasanjo of Nigeria, other regional leaders, as well as key western donors, including the World Bank, gave him confidence the UNDP could generate the requisite support for the land reform program. However, as was previously the case, conditionalities were once again placed on the government. The secretary-general could only persuade the donor community to come on board once "outstanding law and order issues are being brought under control." The government was therefore requested to make a choice between continuing with its fast-track land reform program and adopting "a more systematic, investment-backed approach," which the United Nations supported. In the letter, Mr. Brown conceded the second approach entailed a slow start and the delay of resettlement until confidence-building measures were implemented to secure a resumption of donor funding.

Government through the foreign minister, Dr. I. S. G. Mudenge, responded in March 2001, to Mr. Brown, agreeing with most of his proposals. It, however, rejected the second approach, which would have entailed the abandonment of the fast-track program. It was also put to Mr. Brown that, if the donor community had responded in a timely manner with the required resources to implement the agreement reached at the 1998 Land Donor Conference and the commercial farmers not resorted to legal actions aimed at frustrating the land resettlement program, significant progress could have been achieved by that time. The government indicated a unique opportunity had been missed. At the same time, the government appealed to the United Nations secretary-general "for urgent assistance by the various United Nations agencies, as well as willing donors and

NGOs to assist the resettled farmers who find themselves in dire need to infrastructure and social facilities."

Following yet another round of consultations with the United Nations, the
UNDP resident representative in Harare, Mr. J. Victor Angelo, responded in July
2001 to the government's response to the March 2001 communication by proposing that yet another assessment team to visit Zimbabwe should be set up.
Principally, the assessment team would "produce a comprehensive report with all
necessary technical information and will make recommendations on the possible
establishment of an information mechanism for the land reform program." The
proposed assessment was seen as part of a "possible partnership building process
between the Government of Zimbabwe, the donor community, and local stakeholders." It was further seen that such an assessment would be useful in establishing the facts as far as the fast-track program was concerned. The government
rejected the proposal, which appeared to be a further attempt to delay addressing
a very urgent, highly volatile land issue. The United Nations believed that devel-
opment-related organized land redistribution was the solution to the land ownership conflict in Zimbabwe.

Concerned at the widening rift between Zimbabwe and EU countries led by
the United Kingdom, President Obasanjo suggested that friends of Zimbabwe
and the United Kingdom in the Commonwealth intervene to break the impasse
over the land issue. This initiative was conceived after a meeting between President Mugabe and his Nigerian counterpart on the margins of the Group of 15
Summit in Jakarta, Indonesia, in June 2001. Subsequently, a committee of nine
commonwealth foreign ministers met in Abuja, Nigeria, in September 2001,
under Nigeria's chairmanship. In turn, Zimbabwe reaffirmed its commitment to
carry out its land reform program within the country's constitutional and legal
framework. The undertaking and assurance that no further farm invasions would
occur henceforth was also given. The government also promised to speed up discussions with the UNDP to facilitate the latter's efforts to mobilize international
support for the land reform program. As agreed at Abuja, the committee of commonwealth foreign ministers met in Harare in October 2001, to advance the process. The government proceeded to fulfill the commitments it had made under
the agreement. As a result, a marked reduction of political tension was immediately realized within the country. On the contrary, the United Kingdom did not
honor any of the commitments made at Abuja. No financial or material benefits
accrued to the country following these exchanges.

The fast-track program, launched on July 15, 2000, was designed to be undertaken in an accelerated manner and with reliance on domestic resources. The

program was a fundamental departure from previous philosophy, practices, and procedures of acquiring land and resettling people. The legal framework governing land acquisition had to be significantly amended to consider the rapidly changing policy environment in which fast-track was being implemented. The Constitutional Amendment Number 16 of 2000, as already stated, placed the financial obligation of paying compensation for any improvements on the acquired properties. Similarly, the Land Acquisition Act underwent changes to ensure conformity with the new constitutional provisions. The Rural Land Occupiers (Protection) Act was also enacted to protect land occupiers on land not yet acquired by the government. Although eighty percent of the disarmed and demobilized ex-combatants hailed from rural, agrarian communities, they were deliberately diverted to choose reintegration into civilian life through incorporation into the national army and other state security organs and technical vocational training instead of agriculture due to the unavailability of commercial farming land for reintegration. Twenty years later, the ex-combatants demanded pensions and monthly allowances from the government after realizing they had failed to reintegrate into society through the trade training and cash grant reintegration opportunities. The government bowed down to the ex-combatants' demands. As such, it fell out of favor with the IMF and World Bank. After having realized the "promised land" was not forthcoming through protracted negotiations, the landless natives and ex-combatants invaded and occupied the commercial farms, seizing cattle and equipment.[180]

The 2005 parliamentary elections were held in the midst of chronic food shortages, partly due to the drought as well as the inability of the recently resettled landless and ex-combatants to transform from subsistence to commercial farming. The government allegedly refused organized donor relief food assistance distributed through NGOs, preferring all food to be procured and distributed through the government-controlled GMB. The opposition and the NCA accused the government of handing out relief food to ZANU-PF membership cardholders only. It will be recalled, during the 2002 presidential elections, land redistribution was allegedly used as a vote-buying gimmick. In the 2005 parliamentary elections, selective food distribution was purportedly used as a vote-buying gimmick. The rural electorate favored the Mugabe government for delivering independence and freedom from white domination. The urban population supported the opposition to foster and spearhead regime change in Zimbabwe.

---

180. Ibid.

ZANU-PF accused the British government of supporting the MDC in what was alleged to be a plot to constitutionally effect a regime change in Zimbabwe. During the 2005 parliamentary elections, the ruling party accused those voting for the MDC of being puppets of the former colonial power and traitors. The contesting parties were given equal opportunities to campaign over the electronic media, even though campaigning in the rural areas was nearly impossible for the opposition party. The ruling ZANU-PF won the 2005 elections with a two-thirds majority. The United States, European Union, and the opposition claim the election was not free and fair while the SADC and South African government observers declared differently. According to government and other observers, the voting was free and fair. The opposition alleges intimidation, food blackmail, and rigging of the voters' roll. The opposition has yet to prove these allegations in court. The ZANU-PF government must now turn all the economic indicators from negative to positive growth. The opposition must be able to discount the allegations they are puppets of the commercial farmers, the British, and the European Community. Otherwise, they will be viewed as simple political malcontents, reactionaries, commercial farmer and British puppets with an idea to effect regime change at a cost lower than the pledges made at the Lancaster House negotiations.

The international community is likely to support and fund any political agenda based on economically justified land utilization and economic reforms conducive for investment in Zimbabwe. In the interest of global economic development, the international community, the World Bank and IMF should now make plans to return to Zimbabwe. The land redistribution issue is a southern African regional problem impacting Zimbabwe and is very likely to influence South Africa and Namibia in the near future due to similar historically racial, segregation-based land allocation policies in these countries. Lessons learned from the Zimbabwe land ownership conflict will benefit Namibia and South Africa in conflict prevention through the preparation and implementation of politically and economically justified land reform programs in those countries.[181]

---

181. Ibid.

References

1. Black majority government or meritocracy Bulletin 14 no 4 (1976 p 116-136

2. Among the Matebeles, D. Carnegie, (1894 reproduced 1970 Shaka's Heirs 1971

3. Commonwealth Conference, Nigeria, Lagos 1966, Sir Harold Wilson speech

4. Black majority government or meritocracy Bulletin 14 no 4 (1976 p 116-136

5. Terrorists abduct African students and teachers—Rhodesia Herald 6 July 1973.

6. Avoid secret political deals, Isaya Muriwo Sithole, Financial Gazette 3/11/2004

7. Rhodesian Black groupings in disarray Bulletin 14 no 7-8 1976 p 268-270

8. Zimbabwe Under Siege by Gregory Elich August 26, 2002.

9. Herbert Chitepo, Chairman of ZANU—Speech on a trip to Australia in 1973

10. BBC Hard Talk program interview, Sir Shridath Ramphal in 2002

11. The Zimbabwe Patriotic Front rejoins independence negotiations, October 1979

12. Lancaster House Zimbabwe Independence negotiations 1979-partial record.

13. Zimbabwe Lancaster House Independence Constitution Clause on freedom from deprivation of property—Zimbabwe constitution, December, 1979

14. British Colonialism, Zimbabwe's Land Reform, Settler Resistance-Steve Lawton

15. Constitutional Debate, David Moyo, University of Zimbabwe.

16. Letter of protest from King Lobengula to Her Majesty Queen Victoria

17. Zimbabwe African National Union—Patriotic Front political structure-1990

18. President Kaunda speech on Zambia Broadcasting Cooperation March 31, 1975.

19. The Standard interview with former Zambia, President Kaunda in Harare in 1999

20. Zimbabwe African National Union—Patriotic Front Party Manifesto—2001

21. The Annual National People's Conference—ZANU PF 2000.

22. Democracy and Rule of Law Project of the Carnegie Endowment for International Peace June 20, 2001, Thomas Carothers and Marina Ottaway.

23. Democracy and Rule of Law Project—Synopsis prepared by Gideon Maltz

24. Zimbabwe Democracy and Economic Recovery Act December 5, 2001 approved.

25. ZANU-PF response to Zimbabwe Democracy and Economic Recovery Act 2001.

26. Demobilization and Reintegration in Africa—World Bank released in 1992

27. Journal of Peace, Conflict and Military Studies Vol.1, March 2000, ISSN 1563-4019 Gerald Mazarire and Martin Rupiya.

28. Frank exchange begins on land-Development Bulletin by L.Machipisa September9,1998

29. 45. President Mugabe Speech, Land Reform Donor Conference September 1998.

30. Frank Exchange Begins on Land, Lewis Machipisa, IPS, 9 September 1998.

31. Movement For Democratic Change (MDC) May 1999 Declaration.

32. Uneven Zimbabwe, Patrick Bond's 1998 book

33. Address on independence anniversary, President Mugabe18 April 2000.

34. London Land Negotiations Re-open, Minister John Nkomo, 27 April 2000.

35. Zimbabwe Structurally Adjusted, Steve Lawton, 27.11.2002

36. The Sunday Telegraph Newspaper (August 26, 2002)

37. Zimbabwe and British colonialism bran—by Steve Lawton 27.11.2002

38. The Constitution, Barbara Slaughter and Stuart Nolan 22 February 2000.

39. Referendum on the draft constitution, Presidential address, 15 February 2000.

40. Referendum defeat shakes ZANU FF-B.Slaughter and S.Nolan 22 February 2000

41. The Constitution, Barbara Slaughter and Stuart Nolan, 22 February 2000.

42. Black majority government or meritocracy Bulletin 14 no 4 (1976) p116-135

43. Referendum on the draft constitution, Presidential address.15 February 2000.

44. Constitution negotiations—David Moyo, University of Zimbabwe.

45. Government and farmers in Land Reform Dispute—Commercial Farmers Union Journal

46. Zimbabwe-United Kingdom Relations, Minister Mudenge 15 March 2000

47. New Land Acquisition Act-The Zimbabwe Herald, 6 April 2000.

48. Commercial Farmers Union, impact on Agriculture-land invasions, 23 May 2000.

49. Statement announcing fast-track approach, Vice President Msika, 16 July 2000.

50. Resettlement and Land Redistribution Policies and Procedures.

51. Zimbabwe townsfolk join farm strike, David Blair, The Telegraph, 25 July 2000.

52. Mass job action looms over farm violence, The Financial Gazette, 26 July 2000.

53. Mugabe sued for farm invasions, Andrew Meldrum, The Guardian, 27 July 2000.

54. ZANU-PF seeks to rein in squatters, David Blair, The Telegraph, 27 July 2000.

55. MDC calls for stay-away. by Patrick Bond.

56. Trade unions back general strike, David Blair, The Telegraph, 29 July 2000.

57. At least 3,000 white farms will be seized, Jan Raath, The Times, 31 July 2000.

58. Commercial Farmers Union (CFU), National Stay-away, 1 August 2000.

59. Strike on tomorrow, Zimbabwe Daily News, 1 August 2000.

60. Mugabe to seize more land" Jan Raath, The Times (UK), 2 August 2000.

61. Army mobilized to keep peace, B. Peta, The UK Independent, 2 August 2000

62. Army mobilized for farm invasion, McGreal, The Guardian, 2 August 2000.

63. Strike hits businesses, Hawkins and Mallet, The Financial Times, 3 August 2000.

64. Protest strike halts Zimbabwe, David Blair, The Telegraph, 3 August 2000.

65. Mugabe Dashes Hopes for Reform, Cris Chinaka Reuters, 3 August 2000.

66. SADC looks for the positive, Victor Mallet, Financial Times, 7 August 2000.

67. Government Launches National Economic Revival Program, Herald.

68. Minister of Foreign Affairs meets the UN S G Envoy, 30 November 2000.

69. Government of Zimbabwe—UNDP communications on land redistribution.

70. Zimbabwe Land rights, R.Mukumbira, News and Views on Africa January 2001.

71. Land Acquisition by Grace and Favor, JAG news release, 4 September 2002.

72. Amendments to Land Acquisition Act approved, 11 August 2002.

73. Cry over Land Seizures in Zimbabwe Workers Vanguard 741(8 September 2000)

74. Land Reform and Imperialist Hypocrisy, Workers Vanguard 803 (9 May 2003).

75. Socialist Worker [Zimbabwe], December 1999

76. Socialist Worker [Zimbabwe], August 2000

77. Socialist Worker [Britain], 19 January 2002)

78. Land Reform and Imperialist Hypocrisy, Workers Vanguard 803 (9 May 2003

79. Socialist Worker [Britain], 9 March 2002)

80. Land Reform and Imperialist Hypocrisy, Workers Vanguard 803 (9 May 2003).

81. Zimbabwe Under Siege by Gregory Elich, Mugabe apologist August 26, 2002.

82. Guardian Weekly [London], 21–27 November 2002

83. The Economic Decline of Zimbabwe, Carolyn Jenkins and John Knight 2002.

84. The Life and Ideas of Robert Owen, pp. 73-76, 81, 123-124, 134-135, 164-165.

85. Jailed but never charged with a crime—Davis president of AIA.

86. MDC expelled Socialist by Norm Dixon, Green Left Weekly December 11. 2002

87. Parliament expels Socialist—Norm Dixon Green Left Weekly December11 2002.

88. Mbeki's Zimbabwe comments, Sunday Independent (SA), 14 December 2003.

89. UK and Commonwealth Office—Foreign Policy on Zimbabwe

90. Mbeki's Zimbabwe comments, Sunday Independent (SA), 14 December 2003.

91. Mbeki's newsletter digested in London, Independent (SA),14 December 2003.

92. British sources said Mbeki's newsletter was being digested in London.

93. Mbeki's alleged offensive Sunday Independent (SA), 14 December 2003.

94. Vote-Buying Gimmick, Dzamara, Zimbabwe Independent, 19 December 2003.

95. Land issue history since 1980 New African IC Publications Limited 2001, 2000.

96. President Mugabe address in Gutu—Zimbabwe Harold 18 March 2005

97. Zimbabwe Movement for Democratic on line news Thu March 17, 2005

98. Food shortages in the former breadbasket, Andrew Meldrum, 29 March 2005.

99. Zimbabwe Experiences Exodus of Whites By Michael Hartnack

100.The Daily News (online newspaper), 7 April 2005.

101.Herbert Chitepo ZANU Chairman speech on a trip to Australia in 1973.

102.Lancaster House Zimbabwe Independence negotiations 1979—partial record.

103.Press conference, President, Julius Nyerere of Tanzania on October 16, 1997.

104.Catholic IMBISA Plenary Assembly, President Mugabe, address 30 July 2001.

105.Letter to Zimbabwe Minister of Agriculture—UK Secretary of State Claire Short.

106.Land issue since 1980 (New African IC Publications Limited 2001, 2000).

978-0-595-35632-4
0-595-35632-X